D1563655

Massacre
on the Gila .

MASSACRE ON THE GILA

An Account of the Last Major Battle Between American Indians, with Reflections on the Origin of War

CLIFTON B. KROEBER
and
BERNARD L. FONTANA

The University of Arizona Press, Tucson

About the Authors

CLIFTON B. KROEBER has been active in research in the history of the Lower Colorado Indian peoples since 1958. He joined the staff of Occidental College in 1955 and in 1964 was named Norman Bridge Professor of Hispanic American History. He has become known for his work as a Latin American historian specializing in modern Mexican history. He is author of *Man, Land, and Water: Mexico's Farmlands Irrigation Policies, 1885–1911* and coauthor with A. L. Kroeber of *A Mohave War Reminiscence, 1854–1880*.

BERNARD L. FONTANA, who for sixteen years was ethnologist in the Arizona State Museum, has been field historian in the University of Arizona Library since 1978. An anthropologist and former president of the American Society for Ethnohistory, he is an authority on the history of the Southwest and of its native cultures, having written, coauthored, and edited sixteen books on those subjects, including the prize-winning *Tarahumara: Where Night Is the Day of the Moon* and *Of Earth and Little Rain: The Papago Indians*.

THE UNIVERSITY OF ARIZONA PRESS

Copyright © 1986
The Arizona Board of Regents
All Rights Reserved
Manufactured in the U.S.A.

This book was set in 11/13 Linotron Caslon Old Face No. 2.

Library of Congress Cataloging-in-Publication Data

Kroeber, Clifton B.
Massacre on the Gila.

Bibliography: p.
1. Maricopa Wells (Ariz.), Battle of, 1857.
2. Yuman Indians—Wars. 3. Pima Indians—Wars.
4. Indians of North America—Arizona—Wars. 5. Indian
warfare. 6. War—Origin. 7. Maricopa (Ariz.)—History.
I. Fontana, Bernard L.   II. Title.
E83.8565.K76   1986   973.6′6   86-24974

ISBN 0-8165-0969-7 (alk. paper)

British Library Cataloguing in Publication data are available.

CONTENTS

PREFACE

This book is the result of a project begun in 1961 as an effort to understand an 1857 battle that occurred next to Pima Butte on the Gila River in what is now southern Arizona. The principal attackers, all of whom had come by foot more than one hundred and sixty miles across the Sonoran Desert, were Mohave Indians and Indians known in the literature as Yumas, but who referred to themselves then, as they do now, as Quechans. Except in quotations from other sources where the term "Yuma" appears, we have consistently used "Quechan" in speaking of these people.

The persons attacked in the 1857 battle were the Gila River Pimas and a group known in 1857, as they are to the outside world today, as Maricopas. We have used this designation throughout, although the reader should know from the outset that the term "Maricopa" did not appear in writing until 1846, and that the people thus known are actually a Yuman-speaking amalgam of other peoples who were forced from their aboriginal homelands on the Lower Colorado River beginning in the eighteenth century: the Opa, Kaveltcadom (or Cocomaricopa), Halchidhoma, Kohuana, and Halyikwamai.

Our interest in this single 1857 encounter led us to a broader interest in the history and dynamics of warfare among Yuman-speaking groups and between Yuman groups and other peoples, such as Pimas and Western Apaches. From there, it was but a single step to the still larger question, that of the origin of war generally.

We have used the 1857 battle—a bloody Indian-versus-Indian encounter in which the Quechan attackers were all but annihilated—as a springboard to a consideration of war and of its immediate and ultimate causes. It will be for the reader to decide how well we have succeeded in arriving at new insights and understanding.

Along the way we have become indebted to a great many people and institutions, not the least among them the late Joe Giff, a Pima Indian who gave us a tour of the 1857 battleground; Nicholas P. Houser, who went searching for oral history in our behalf; and Kieran R. McCarty, who piloted us in a small plane over the scene of the 1857 calamity. We single out for special thanks the libraries and librarians of the University of Arizona, especially its Special Collections division; the Southwest Museum, Los Angeles; the Huntington Library, San Marino, California; the Sharlot Hall Museum, Prescott, Arizona; the Arizona Historical Society, Tucson; the Bancroft Library, University of California, Berkeley; Sonoma State College, Rohnert Park, California; Occidental College, Los Angeles; and the University of California at Los Angeles. We need also to acknowledge help from the Doris Duke American Indian Oral History Project at the University of Arizona as well as general support from our respective institutions, Occidental College and the University of Arizona. None of this would have been possible without such support.

CLIFTON B. KROEBER
BERNARD L. FONTANA

Massacre
on the Gila

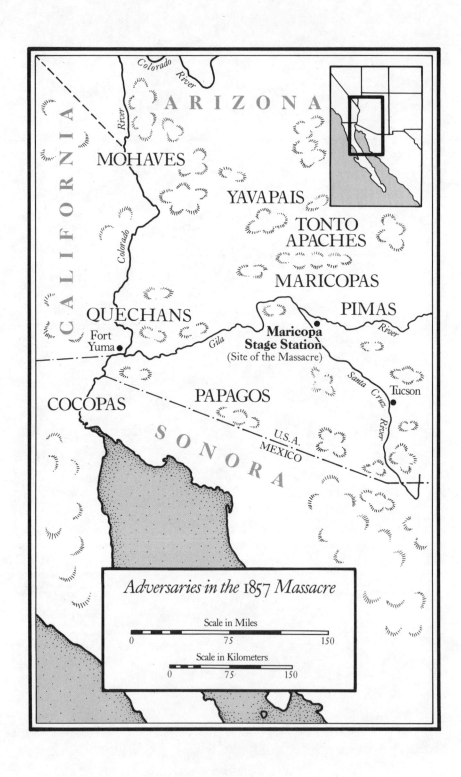

Adversaries in the 1857 Massacre

The Eyewitness

I saiah Churchill Woods swore. It was just daylight, August 31, 1857. And here he was, thirty-six miles north of Tucson, New Mexico Territory, with R. W. Lane, five other men, twelve mules, and a carriage that was a "complete wreck."[1] During the night the perch of the carriage, the pole connecting the fore-gear and hind-gear, had broken and he and his men had spliced it in the dark using mesquite branches and ropes. But in the first gully, at 2:00 A.M., it had broken down again, this time worse than before.

Now, at dawn, they took careful stock of the damage. By taking out one of the standards supporting the top of the carriage and wrapping that and a piece of broken whiffletree tightly with rawhides soaked in water, they managed to get the coach into serviceable condition provided they did not overload it. So Woods left three of his men on the road with mules while he, Lane, and two others nursed their rig to the banks of the Gila River north of Tucson about seventy miles.

All this effort was in behalf of mail service. In 1857 James E. Birch was given a contract to carry United States mail between San Antonio, Texas, and San Diego, California. Birch sent Isaiah Woods to San Antonio as general superintendent of the whole operation. Two years earlier, Woods had been well known as a partner and manager of the San Francisco branch of the Adams express company. Unhappily, both it and the bank failed in the general banking crisis of 1855 and a great many people lost

3

large amounts of money, including $300,000 that was never accounted for. Culpable or not, Woods did nothing to enhance his reputation for honesty when he fled responsibility and criticism by sailing for Australia in September 1855.

Precisely when he returned to the United States is not clear, but by June 1857 he was hired in New York by Birch—a major stockholder in the California Stage Company—to take charge of the fledgling San Antonio and San Diego Mail Line. Woods was, after all, an experienced expressman, and it was that background which had brought him to a camping place alongside the Gila River where he awakened before sunrise, Wednesday morning, September 1, 1857.

The road Woods and his companions followed downstream toward the west skirted the southern edge of the Gila. It had been opened to wagon travel nearly eleven years before, the first time in November 1846 when Gen. Stephen Watts Kearny and his Army of the West, with pack mules and horses to pull two small cannons, moved toward southern Alta California as rapidly as the terrain would allow. They were hurrying to fight Californios in a campaign that was part of the United States and Mexican War. A month later Lieut. Col. Philip St. George Cooke led his battalion of 339 Mormon volunteers over this same part of the route. They, too, were headed for southern California and the war with Mexico. Kearny's march had taken him along a tortuous path paralleling the Gila River down from New Mexico's Gila Mountains. Cooke's pioneering road had come northward from Tucson, joining Kearny's cannon tracks eight miles upstream from the Pima Indian villages.[2]

The Mormon Battalion had fifteen wagons as part of its equipage. One result of the travels of these soldiers was the opening of what three years later came to be called the "Southern Overland Route" to California's gold fields, a wagon trail that tempted thousands of Argonauts to try their skills and luck over its often waterless course. Before wagons, Spanish missionaries, soldiers, and settlers had ridden horseback and walked on foot from Tucson to the Pima settlements and down the Gila to its junction with the Colorado River. And before horses, the same route had been trodden by Indians for countless hundreds or even thousands of years.[3]

By 1857 the route had become sufficiently established to make it a natural for the San Antonio and San Diego Mail Line. The stretch in the vicinity of the Pima villages was pleasant enough. Cottonwoods, common mesquite, and screwbean mesquite lined the river and its tributary drainageways, and in places these larger trees commingled with acacias, both whitethorn and catclaw.

Twelve Indian communities were stretched out for perhaps as many as twenty miles along the Gila, the first ten, or easternmost, being Pima and the two immediately below them belonging to the Maricopas.[4] It was here where natives cultivated the lowlands, where the sand and fine clay had a darker tint than the surrounding earth. There were dozens of small fields, each about one hundred and fifty feet on a side, fenced off by rows of brush and irrigated by a simple but fairly extensive system of ditches. All these fields were barely within, or very near, the river's natural floodplain, a narrow band of cultivation in which wheat, corn, beans, cotton, melons, pumpkins, and other squashes were the most important crops. Pimas wove blankets out of yarn spun from their cotton; both groups raised their own food as well as a surplus for trade.[5]

Isaiah Woods and the others had set off from their campsite that September morning before sunrise. They reached the first Pima village just as daylight warmed its way across the desert. They were greeted by Pimas from whom they bartered corn and a little wheat to feed the mules and beans and a pair of chickens for themselves. Woods paid with cotton cloth and a few bells he had bought in Tucson.

By breakfast the overland mailmen had driven their mended carriage beyond the Pima settlements to a spot known as the Maricopa Wells, situated next to the two Maricopa villages. During the preceding years travelers had used shovels and their own labor to dig several holes from seven to ten feet deep and into which water rose to within two or three feet of the surface. The site was later selected by the mail line for a station, and this watering place on Cooke's wagon road came to be known officially as Maricopa Wells.

Woods looked around as he ate breakfast. Within clear view of the wells, and less than a mile to the east, were two rocky prominences rising a couple of hundred feet above the surrounding plain. These eventually came to be marked on maps as Pima Butte. To the west, between two and three miles away, lay a short, high, and steep-sided range, the Sierra Estrella. Northward, across the Gila, was a long, low-lying string of hills, later to be called South Mountains by residents of Phoenix, Arizona. Closer at hand, and a little downstream, thickets of mesquite and screwbeans grew densely at the junction of the Gila and north-running Santa Cruz River—although it was a rare occasion when the Santa Cruz flowed its way above ground to reach the bed of the Gila. For many miles to the south, the land was flat.

Indeed, this part of the Sonoran Desert was typical of its other regions: a great plain covered with creosote, bursage, salt bushes, and cactus; trees marking the paths of the arroyos and rivers where these channelled gently into the soil; and level vastness interrupted by short, abrupt, and narrow mountain ranges and occasional isolated volcanic hills.[6]

There were other people at the wells. This was the third trip from east to west for the mail line, and company employees, mules, and equipment had been stationed here for more than a month. Isaiah Woods sat down to rest beneath a large mesquite tree and to wait the arrival of the man whom he had assigned as station agent.

Below the place he was sitting, a short way to the north, he noticed a bonfire. Then another, and still another. The burning grass and limbs poured thick white smoke into the morning sky. Signal fires, he thought. But signaling what, no one at the wells seemed to know.

Still more bonfires blazed, each a hundred yards or more from the others. The sound of shouting voices came from the direction of the fires. In the early morning light and through the trees people could be seen running. Then it became clear. The flames were leaping from the Maricopas' dome-shaped brush houses that had been set to the torch. The Maricopas' villages had been attacked by other Indians and a battle was taking place! There was no sound of firearms. The weapons were clubs and bows and arrows. This was Indian versus Indian, and Woods and the others at the wells had a ringside seat.

The mêlée continued for some time. Most of the Maricopa houses in at least one of their two villages were fast burning to the ground. People ran in all directions and shouts and screams became more identifiable. The Indian attackers, who were chiefly Quechans and Mohaves, were on foot. A few Maricopas who had horses managed to mount their steeds and ride full speed in the direction of the upstream Pima villages. One old Maricopa, his hair mostly grey, rode his horse to the wells. He was nearly hysterical, and saliva ran down the sides of his chin as he spoke. He explained in perfectly clear Spanish that his wife had been killed by the attackers. Would the white men, he wanted to know, come help the Maricopas in their struggle? They would not. It was not their fight. They had no wish to provoke the animosity of the Quechans; the road to San Diego passed directly through their territory. Neutrality was the best policy.

Disgusted, the old man turned his mount and rode off toward the east in the direction of the Pima settlements.

There was a lull in the fighting with both sides regrouping. It was a fatal lull for the Quechans and for some of the Mohaves. Other Mohaves as well as Yavapai and Tonto Apache allies elected to leave the field of battle and to return to the north and northwest. The Quechans and a segment of Mohaves, however, lingered to savor their victory, and as they lingered a small army of Pima warriors, many on horseback, joined their Maricopa neighbors in the attack.

The battle was now completely one-sided. A census taken the next year reported 500 Maricopas living in their two villages, "El Juez Tarado" and "Sacaton" in Spanish—probably the places called "Hínămâ" and "Tcóûtcǐk Wútcǐk" by the Pimas. Three hundred of this number were women and children, leaving 200 men capable of bearing arms. And the eight Pima villages were inhabited by 4,000 Pimas, of whom at least 1,000 were potential male warriors.[7]

Whether there were 1,200 Pimas and Maricopas in the field or fewer than half that number, they now had to contend with comparatively few Quechans and Mohaves, 104 of them in Woods' estimation, and all of them on foot. Surprise was no longer on the side of the invaders who had hiked at least one hundred and sixty miles across the desert from their respective homes on the Colorado River. It was now broad daylight; they were tired; and they were surrounded by revenge-seeking Maricopas and their Pima allies. All they could do was stand and fight to the death or attempt to flee for their lives.

What followed was near total annihilation of the Quechan forces, and all the Mohaves died who had stayed to fight. They were lanced, shot with arrows, and clubbed to death. Woods placed the number of survivors at eleven. Other accounts, second hand and perhaps less reliable, put the number at from one to seven. Those who escaped had fled into the rocks of the Sierra Estrella where horses could not follow.

When the battle ended, sometime before three o'clock that afternoon, the old Maricopa who had lost his wife during the dawn attack reappeared. Woods and others spoke to him in Spanish, only now he professed not to understand a word. Why should he, after all, talk with those who had refused him when help had been so desperately needed?

The Maricopas and Pimas were not so preoccupied by that day's battle that they overlooked the fact that the San Antonio and San Diego Mail Line was planning to build a station at the wells. The Indians regarded the grass, water, and surrounding land as theirs. Before Woods departed that day he agreed that when he returned he would discuss with them payment for their protecting the station as well as fees owed for grazing the company's mules on their range.

By 3:00 P.M. the employees who had been left behind on the road from Tucson arrived in camp. The superintendent stationed two men at Maricopa Wells, leaving them with two mules and accoutrements, a few rations, and with a few beads, a little cotton cloth, and a little money for barter. With Lane and two others he then set off for San Diego. They crossed the Colorado River at Fort Yuma on September 5 and arrived safely in San Diego three days later.

Happily for posterity, Isaiah Woods was a highly literate man who kept a day-by-day journal of his trips for the mail line. In March 1858, he sent a report to A. V. Brown, Postmaster General of the United States. It concerned "the United States overland mail route between San Antonio, Texas, and San Diego, California," and consisted for the most part of extracts from his journal. The battle is recounted in two paragraphs:

> September 1 [1857]. —. . .Camped for breakfast at the Maricopa Wells, which we have since selected as the site for our station; remained at the wells until 3 P.M. waiting for our agent to come up whom I yesterday left behind on the road. Finally he came along and we prepared for a start. While camping at the wells I was witness to the largest Indian battle of the times. The Yuma [Quechan] Indians, aided by the Mojaves and Tonta Apaches as their allies, attacked the Maricopas just before daylight this morning. The Maricopas and Pimos are strongly allied together. The former being comparatively few in number, are rather under the protection of the more numerous Pimos. The Maricopas are the more western of the two tribes, and as the Yumas approached from down the river, their villages were consequently the first attacked. Some warriors and their families were killed, and their huts fired before the presence of the Yumas was known. We saw huts blazing and thought they were signal fires. Besides warriors on foot, every Indian that could get a horse was in the fight, many of them going a half dozen miles to reach the battle ground. One aged chief, whose wife had been killed by the Yumas, rode furiously up to our camp, foaming at the mouth, and begged of us in good Spanish to aid them against the Yumas; of course we declined. When the battle was over he refused to speak or understand a word of Spanish.

The principal fight was along the bank of the Gila, not half a mile from our camp. One hundred and four Yumas left their villages at the junction of the Gila and Colorado, led on by a young and ambitious chief, whose new dignity required some striking act to dazzle his people. He and ninety-three of his warriors were killed within an half hour, on the side of a hill in plain view from the spot where I was reclining under a tree.

We started from Maricopa Wells at 3:00 P.M. and drove all night. . . .Made 69 miles today.[8]

ONE

The Battle:
White Men's Versions

Woods left posterity the only eyewitness account of the last major battle fought in the American Southwest between opposing forces made up solely of Indians. He had no reason to reflect, a spectator sitting beneath a tree in what was then southwestern New Mexico, that here was the end of an epoch in the history of humankind. It is likely that for more than 10,000 years the aboriginal peoples of this vast and arid region of the New World—encompassing what is now the southwestern United States and northwestern Mexico—had engaged one another in pitched battles, whether for joy, spirit, territory, food, captives, other booty, or revenge. Then, beside Maricopa Wells on a Wednesday in 1857, it had all come to a close.[1]

True, there were later other skirmishes and raids and more warfare involving Indians of the Southwest. Campaigns against Walapais, Yavapais, Navajos, and Apaches come to mind, struggles that culminated in 1886 with the final surrender of Geronimo. But these events were essentially those involving white men—often with Indian allies—fighting Indians. Or they were battles of a much smaller scale than that represented by this late-summer carnage beside the banks of the Gila River.[2]

Why such an event has gone largely without notice in the annals of American Indian history calls for some explanation. By any standards, the battle was a large one. No mere raid, it was an episode of warfare. There were at least 400 men involved—some say as many as 2,000—and casualties ran high. Any fight that leaves more than eighty human beings dead on the field places it near the top in the rank of bloody frays.

The battle has been generally ignored in spite of its magnitude because it was one of Indian versus Indian. It grew out of ancient enmities that had nothing directly to do with Indians' attitudes toward white men. It seems that no white men took part in the fight; no white men were threatened by the immediate or ultimate outcome; it was simply not a white man's affair.

Coupled with this is the fact that in 1857 the non-Indian settlement nearest the Pima and Maricopa villages was more than eighty miles away in Tucson. There were very few non-Indian witnesses to the battle or to its immediate aftermath and even fewer who ever reduced their knowledge to written form. It was mere coincidence that the San Antonio and San Diego Mail Line had been given an 1857 contract to carry mail between these two cities. Otherwise, Isaiah Woods would not have seen the battle nor have had any reason to file a report of his day-to-day travels. And although the fight took place along the principal overland route to southern California, by 1857 much of the gold fever had subsided and there were fewer emigrants using the wagon road pioneered in 1846 by Lieutenant Colonel Cooke.

The end result seems to be that there are fourteen reports of the battle of 1857 by white men who saw or heard of the event and its aftermath at the time or up to even six years later. Their accounts are uniformly brief, some merely a sentence or two, the longest being only five paragraphs.

Woods' arrival in San Diego on September 8, 1857, was right on schedule. This was no small feat, and the San Diego *Herald* of September 12 paid proper attention:

> The mail that left San Antonio on the 9th of August, arrived here on Wednesday the 8th instant, making the time in just 30 days!!—the time of schedule exactly. What will the abolitionists and other croakers who have opposed this line simply because it comes over the Southern route, say to this? Will they acknowledge, now, the superiority of our route over *all* others? Over what other route across the continent, we would most respectfully ask, can a trip be made in even 50 days? And this mail was brought 1,400 miles in wagons.

The mail party also brought with them an account of the battle that had taken place on the Gila, and the same article in the *Herald* became its first announcement to the public at large:

> The principal item of news is the intelligence of a battle between the Pimos and Maricopas on one side and the Yumas and their allies on the other.
>
> It seems that the Yumas, aided by a few Apaches, Mojaves, and two other tribes who live on the Colorado and its tributaries, came in the early morning to the Maricopa village, which is the most westerly one, burned some huts, destroyed as much corn as they could find, killing one man and two women. The Pimos and Maricopas immediately mounted an attack [*sic*] them, succeeding after several hours fighting in driving them off.—The Pimos reported a loss of 17 on their side and 30 on the part of the Yumas. The mail party saw the fighting and could plainly see the Yumas give way and run up the mountain, where the horsemen of the Maricopas and Pimos could not follow them. One old chief was very anxious the mail party should mount and aid them in driving off the Yumas. The Indians reported 1000 engaged on each side; probably 200 would be a nearer estimate. The Yumas must have made a direct march to the Colorado, as the mail party saw some along the Gila.[3]

This account, a little different from that recorded by Woods in his journal, was probably one given the newspaper by R. W. Lane. Lane was described by the *Herald* as "the pioneer conductor," and it was he who had been in charge of the first lap of the San Diego to San Antonio mail run which had been inaugurated on August 9.

John N. Hinton, an emigrant en route to California, arrived at Maricopa Wells about ten days after the battle had taken place. Forty-nine years later he recalled, "The old chief took us over the battle ground and explained the whole battle in pantomine. The Pimas and Maricopas joined forces and surrounded the Yumas and almost exterminated them."[4]

And at Fort Yuma, on the California side of the Colorado River near which the Quechans had their settlements, official notice was taken of the September 1 conflagration. Captain H. S. Burton, Third Artillery, commander of Fort Yuma, wrote to the California Superintendent of Indian Affairs on September 16:

> . . . Some commotion has existed among the Indians living near the Colorado that indicates trouble among them. Actual hostilities

have commenced among the Yumas, Mohaves, Chimiwagwahs [Chemehuevis], Yumpi [Yavapai], and Tonto Apaches on the one side, and the Pimos, Pa-pa-gos and Maricopas on the other.

. . . between 6 & 700 strong [of the former] attacked the Maricopas.

It seems that the Pimos and Maricopas were advised on the intentions of the Yumas &c. by four *Cocopas*—and met their enemy with 1000 or 1200 warriors.

The Yumas and their friends were totally defeated with great loss.

The Yumas living around the Post lost between 60 & 70 fighting men and the other tribes suffered in proportion.[5]

The Cocopas had long been enemies of the far more numerous Quechans who lived above them on the Colorado River. It is not surprising that Captain Burton heard that Cocopas had had a hand in the defeat of their enemies by the Pimas and Maricopas, although it seems clear from accounts of the mail riders that the Maricopas had indeed been taken by surprise and had not been forewarned of the Quechan and Mohave attack.

News of the battle reached San Francisco before the month was out. That city's *Daily Alta California* ran a story on September 28:

By arrivals in town from the Pimo villages, as well as by the way of San Diego, we learn that quite a serious engagement took place between the Pimo Indians on the one part, and the Yuma and other Colorado river Indians, aided by a number of the Apache tribe. Some time since the Pimo chief sent word to Colonel Burton, U.S.A., in command of Fort Yuma, that his Yuma Indians were becoming insolent, and that he must take care of them, or he (the Pimo) would be compelled to go down and chastise them.

It would appear that this caution was not received by the Yumas, or at all events, it was not heeded, as not long after that the Yumas and other river Indians, with some allied Apaches, entered the Pimo country, and killed some women and children.

As soon as the alarm was given, the Pimos were called to arms, and mounting hastily pursued the intruders. On overtaking them, a fight commenced which led to an action, seldom equaled in Indian warfare. It is reported that 150 or 160 of the allied Indians, being nearly or quite the entire party, were left dead on the field. The Pimos lost some 25 men in the battle.[6]

By the time the story reached San Francisco, the Maricopas, the real objective in the Quechan and Mohave attack, had been filtered out of the account.

The San Antonio and San Diego Mail Line agent at Maricopa Wells forwarded a report on the battle to his company's office in San Diego through the company rider. He arrived in San Diego on September 30, and on October 3 the *Herald* published an account:

> Despatches received from the Company's agent, at the Maricopa Wells, are full and more accurate than any previous information we have received of this Indian fight. . . .
>
> At the time of making this inroad, the Yumas and their allies, the Mojaves, appropriated the corn and melons stored by the Maricopas, indeed, whatever property they could find, attempting to secure it on their retreat, but when the pursuit became hot they scattered everything along the road, intending to destroy it, but much was afterwards secured and gathered by the Maricopa squaws.
>
> It is said there were two hundred Mojaves in the fight, who deserted the Yumas before the fighting really commenced. A great peculiarity in the mode of warfare practiced by the Pimos and Maricopas, is the fact of their not scalping their enemies, as is the custom with nearly all the wild Indian tribes of this country. It seems from the best information we can obtain, that they cut off a small lock of hair from such enemies as are killed in battle.
>
> One custom prevails among the Maricopas and Pimos, the same as we stated last week respecting the Yumas, namely, that they destroy all the property of the warriors killed in battle, as indeed they do of those dying naturally. This custom is a religious one: they consider the warrior will need his horse, his bow and arrows, and some food, until he can hunt or raise corn by planting, also his clothing and ornaments, as much in the next world as he did in this. . . . From all accounts it would appear that this battle, in which the Maricopas and their allies the Pimos so bravely defended their homes, destroying nearly the whole force which came into battle against them is the largest Indian fight which has occurred in this region for many years.[7]

On November 10, 1857, Lieut. Sylvester Mowry sent a report to the Commissioner of Indian Affairs in Washington, D.C. He had been sent to the area acquired by the United States from Mexico as a result of the 1848 Treaty of Guadalupe Hidalgo and the 1854 Gadsden Purchase to give an account of the region's Indians. His dispatch to the Commissioner noted that the "late battle between the Pimos, their allies the Papagos, and Maricopas; and the Indians of the Colorado River combined with the Apaches, is probably the greatest Indian battle fought on the Continent for many years past." He continued:

The following account of the fight is from a letter received by me from an Officer of the 3rd Artillery now at Fort Yuma.

"Fort Yuma Sep: 16. 1857.

"The Yumas have been most dreadfully beaten by the Maricopas, Pimos, and others. They have lost not less than *two hundred* of the flower of their chivalry. The opposing parties were, on one side, the Yumas, Mohaves, Yampais [Yavapais], and Tonto Apaches; and one or two Dieganos [Diegueños]; on the other, the Maricopas, Pimos, and Papagos.

"The former party commenced the attack, by burning some wigwams, and killing women and children belonging to the Maricopas. The great battle was fought near the Maricopa wells. (About 160 miles above the mouth of the Gila). There were probably about fifteen hundred engaged on each side. The Yumas and allies were completely routed.

"We have not heard full accounts and know nothing of the losses of any tribe except the Yumas. Scarce one of them was left to tell the story: in fact, they knew nothing of the affair until we told them. We learned it from the Texas mail party. All the Yumas are in mourning.

Another letter says: "The Yumas and Mohave suffered severely. Our old friend, Soll Francisco, who acted as our agent in rescuing Olive D'Otman [Olive Oatman] from the Mohaves, a year since, was killed. Out of about one hundred Yumas who went to battle, only some six or seven returned."[8]

On November 25, 1857, twenty-four-year-old Silas St. John arrived at Maricopa Wells with a herd of stock for the San Antonio and San Diego Mail Line. He continued to work for the overland mail company until October 1, 1859, when he became United States Indian agent for the Pimas and Maricopas. St. John spent most of the rest of his life in Arizona, and in 1912—stout and still looking hale and hearty—he was Assistant Superintendent of the Home for Aged and Infirm Pioneers in Prescott, Arizona.

Probably that same year, someone interviewed St. John or perhaps he wrote down his own reminiscences. Either way, there is a manuscript in Sharlot Hall Museum in Prescott which includes his version of the battle:

. . . The invaders were estimated to number from 250 to 400 warriors—about one half Yumas and the rest Tonto and Mohave Apaches, with a few Cocopas. . . . They had reached the western end of the valley in which are situated the villages of the Pimas and Maricopas unobserved, and at early daylight of the morning of November 23d the force deployed to surround the westernmost village.

It is supposed that one of the Cocopas—who are closely related to the Maricopa managed to convey intelligence of the intended raid to the Maricopas—enabling them to prepare for the fight; and nearly one thousand mounted warriors were in the saddle surrounding the enemy before they reached the village.

The valley at this point was at that time covered with a heavy growth of mesquite under the cover of which the defending forces gathered unobserved, as the invaders failed to send out new scouts. At the north end was "Candela"—a veteran war chief with about 300 men. Next came "Cuchillo del Mundo" with a force of about 400—these all Pimas, while south of the line were about 300 Maricopas under "Juan Echevaria." All of these were mounted. As they rode out into the open the invading force was panic struck; turning to retreat they covered nearly two miles as they were strung out. The mounted force rode down on them in an enfilading movement—thus covering nearly the whole line; doing fearful execution with their battle clubs. . . . Those who reached the Estrella mountain escaped by ascending the precipitous rocks where the horsemen could not follow.

There were no fatal casualties to the Pimas and Maricopas; a few arrow and lance wounds—none very serious. The battle lasted less than half an hour, and was the last raid made by predatory tribes upon these semi-civilized Indians. Antonio Azul was then chief of the Pimas, but as he was only twenty-five years of age the command was taken over by the older and experienced subchiefs.[9]

Starting from Fort Yuma in January 1858, Lieut. Joseph C. Ives led a United States surveying party up the Colorado River. He took on board his boat a Quechan named "Capitan," a "young chief who had signalized himself by escaping unhurt" from the 1857 battle. Because he had been on the river in 1853, Ives was well acquainted with the Mohaves, including subchiefs Yara tav and Cairook. Based on what he heard from them, from Capitan, and no doubt from others at Fort Yuma, he offered a version of the Gila River fight:

> . . . The Yumas . . . prepared for a secret attack upon the Pimas' and Maricopas' villages. They notified the Mojave of their intention, and a large number of picked Mojave warriors united themselves to the party. The intended victims of the enterprise had meanwhile—through the offices, as is supposed, of the Cocopas—got wind of the meditated attack, and not only mustered the whole of their own force to repel it, but obtained assistance from the Papagos—a warlike tribe living within the province of Sonora. It was in the month of September, 1857, that the invading force, numbering between one hundred and one hundred fifty of the most distinguished Yuma and Mojave warriors, set out for the Pima villages, under the guidance of a prominent and ambitious Yuma chief. They held no suspicion that their movement was anticipated, and the unprotected appearance of the first village they entered convinced them that they had been successful in effecting an entire surprise. The few inhabitants that were sauntering about fled in apparent terror, and were hotly pursued. The attacking party followed them beyond the entrance of a small cañon, where they suddenly found themselves surrounded by an overpowering force. They attempted to fly, but finding that impossible, fought bravely to the last. The advantages of position and numbers were, however, altogether against them, and rendered resistance hopeless. The contest lasted less than an hour. Out of the whole number of assailants, only three or four escaped to carry to these tribes the bitter tale of discomfiture.
>
> The moral effect of the defeat will long be felt. The very name of a Pima or Maricopa now inspires the Yumas and Mojaves with chagrin and dread. . . .
>
> The Mojaves preserve constant friendly relations with the Chemehuevis and Yumas, and were allied with the latter in the attack upon the Pimas and Maricopas, last September. At that time they lost one of their five chiefs and a great many of their best warriors. The Cocopa Indians they bitterly hate, and make forays into their country, slaying and taking prisoners. The unwarlike habits of that tribe have not permitted them to offer much resistance to these incursions, but they avenged themselves by giving warning to the Pimas, which resulted in the wholesale slaughter of the attacking force. The animosity of the Mojaves against the Cocopas has

been raised to the highest pitch by the disaster which befell the war party from this intervention of their despised foes. [10]

What transpired on the battlefield that day left grisly remains in its wake. And the engagement should be added permanently to the list of Indian massacres, for a massacre is what occurred.

Emigrant John Hinton wrote, "We found ninety corpses lying in one spot. There was but one out of the 100 Yumas lived to get back to Fort Yuma. These bodies were lying in all positions. It was a little over a week after the battle took place, but there was no stench from the bodies; they seemed to be drying up." [11]

The station agent left at the wells by Woods ". . . went over the battle ground himself, and counted fifty-five dead Yumas along the road, pierced full of arrows." The San Diego *Herald* of October 3, 1857, went on to elaborate:

> The Pimos and the Maricopas leave their dead enemies to the crows and coyotes, religiously refusing to touch the bodies, but allowing them to be exactly in the place and position they fell. They have the same scruples respecting all the property belonging to them, so that the bows and arrows and other implements of warfare, together with their clothing, such little as they had, were untouched on the dead bodies of the Yumas. [12]

California-bound James Hamilton camped within a few hundred yards of the site less than two months after the battle. "The bones, hair, and arrows," he told his wife in a letter, "are strewed all along for two miles." [13] And mail company employee Silas St. John later recalled, "Seventy-two corpses lined the trail when I visited it on the 25th [of November, 1857]—all with their skulls crushed." [14]

Major Enoch Steen, commanding at Fort Buchanan near the United States and Mexican boundary, wrote on November 2, 1857, that "these Indians [Pimas and Maricopas] were attacked by the Yumas and two other tribes living on the Colorado and Salt Rivers.—In the fight they killed Eighty nine of the Yumas." Steen recommended that the Pimas and Maricopas be given 500 rifles, 2,000 pounds of powder, and 5,000 pounds of lead that they might be enabled to improve their fighting against "the Gila Apaches." [15]

Captain John C. Cremony was with a unit of California Volunteers when he visited Maricopa Wells in 1862. He reported "the ground was strewed with the skulls and bones of slaughtered warriors."[16] A fellow member of the California Volunteers, George Washington Oaks, said "there were plenty of skeletons scattered around. Old Paulino Weaver, who was our guide from Fort Yuma, had helped the Maricopas in this fight a few years before and told us about it. He said only one or two Yumas got back to the Colorado."[17] And two years afterward, John Ross Browne was there. He wrote for *Harper's New Monthly Magazine* that "the bones of seventy-two Yuma warriors still moulder on the plain," making one suspect this part of St. John's "reminiscence" was based on a reading of Browne's account.[18]

Regardless of the exact numbers of dead, it is clear that the river and desert next to Maricopa Wells had been turned into a charnel house. The effects of the battle on the losers were devastating. At least sixty and perhaps as many as one hundred and fifty able-bodied Quechan men—to say nothing of the Mohaves—were killed in the engagement. This is a sizeable proportion of adult males in a tribe whose total population was no greater than three thousand. The Quechan attackers had been all but wiped out.

More than six months after the battle, Lieutenant Ives tried to enlist the aid of Mohave warrior Yara tav as a guide for his surveying expedition, but "when he learned that we might have to pass through the villages of the Maricopas, on the return route, he positively refused; making no secret of his terror at the idea of encountering any members of that tribe. I told him we could protect him, but he thinks if they could slaughter so easily a hundred of the best Yuma and Mohave warriors, our little party would stand a poor chance against them."[19]

The battle on the Gila was over, but the memory of it would survive. Sylvester Mowry said it best: "The Pimos have . . . inflicted a blow upon their enemies which their children and their children's children shall recount and mourn around the camp fire."[20]

TWO

The Battle:
Indians' Versions

They called him Tcókŭt Nak, "Owl Ear." His long hair, partially braided, hung slightly below his shoulders, held back from his face by a piece of cloth rolled into a headband. He wore a long-sleeved shirt, four-button vest, and white man's trousers, typical clothing for a Pima elder living on the Salt River Indian Reservation in the early twentieth century. He sat on a wooden chair holding a four-foot-long, notched stick between the thumb and forefinger of his right hand. Each notch represented a calendar year.

Tcókŭt Nak raked his thumbnail across a notch, and began speaking in Pima, "This notch means. . . ." And he went on to recount that year's outstanding event as determined by tradition. Jacob Roberts, another Pima, took the stick from him and stuck his thumb into the same notch before translating the story into English. Frank Russell, a thirty-three-year-old anthropologist, wrote down the English words as Roberts spoke them.[1]

Owl Ear was a keeper of the stick, one of the very few still surviving among the Pima Indians when they were visited by Russell between 1901 and 1902. The young ethnographer, in fact, had been able to find only five such sticks, and, of those, two were "told" to him by their possessors. These calendar sticks had rudimentary characters incised on them, each year's characters separated by a notch. To the keeper of the stick, these

were mnemonic devices, indentations to help him recall by touch the
events for a particular twelve-month period.

Owl Ear's stick began in 1833—34, and for each year he recited various
accounts: raids, warfare, meteoric showers, hunts, successful harvests,
floods, and horse thefts. Then he came to 1857—58. Roberts translated;
Russell wrote:

> In the summer the Yumas came again, accompanied by the Mohaves.
> They sent scouts ahead, who found the Maricopa women gathering
> mesquite beans. They killed all the women except one, whom they
> kept to act as a guide. She was the sister of a well-known Maricopa
> warrior, and they compelled her to lead them to her brother's home.
> When they reached it she was killed with a club and the man was
> chased, but he was as good a runner as he was a fighter and they
> could not catch him. A Yuma told him to stop and die like a man,
> but he answered that if they could overtake him he would show them
> how to die like a man. The Maricopas fled from their village and the
> Yumas burned it. Messengers went to all the villages that day and
> under cover of the night the Pimas and Maricopas gathered. They
> kept coming until late the next forenoon. They found the Yumas
> encamped near the river at a spot where they had assaulted some
> women and a Pima had been killed while defending them. The
> Yumas had spent the night in singing their war songs. Now and
> again a medicine-man would come forward to puff whiffs of smoke
> in order that their cause might find favor with the gods. The Pima-
> Maricopa council ended about noon and it was decided to surround
> the Yumas and to make special effort to prevent them from reaching
> the river to obtain water. Formed in a semicircle, the Pimas and
> Maricopas shot down the Yumas upon three sides. Soon the Yumas
> began to waver and become exhausted from thirst in the heat of the
> day. They made several attempts to break through the line, but
> failed, and finally gathered in a compact body to make a last attempt
> to reach the river. At that moment the Pimas and Maricopas who
> were on horseback rushed in upon the enemy and rode them down.
> After a hand-to-hand combat the Yumas were all killed except one,
> who was stunned by the blow of a club and lay unconscious under a
> heap of dead. During the night he recovered his senses and escaped.
> This was the bloodiest fight known, and the Yumas came here to
> fight no more.[2]

Although Owl Ear was certainly alive in 1857 when the battle took
place, nowhere in Russell's book about the Pima Indians is it suggested

that he personally had been involved or had been an eyewitness to the event. Several facts, however, make his version noteworthy. The first is that it was carefully written down by an experienced field recorder, Frank Russell, and that it was told—presumably by rote memory—with the aid of a calendar stick. Regardless of whether Owl Ear learned the story from a previous keeper of the same stick or from someone else, he lived on the Salt River Reservation east of Phoenix, Arizona, where there was a community of Maricopa (Halchidhoma) Indians, many of whom almost certainly had taken an active role in the fight.[3] Finally, Owl Ear's story was written within forty-four years of the event, making it the earliest recorded full-blown Indian description of the excitement of that day. It was not, fortunately, the last such description.

In 1929, anthropologist Leslie Spier worked among the Maricopas, learning from them as much as he could about their history and aboriginal culture. He discovered, among other things, that the Indians called Maricopa were in reality a composite of several Yuman-speaking groups of Indians who in former times had lived on the Colorado River and along the lowest reaches of the Gila. These groups had been driven from these earlier homes, starting in the late eighteenth century, by those other Yuman speakers, the Quechans and Mohaves. By 1857, all of the former— the Maricopa proper, the Halchidhoma, the Kohuana, the Kaveltcadom, and Halyikwamai—had apparently consolidated themselves into the two Maricopa settlements immediately downstream from the Pima villages on the Gila.[4]

Just as a few Pimas had done, some Maricopas had kept calendar sticks. In 1929–30, the sole remaining example was in the hands of an elderly man whose father was Kaveltcadom and whose mother was Kohuana. He had begun to keep the record in 1873–74, having learned the earlier events from another Maricopa of mixed heritage, an old man who lived on the Salt River Indian Reservation. As Spier discovered, the account of 1857–58 was brief: "The Yuma came to Sacate to fight." Sacate was another name for one of the two Maricopa towns.[5]

Spier's principal informant, a man named Kutox, was born about 1848 near Maricopa Wells. "The second time the Yumas came here," he told Spier, "I was about nine years old [1857]. I can remember it pretty well." And he continued:

There were about three hundred Yuma with a few Yavapai and Mohave. We heard them coming early in the morning. All our women and children fled to *viva'vis* [Pima Butte; literally, "solitary mountain"]. This time the Yuma and Mohave did not push on, but stopped at the first house of the village. Some were sent to the houses to collect all the food stored in them. Then they prepared something to eat, since they had come without eating. They remained there all morning.

Our men then tried to scare them away. But instead of retreating the Yuma advanced. The Maricopa of this village sent for the Halchidhoma and Pima again. Then the two parties clashed. But when the Yuma saw the horsemen arriving one by one, lines of them converging on the battle, they thought they were lost. At noon they fled. This time, instead of forcing the Yuma down the river, the allies drove them south [southwest?] to the mountains [Sierra Estrella?]. The slain lay in piles, struck down as they fled. Only a few were left. These went on southward until they almost reached the foot of the mountains. The Maricopa left it to a few clubmen to finish these Yuma, but when they saw they might escape, the horsemen ran them down, so that those with clubs could beat them to death. Not one escaped this time.

Six years after this they made peace. I was sixteen years old then.[6]

In 1921, Edward Winslow Gifford, a University of California anthropologist, visited the Yuma Indian Reservation. One of the Quechans with whom he spoke was Joe Homer. Homer provided Gifford with an account of the 1857 holocaust, the earliest Quechan version in print. It was told to Homer by an old man in 1916. Homer, moreover, insisted that the Cocopas had no involvement in the Yumas' defeat, that the Maricopas and Pimas had been solely responsible. His discussion of the entire affair concludes with a description of the battle:

. . They journeyed for nine days before they reached the Maricopa camp. Just before dawn they attacked the Maricopa. They killed many of them but some escaped. The war party remained all day at the Maricopa camp. Those Maricopa who escaped carried messages to the other Maricopa and to the Pima. Meanwhile the Mohave and Yuma who had suffered from hunger, thirst, and fatigue on the journey, remained at the Maricopa village to enjoy the maize and blackeyed beans of the Maricopa.

Meanwhile the Maricopa and Pima gathered their forces. The Mohave took the maize and beans which they had cooked and crossed the Gila river, following the track of the escaped Maricopa.

The Yuma followed them without much food. On the south bank of the Gila, at a place called Avivava [Pima Butte], they were met by the Maricopa and Pima forces. The Maricopa began the attack. Later the Pima who were mounted and had rifles joined them.

The Maricopa leader stood in the middle of the line and asked: "Which of you are the Yuma?" Apparently he could not distinguish Yuma from Mohave. The Algodones man [i.e., a Quechan from Algodones] said: "I am here, to the right of the Mohave. I am a Yuma." The Maricopa approached close to the Yuma troops and pulled out one man, whom they stabbed to death with a steel bladed spear. Then followed club and spear fighting between the Maricopa and Yuma who fell dead in pairs. The Maricopa tried to drive out the Yuma but they stood their ground, determined to die rather than yield. "Do not bother the Mohave," the Maricopa said, "let's settle with the Yuma." Most of the Mohave ran away, only a few who stayed with the Yuma and died. All but seven of the Yuma were killed. Most of the fighting was between the Maricopa and Yuma rather than the Pima and the Yuma.

After the fight the Maricopa cried for their relatives, while the Pima clubbed the wounded Yuma. Two of the Yuma who escaped climbed a mountain near Maricopa station. They stayed there in hiding. In the evening five wounded men joined them. Meanwhile the Maricopa continued to mourn for their dead.

During the battle the Pima had avoided hand-to-hand fights, such as the Maricopa and Yuma engaged in. With their horses and rifles, however, they cut off the retreat of the Yuma. There are said to have been ninety or one hundred Yuma in this expedition. Among the slain was the Algodones man who was responsible for the expedition. No attempt was made on the part of the Pima and Maricopa to prevent the return of the seven fugitives, for they wished them to return and tell the Yuma what had happened.[7]

After the Quechans, the losers with the biggest stake in the outcome of the battle were the Mohaves. In 1925, Alfred L. Kroeber put a Mohave version in print:

The last great fight of the Mohave occurred in 1857 or 1858, a short time after their successful raid against the Cocopa, the celebration of which has been described. The same five leaders were at the head of this more disastrous expedition, which was directed against their hereditary foe, the Maricopa. The Mohave, in a party whose numbers are not exactly known but estimated by themselves at about 200,

were joined at Avi-kwa-hasala by 82 Yuma and a considerable body
of Yavapai and a contingent from a more remote tribe whom the
Mohave call *Yavapaya-hwacha*, "traveling" or "nomadic Yavapai,"
and the description of whose appearance and manners exactly fits the
Apache. The Maricopa summoned the Hatpa or Pima, "a large
tribe of many villages," as the Mohaves found to their cost. The
battle took place at Avi-vava [Pima Butte] in an open plain. The
Apache fought fiercely for a time but fled when things turned against
them, and escaped without a fatality. The Yavapai followed but lost
seven. The majority of warriors of these tribes were probably
mounted, whereas the river nations [Mohaves and Quechans] fought
on foot. A part of the Mohave and all the Yuma were surrounded
and exterminated after a most determined hand-to-hand fight. Sixty
Mohave fell and 80 of the 82 Yuma—Humara-va'ache and
Kwasanya being the only survivors of the latter. The Yuma refused to
flee and stood in a dense mass. When the foe charged, they attempted to grasp and drag him into their body, where he was hacked
to pieces with great knives. [8]

Mohaves told Kroeber that it took eight days for their survivors to get
home from Pima Butte, one night spent sleeping in Maricopa country, five
in Yavapai country, and one in Walapai lands before reaching home in the
Mohave Valley. [9] The straight-line distance is about one hundred and sixty
miles, much farther on foot. And it is all desert.

The Quechans and the Mohaves had not been the only losers. There
were Northeastern Yavapai, Southeastern Yavapai, and Western Yavapai
who also had gone home in defeat from the Pima Butte battleground.
These three Yavapai groups, clearly recognized as such by the natives
themselves, used and occupied distinct tribal territories in west-central
Arizona. All spoke mutually intelligible dialects of the same language. All
Yavapais were friendly toward one another, even as they were hostile
toward the Maricopa and Pima.

Again it was anthropologist E. W. Gifford who collected a version of
the fight from a member of one of the losing groups. In late December
1929 and early January 1930 Gifford spoke with seventy-year-old Michael
Burns, a Southeastern Yavapai. Burns told Gifford that no Yavapai then
living had taken part in the 1857 battle and that he had learned about it
from his mother's brother who had been a participant. Gifford summarized the story:

Some time before the Yuma-Mohave campaign against the
Maricopa, the Maricopa had sent 100 of their men against the
Yuma. None returned. The Maricopa therefore looked forward to a
raid by the Yuma, so that they might avenge their kinsmen.

Now the opportunity had arrived. With the Yuma were their
allies, the Mohave, the Yavapai (of all three tribes), and certain
Apache. [The informant placed the scene of action near Laveen and
the time in the afternoon. Actually, it was near Pima Butte, between
the Gila and Santa Cruz rivers.] The Yuma and Mohave were
anxious to press on ahead of their Yavapai allies in the hope of
surprising and slaughtering the Maricopa without Yavapai aid. In
the morning the allies had destroyed two Maricopa camps. During
the fray some of the Yavapai were wounded.

The Yuma warriors numbered 40, the Mohave 75 or 80, and the
Yavapai 1500 [*sic*]. Opposed to them were Maricopa, Pima, Papago,
and Mexicans, the last armed with guns.

In the afternoon action the Mohave, Yavapai, and Apache took
fright and climbed Pima Butte (the Avivava of the Yuma and
Maricopa). The reason for this debâcle was that their vanguard
mistook their rearguard for enemies and were seized with panic,
thinking they were about to be surrounded. They therefore fled up
the hill and did not attempt to reenter the battle to help the Yuma,
who were surrounded.

Perhaps their panic was in part induced by evil omens in the
morning, for when the Yavapai warriors were marching down to the
battlefield, a deer fell down before them on the desert, bleeding from
its mouth and nose without having been shot. This was an omen of
disaster and some turned back. The mastava [leader] said cowards
should go home, but the remainder should go on. At the river a
hawk fell dead before the warriors, and still others turned back.

The Yuma warriors wore distinctive war paint, so that the
Maricopa had no difficulty in recognizing them. Their faces were
painted black, their bodies red. The Mohave were painted dif-
ferently. The Yuma had long hair adorned with feathers, and wore
red calico around the waist. They were all large handsome men. The
Yavapai went into battle nearly naked, wearing only the breech clout
and no leggings. Very few were painted. The mastava alone wore
eagle feathers.

The Maricopa killed all but one of the Yuma warriors. He was
struck on the head with a club, wielded by a mounted Maricopa.

The blow knocked him into the waters of the Gila, down which he floated to safety. The battlefield was named by the Maricopa to commemorate the annhilation of the Yuma.

No Yavapai were killed, but some were wounded, though apparently very few participated. The wounded lay on the battlefield until dark, then slipped away. Meanwhile, their comrades arrived home and reported them dead. Their houses and property were burned at once and mourning commenced. In two or three days these wounded men arrived to the astonishment of all.[10]

Many accounts include Apache Indians among those who attacked the Maricopas, but there are no known Apache versions of the battle. It is clearly documented that various bands of the Western Apache tribe were frequent raiders of the Pima villages, and since by the mid-nineteenth century the Maricopas and Pimas had become allies, the former became involved in Apache warfare as well.

There is no reason to doubt that at least a few Apaches may have been present at the battle on the Gila. The Tonto Apaches were the immediate neighbors of the northernmost band of Southeastern Yavapai; the eastern neighbors of a second Southeastern Yavapai band were the San Carlos Apaches. Many Tonto Apaches were part Yavapai in blood. Even though Yavapai and Apache are wholly unrelated languages, many members of both groups were bilingual. Yavapais and Western Apaches are known to have fought together against Chiricahua Apaches, Pimas, Papagos, and Americans. They could well have fought side by side on September 1, 1857.[11]

If there are no surviving oral traditions among Western Apaches concerning the battle, the event has not been altogether forgotten among modern Pimas and Maricopas. Pima Indian Anna Moore Shaw in 1968 published a version in a collection of Pima "legends." The protagonist in her story, interestingly enough, is the Quechan instigator of the attack, "Chief Hawk." And her version also depicts a much more formalized battle than the versions of anyone else:

As the Yumas neared the first village, they met three squaws whom they recognized as Maricopas. Since their language was somewhat similar, the Yuma chief asked, "Where are you going so early in the morning? Tell us where we may find your brave warriors."

The women were afraid and ran for safety. "We're going out to gather mesquite beans. The warriors are over there," called one of the women over her shoulder, pointing toward the first village.

Some of the Yuma warriors chased the women, who ran as fast as they could and disappeared into the dense mesquite growth.

A Maricopa warrior who had awakened early was outside tending to the baby while the mother was cooking breakfast; noticing the cloud of dust made by the invading Yuma tribe, he ran, carrying his child, to warn the nearest Pima village with shouts of "Enemy! Enemy!"

When the Pimas heard the warning, they sent a young brave on his fastest pony to relay the warning to the Pimas living further up the Gila Valley. The news spread like wildfire. It did not take long for the Maricopa and Pima warriors to come full speed on their ponies to meet the invading Yuma warriors.

The women and children ran to the nearest mountain for safety.

When the opposing tribes gathered at the place where the battle was to take place, the Pimas through the interpretation of a Maricopa warrior agreed to fight according to a plan proposed by the Yuma chief.

Two straight lines were marked on the ground about three feet apart, one by each of the opposing chiefs. Then they placed their men on the lines facing each other, the Yuma warriors, armed with bows and arrows, on their ponies. The agreement was that each force was to remain on its side of the marked lines.

When everyone was ready, the warriors struck at each other with their weapons. The swift arrows of the Pimas and Maricopas proved too much for the Yuma warriors and one by one they fell to the ground. In the din of battle the lines were soon forgotten, and warriors were running all over the battlefield.

Soon only a handful of Yuma warriors remained. Chief Hawk bravely stood his ground with the help of his brave young son who snatched some of the flying arrows and used the bow of a fallen Pima warrior to shoot back at the Pimas.

Finally father and son fell at the hands of the Pimas whom they had come to conquer. The handful of Yumas who were left ran toward the east end of Komatke Mountain for safety, but were quickly run down by the Pima warriors on their ponies. One survivor alone escaped, and he returned home by swimming down the Gila River. He told his people about the terrible battle.

Thus did the haughty chief meet his tragic end along with his son and his noble warriors.[12]

Luke Perchero, a Maricopa who was seventy-eight years old when he spoke into a tape recorder in September 1970, had heard about the battle and was willing to share his knowledge with posterity:

> . . . And then the Yumas came over to fight. . . . They came over, but they gonna get killed. And the Mohaves, they coming this way, too. And they meet together somewhere and they don't know each others and fight. Not the Maricopas. But they fight with Mohaves.
>
> Well, they line up, Maricopas, they line up. They waiting for them to come. They line up and they come. And the chief had to speak, you know, to them, whatever they gonna do to them, because this Maricopa in this dream he saw everything already. They gonna get ready for these . . . Yumas. So they did. They use bow and arrow and some using sticks, you know, and they fight right there.
>
> Then the Yumas began to go off from the place. It's a lot of brush and everything they have to go under there, and people just shoot them with bow and arrow. Then just a few more, then some got a horse, you know, then they went through and got them all. And then four of them [Quechans] left. So he's going to let them go, go home to tell the people what they done with them. So they let 'em go, four of 'em. . . .
>
> Well, that's what I heard from there, you know. These Yumas, from there, they don't fight no more, and some people from here they get married there and we have some women here, too, around here now. So I don't want to bring this up. They might fight again [laughter]. That's all I have. [13]

Another elderly Maricopa spoke of the battle in 1970. She was Ida Redbird, a woman who had been one of Leslie Spier's informants in 1929 and who later became a regionally renowned potter. [14] Before she died in the 1970s, like Luke Perchero she left a tape-recorded account for others to share:

> [The Quechans came] from Yuma, and then the Mohaves from Parker. . . . And it's always on a stormy, rainy night when they know that everybody would be in their home. And so that's how it happened. They all came.
>
> And somehow someone heard them coming. They said it made a lot of noise, though. So he went and investigated and here they were, all just coming down. And so he sent out the warning to the people and they all got out and took their children and they all ran for safety. And when all the men gathered in a group, waiting for them,

and so they started fighting. And then word was sent to the Pimas over in Casa Blanca, and so here they come. And then another word was sent on to Blackwater and places like that [i.e., Pima villages], you know. And here they were coming and it was almost daylight when these people were coming in, coming in, and so they know they gonna be just all killed and the Mohaves backed out and they all dropped off and went home. And so that left just the Yumas alone. And they were fighting, fighting. And about noon they were still coming on horseback. Oh, these Pimas were just riding down!

And so they knew that they were going to all be killed. So they drifted down . . . right there where that Gila River is. And then, of course, the bank was kind of high. They all dropped down and they all raced on, raced on. And then these Pimas with their horses just went over them, knocked them down, clubbed them down and all that until just about four of them. The understanding was that only four of them were left alive. Then they went back.

And then, during that time when the warning was sent out, why my grandchildren's great-grandmother was getting out. Instead of getting out, well, she was gathering some stuff that they thought they might take it. So she went out and just right then at the doorway she was taken a prisoner. So they carried her down with them. And then a Pima went and shot her, thinking that it was an enemy, I guess. But then they got some men to tend to her, so she was all right then, you know. She suffered but then she was all right after.[15]

In August and September 1970, anthropologist Nicholas Houser visited the Fort Yuma Reservation at Winterhaven, California, in what proved to be essentially a vain attempt to collect tape-recorded accounts of the 1857 battle from elderly Quechans. He talked with six people, and while they spoke of battles, enmities with Cocopas and Maricopas, omens, and of many other things, no one offered precise details of the final battle in which so many of their forebears had been killed. Whether this indicates the battle and its painful consequences has been pushed out of tribal memory or if it means simply that Houser failed to interview the right people or to ask the right questions we have no way of knowing. It is possible the people with whom he spoke were not descendants of the Algodones Quechans and therefore had little interest in the affair. In any case, we are left with no succinct modern version of the battle on the Gila as related by Quechans.[16]

Perhaps one of the most vivid "Indian" accounts of the battle is a fictionalized version written by Alfred L. Kroeber. It is clearly based on the story of the fight published by Kroeber in the *Handbook of the Indians of California*, and reprinted on pages 25–26 of this book. But it is also based on Kroeber's extensive knowledge of Mohave warfare, history, and other aspects of Mohave culture.

In this tale, "Earth-tongue" is the Mohave hero. Kroeber takes him through virtually all the stages of his life in this biography of a composite, make-believe Mohave man, one who had been an important warrior among his people. In his later years, Earth-tongue became active as a curer. Kroeber writes:

> Fighting interrupted these [curing] pursuits. It was a summons from the Yuma, this time against the Maricopa; and two hundred of the Mohave responded. The seventh night they were on Maricopa soil and met eighty Yuma by appointment; and in the morning advanced to attack. But the Maricopa had got wind of their presence, and when the fight opened were reënforced by a vast number of the Pima. The Mohave and Yuma exhorted one another, and though man after man fell, gave ground slowly, fighting back outnumbered
>
> At last the enemy ran all in a body against them. Part of the Mohave broke before the shock and fled to the north, ultimately escaping. But sixty of them formed with the Yuma on a little knoll near the Gila, where they stood in a dense mass. As the Pima and Maricopa dashed against them, they dragged man after man struggling into their midst, where he was dispatched with fierce club blows on his head or thrusts into his face. Twice, Earth-tongue leaped out to grasp an opponent and fling him over his back, thus protecting his own skull, while his companions beat the struggling foe to death. The fighting grew wilder. The Pima no longer drew back to shoot but swirled incessantly around and into the dwindling cluster at bay. At last the shouts ceased; the dust began to settle; and all but two of the Yuma, and every man of the sixty Mohave, lay with crushed head or mangled body on foreign earth.[17]

THREE

Armed Conflict: Conceptions, Personnel, & the Warpath

Anthropologist Anthony Wallace has written: "War is the sanctioned use of lethal weapons by members of one society against members of another."[1]

It is, of course, much more than that. The waging of war involves highly ritualized behavior. There are prescribed codes of dress for the warriors; there are norms of ideally prescribed actions, certain minimum and maximum limits being set on the ways in which the ultimate goal of warfare—that is, winning—can properly be achieved; there is a leadership structure that is unique to that aspect of society. So does each culture offer its own conceptions of armed conflict, classifying it in such categories as "pitched battles," "raiding," and "warfare." War also has its supernatural side. *"Gott mit uns"* or "no heathens in the foxholes" are typical slogans. War, after all, is usually a matter of life or death.

Each society has its own rules governing war, with no two sets being precisely the same. Such rules partially are the products of tradition, environment, technology, the lessons of history (past successes or failures), demography, and of more general values held by most members of the society. To understand a war, or even a particular battle, requires a knowledge of the rules which govern its participants.

The protagonists at Pima Butte represented six societies: Quechan, Maricopa, Mohave, Yavapai, Pima, and Western Apache. Of these, the Quechan and the Mohave on one side and the Maricopa and the Pima on the other were by far the most significantly involved. Their men accounted for most of the warriors—the exaggerated claim of 1,500 Yavapais notwithstanding—and whatever battle strategies were used can be attributed to the leadership of these four groups.

Despite centuries of enmity between the Maricopa and the Quechan and Mohave, all three tribes were culturally similar. Their languages, linguistically a part of the Yuman family of the Hokan phylum, were mutually intelligible; their traditions in religion, government, economics, and social structure differed in detail rather than in kind. They comprised the Up River Yumans, bearers of a broader cultural heritage which included the Upland Yumans (Walapai, Havasupai, and Yavapai), Delta River Yumans (Cocopa, Kohuana, and Halyikwamai), and Southern and Baja California Yumans (Diegueño, Kamia, Akwa'ala [Paipai], Kiliwa, and Nyakipa).[2]

It should be stressed further that the Maricopa were not originally a "tribe" in the formal sense of that word. "Maricopa," as already noted, was a label which by 1857 had come to be applied carelessly to an amalgam of Up River and Delta River Yumans who had come to rest on the Gila River as immediate neighbors of the Pimas. Until they were assimilated, and defined away by outsiders, these "Maricopas" were the Kohuana, Halyikwamai, Kaveltcadom, Halchidhoma, and Maricopa proper. The latter were also known as the Opa, but they refer to themselves as the Pee Posh.[3]

The Pimas, on the other hand, were alone among the 1857 Gila River combatants as representatives of a broader "Piman" heritage, a linguistic and cultural base shared with other Pimans living farther to the south: Papagos, Lower Pimas, Tepehuanes, and Tepecanos. And just as Yuman languages are Hokan, Piman languages are a part of the much larger Aztec-Tanoan phylum. The Gila River Pimas, or "Gileños" as they were sometimes called by Spaniards and Mexicans, were the northernmost Pimans, some of whose numbers lived as far south as northern Durango in Mexico.[4]

Yumans and Pimans were alike in that nearly all of them were *ranchería* peoples, Indians who lived in widely scattered settlements of brush houses which were rarely closer than shouting distance. They were part-time farmers who raised summer crops of corn, squash, and beans, planting either in the floodplains of rivers or in fields that could be watered by rainfall spread out at the mouths of normally dry arroyos, or mountainside gullies that served as pipelines to intermontane valleys. Although it is impossible to say with certainty, it appears that canal irrigation was introduced among the Pimans, along with wheat, by Spaniards. It also seems that it was only in the Anglo-American period in the second half of the nineteenth century that Colorado River Yumans adopted this technique for watering their crops.[5]

Ranchería peoples had to supplement their agricultural products with the fruits of hunting, gathering, and fishing. Indeed, wild plants and animals almost always provided the mainstay of their diet. The result was a form of village life that might best be described as "semi-sedentary," mobility ensuring that people could get the most out of their essentially arid environment. Villages were easily relocated. Material possessions were accordingly scanty. Government was uncomplicated. Except in warfare, government tended to be at the local level. Leaders were selected largely on the strength of personality rather than inheritance. There were shamans or medicine men (and women) whose power came to them through dreams, but there were no priests with autocratic authority.[6]

Beyond these very general similarities, among all ranchería peoples were important differences. Any explanation for the massacre of 1857 requires at least some understanding of those differences as they apply to concepts of warfare as well as military paraphernalia and dress.

RAIDING AND WARFARE

The Quechans recognized two kinds of war parties: *axwe hava'ig metapui* (going to the enemy, seeking battle), were large expeditions; and *axwe-om' an axwaiv* (waking the enemy, state of enmity) were small raiding parties.[7] Likewise, the Mohave distinguished between larger war expeditions intended for pitched battles (*kwanatme*) and small raiding parties of from ten to twelve warriors (*hunyu*).[8] Maricopas fought "two quite different modes of warfare," those characterized by formally arranged pitched battles and by forays, "a quick blow and a speedy return." The former were "preceded by challengers who first pranced up and down shouting insults at their opponents, until they clashed in a single combat, followed by a general mêlée in which foemen stood against each other until they were clubbed down."[9] This is similar to the practice of Western Apaches who went on raids "to search out enemy property," but who indulged in vengeance warfare to "take death from the enemy." Raiding parties consisted of from five to fifteen men who moved in stealth and who tried to avoid combat; war expeditions had as many as two hundred men whose aim it was to kill enemies and even destroy their settlements.[10]

Least serious in its effects was the small-scale, hit-and-run raiding that went on between Yavapais and Apaches against Pimas, Maricopas, and Papagos. Sometimes a single man made the raid. The objective was theft rather than injury to persons. When one of these small raids was aimed at killing, the attackers often were satisfied with ambushing a single person at some distance from a settlement. So far as is known, none of these raids was intended to overwhelm a whole village, and attackers would strike at isolated groups of a few families at most. Usually the raiders had no interest whatever in making their presence widely known, in staying long, or in doing any real fighting.

Terrible as such raiding could be for the victims, these were irritants rather than threats to the existence of a tribe, and raids were frequently broken off at the sight of mounting opposition. An attack that seemed risky might be discontinued at the last moment. Such attacks could also be cancelled at the sudden appearance of bad omens. Many small raids were probably terminated after one enemy had been killed or some bit of booty spirited away.

It seems reasonable to believe that small raids constituted most of the "warfare" of these Indians and to conjecture that "war parties" left home without fanfare or ceremony, with the idea of maintaining secrecy and quiet throughout the expedition. If possible, clashing with the enemy was avoided unless it looked as if staging a surprise battle would bring success. Small raids probably netted the trickle of captives who were later sold as slaves to Mexican settlements.[11] Large raids were too infrequent and too seldom successful to have brought in many captives. These suppositions seem to point to more small-scale raiding than was ever recorded in historical accounts by Anglos.

The second kind of warfare was more large-scale, such as attacks by Yavapais and Apaches on Pima and Maricopa villages; by Apaches on Papagos; and by Gila River Indians on the small and moveable camps of Yavapais or Apaches. By the 1850s, raids on a similar scale were waged between Cocopas and Quechans. Such large groups occasionally went from Quechan country against the Gila River villages, and sometimes from the Maricopa villages into the territory of the Quechans.

Larger raids probably had revenge as a principal motive with destruction of the enemy as the primary objective. Small settlements could be wiped out. Yet, except in favorable circumstances, attackers were probably not numerous enough to kill all the defenders who hastened from nearby camps. The raiders retreated lest the tables be turned and the attackers themselves be killed to the last man.

Even so, the raids often were not driven home with the vigor one might expect from attackers who find everything in their favor. So it was with one successful raid by Maricopas against a Quechan village at a time when the Quechans were in a weakened condition after prolonged hostilities against neighboring Cocopas. Quechans lost so many people that they abandoned their village and left the Colorado River for a time. The Maricopa aggressors made no attempt to pursue the fleeing Quechan families to kill as many people as possible.[12] Caution, fatigue, or satiated vengeance may have deterred attackers.

The Cocopas suffered a disadvantage in having no central institutions to unify them. They settled in small groups of two or three families which left them more vulnerable to attack. A unique element in their warfare with the Quechans was that they lived so near them that individuals from opposing tribes sometimes became friends or married across tribal lines. These individuals opened the way for more than the anonymous hit-and-run raiding by other peoples. Quechans and Cocopas practiced mutual deceit and treachery, inviting their enemies to peace meetings that turned into ambushes or slaughters of the guests.[13]

This kind of relationship did not develop among the other contending tribes. For instance, although Yavapais and Gila River villagers lived in adjoining territories and gathered food in the same areas at different times of the year, the Yavapai are believed to have avoided the Gila whenever possible.

Finally, Quechans and Cocopas had by the 1840s and 1850s begun to send large numbers of warriors in their raids against each other. The Cocopas twice staged raids of more than a hundred warriors, and one Quechan war expedition is reported to have numbered from 250 to 300 men.[14]

The only other known form of hostility was ritual battle. Only the Quechans—with Mohave help on occasion—and the Maricopas are known to have engaged in this type of warfare. What distinguished the "battle expedition" from other sizeable raids was the issuance and reception of a formal challenge which made it clear that the attackers were coming to seek out their enemy's fighting men. So far as is known, these challenges were not issued long in advance. They came after attackers recognized that their approach had been detected. Or, having made a surprise raid, the attackers might choose to stay in the vicinity and issue a challenge to other, larger numbers of enemy defenders hurrying to the scene. The presence of warriors bearing the symbolic feathered stave was indication of an impending battle among most of the Gila-Colorado people.

Although Yumans seem to have thought of armed conflict in terms of raiding or warfare, confrontation was not always planned nor was the outcome always predictable. On occasion, they engaged in large scale, hand-to-hand fights to a finish when large raiding parties became trapped by numerous defenders. To most observers the tactics in such cases would probably have been indistinguishable from those of ritual battle.

Stated another way, defenders who appeared in large numbers could issue their own challenge to the attackers whom they had surprised. If the challenge was accepted, the battle could proceed along the same lines as it would had both sides attended to all the prescribed formalities. One Maricopa's account describes some of the possibilities for last-minute decisions affecting the nature of these large confrontations and reveals some of the undercurrents of personal feeling that permeated these events:

> The Maricopa started to war with the Yuma. They reached the Colorado late in the afternoon. Two or three Yuma, who were fishing . . . saw the Maricopa approaching. These men told them to stop and go home, else they would be annihilated. Even the bravest warriors declared that they should return, since the Yuma already knew of their coming. Some of our people urged the older men to fight. They took willow limbs and beat them to force them to do it. They had not yet decided whether to go on, when two Yuma came up carrying a Maricopa scalp. They bore it on a long pole, dancing up and down on the bank. The only elderly Maricopa declared the scalp was that of his brother. He said that even though he went alone, he was going to fight the Yuma. So all declared they would fight on account of the scalp. These were the best warriors we ever had. All said they would fight because if they retreated it would be to their shame. They started . . . across the Colorado. The Yuma had long poles for clubs, a little above their head in length. Every man, woman, and child had such a staff. Before the Maricopas crossed, they saw the Yuma carrying torches; going off to collect their forces.

This continued all night. Toward morning the Maricopa knew the Yuma had all collected opposite. They knew they would be killed, but determined nevertheless to fight them. Better to kill an enemy and be killed in turn than to return without fighting.

Where they crossed the river were some Yavapai armed with bows on the bank in front of the Yumas. A great many of our best men were shot as they were crossing.

They marched too close with the enemy. Some had hip-length clubs but those were not long enough. Before they were close enough to use them, the Yuma beat them down with their long staves. Our men, striking at legs and hips, brought some of them down. But as the Yumas had much longer clubs, they knocked down a good many of our men with one blow. The Yuma had all put mud over their faces and bodies, down which they scratched lines with their fingers, so that they should recognize their men in the fight. Both sides came up in several ranks, until they stood so thick one could hardly get through. As those in the front rank were knocked down, the men behind would step into their places.

Our men had a few horsemen with them, perhaps twenty or fewer. These rode once through the mob of Yuma and once back again. They charged through twice and no more. No one knew what became of our horsemen; perhaps the Yuma pulled them down and killed them.

This left our clubmen standing in a group, surrounded by Yuma men, women, and children. The battle began about nine or ten in the morning and lasted until late in the afternoon. By that time all our people had been killed except two or three of the two hundred who went there. These few crawled back under their men's legs as they fought. . . . That is how they were saved. It is shameful to tell this, for these were the very ones who coaxed the others to give fight.[15]

The record is clearest when a formal battle was preconceived. Battle ritual included ceremonies conducted at home before the warriors' departure and dictated behavior during and after battle. Form and ceremonial demanded a national exhibition, a public performance requiring that each participant stand forth and, eventually, risk his life in circumstances he could not control. His proper behavior would bring credit to his tribe and to himself. Cowardice or failure to act properly could bring shame on his own head and might bring defeat to his tribe.[16]

CIVIL LEADERS AND OTHERS

Ranchería peoples recognized "peace and war conditions as sharply distinct realms, and the organization for each as necessarily separate." In civil affairs these villagers looked to one man as the moral leader of the group, one who "gained recognition through stability of character and speaking ability," and the basis of whose authority rested on his "capacity for learning and repeating the phrases which his people regarded as proper and wise, and which constituted a body of traditional knowledge of the truth . . ."[17]

Each settlement would probably have one such man, "but also there [sometimes] were men whose leadership was recognized beyond their own rancherías and who, as among the Yumas, were looked to for advice and wisdom by people over a wide area."[18] So it was with the Quechan, the Mohave, and the Maricopa, and so with the Cocopa of the Colorado delta country except that they had no real unity among rancherías and therefore no preeminent moral figure among them.

This civil leader was neither an executive nor a commander. He was a repository of wisdom and a source of the group's well being. He was often the judge in disputes, but he worked with mild suasion wherever possible. In any case, he never made or carried out a "judgment" purely on his own. He conferred with the other ranchería leaders because all major decisions came from a group who in turn embodied and invoked the wisdom and custom of which all members of the culture were well aware. The civil leader's advice might merely point the right way to approach the supernatural, with the actual ritual being prescribed by a specialist. Although "sometimes possessed of special supernatural powers, he was not necessarily such a specialist."[19]

He was above all the recognized master of moral exhortation, the preacher who kept before people the right course of action. He "embodied the tradition by which they [the people] lived and from which they derived security. . . . He was surrounded by ritual and his discourses were sacred, even though outside of public meeting he dressed like everyone else and cultivated his fields and lived like the usual family man." By and large, "his authority depended on his saying what everyone knew was right, not on esoteric or special knowledge. . . . In a public meeting a course of action was stated and repeated, a way of action plotted out, until all the men present, normally all the men of the ranchería, could see its wisdom. The rest depended upon the cohesion and solidarity of the community; if it was strong the ranchería acted in unison."[20]

Anthropologist Edward Spicer emphasizes that the leader "functioned as an interpreter to others of the unalterable right path which he had spent long years learning to follow and which he knew was laid out by the supernatural powers in whose hands the community's welfare lay. . . ."[21] And for some of these Yuman peoples the right way to act, the proper decision to make, had been set clearly before them all their lives in the long song cycles with interspersed stories which taught them at once their history, the moral rules for a proper life, and the specific identifying customs, geographic lore, and social framework that made them Yumans. That literature and song "defined a relationship between people and land . . . showed how the tribe was rooted in a very specific locality. These roots were implanted and fixed by higher beings than men. They had existed from the beginning and could not be conceived as alterable by men," since the Creator of the people had set them down in such detail and with such finality.[22] For the Mohave the word *sumach*, meaning "roots" or "good roots," evokes this concept of each Mohave with all others as part of the life to be lived well and properly.[23]

Like some of the other ranchería peoples, the River Yumans expected the civil leader, the moral guardian, to stand apart from war save in situations where all lives were in immediate danger. Where these River Yumans may have differed somewhat from other ranchería peoples was that a warrior of proven skill, a war leader, often became the moral leader of the community. He might therefore continue to show a lively interest in armed conflict, although he might personally no longer take part. It is barely possible that some of these men combined moral and military leadership in one person, although such a case was never recorded. It is perhaps enough to say that nineteenth-century Quechan and Mohave moral leaders—and perhaps moral leaders of the Maricopa and Cocopa as well—had all been leaders in war before they arrived at the dignified position of civil leadership. Among the Mohave it is clear that the moral leader of the tribe must have been a trained warrior in order to reach that highest position of prestige.

At some point in deliberations over a potential raid, decisions and arrangements were made by warriors and religious figures, shamans who specialized in wartime problems.[24] Until a final decision was made, there was ample opportunity for argument about details of the general plan. A plan submitted by the war leader could meet with general disfavor, and an altogether different enterprise could be proposed by some other warrior whose ambition it was to lead the coming war party.

There were, indeed, likely to be conflicting proposals, each one drawn from a different view of the best target to strike, the best time to launch the attack, or the most favorable route to follow to reach the objective. Young men chafed at the conservative views of their elders. And there were those who wished to displace the tribal war leader by outshining him in small raids or by persuading the council to let them manage a major enterprise of war. They hoped to demonstrate that theirs were the better predictions and choices and that the war leader had strayed into mistaken thinking. Here was plenty of opportunity for bold men to sway people with their oratory and thus to bring a tribal contingent to launch a raid or even a formal battle expedition. As Spicer says, "the best combination for a war leader was bravery and effective magic,"[25] and many candidates stepped forward to prove that they had a good supply of both.

In all likelihood, most River Yuman warriors reached the point of proposing campaign plans after a period of years of success in fighting against the enemy. In this way a man could gain a "slow increase of authority," and could win recognition as one of the most dependable and bravest of fighters and ablest of planners. This kind of testing experience clearly existed for the Cocopa, the Quechan, and the Mohave, who recognized the status of the warrior (*kwanami, kwinemi*) as one having a special role in the society, who was accorded respect during his lifetime and a special mourning ceremony at his death. The Yavapai gave abundant recognition to warriors, because the prominent man in the civil affairs of each small group was also the leader in war, the *mastava*. Other men leading small raids could accumulate the kind of reputation needed to advance eventually to the post of *mastava*. The Maricopa, too, had a moral leader in their community, and probably several village leaders, as well as a war leader.

For all these fighters leadership of a small raid was much easier to attain than any of the other prestigious roles open to them in the society. In Yavapai country, for instance, a small raid might be undertaken whenever people were without food. The leader could be any mature man who wished to step forward to meet the need. Only for the much larger expeditions that went forward for purposes such as taking revenge did one *mastava* issue a call for a meeting of other groups of men, each with its respective *mastava*. Neither the Yavapai nor the Maricopa had any special status or title for warriors. Any man old enough to have passed the initiation rite was considered competent to take part in a raid or expedition. [26]

All these people were careful to provide an important role for the specialist they counted on to divine by religious means the best objectives, routes, and tactics for an expedition. For some of these peoples, that specialist might be a shaman called in to refine or to verify the project already conceived in the vision of a war leader. Among the Cocopa, this specialist was on hand when discussion preliminary to armed conflict was far enough along that decisions had to be made concerning which tribe to attack and where to locate the enemy. The shaman listened to the outline plan before asking all the men present to report to him their "dreams" concerning this war party. He then retired from the meeting to enter his own psychic "dream" experience, and he returned to inform the war leader where the enemy could be found, what they would be doing, and when was the best time to attack. [27]

Joint planning for warfare, as all other important matters among the Yumans, was done in the light of dream-vision experiences reported by people who possessed the special capacity of undergoing these "power-giving" dreams. Individual warriors could in the meantime decide whether to go on the expedition or to avoid it based on their own simpler dreams—ones applying only to themselves—or on the basis of other favorable or unfavorable portents.

Among the Quechans, any suggestion for a tribally sanctioned war party was discussed at length in a meeting of the civil leaders, or *paxatan,* of the various villages. One of the reasons for a conference of leaders has to do with the social structure of the Quechan tribe. Jack Forbes believes Quechans were once comprised of bands whose repeated gatherings developed into a grouping of villages and ultimately into something akin to a nation or, at least, into a sense of national unity among the people. [28] In any case, by the mid-nineteenth century each village recognized one or more senior civil officers (*pipá taxan*) who had to be consulted if the people were to be involved in any common project. In addition, there was a tribal moral leader (the *kwoxot*) who could convene such general meetings of the prestigious men from all villages north and south of the Yuma crossing of the Colorado River. And there was a tribal war leader as well. At the meeting, whoever had "dreamed" the proposed expedition would argue for his view volubly and, sometimes, almost endlessly. Discussion might continue indefinitely if there were many contrary views or if an alternative project was proposed by some other man. At some point the group would come to a feeling in favor of one project or against them all. If a single plan was accepted among them, the *kwoxot* would take the opportunity to discover whether the moment for this particular enterprise was promising or not.

He did this by carefully looking through enemy scalps in his official care. He examined scalps that came from those to be attacked. Shiny, bright scalp hair promised trouble for a Quechan war expedition at that particular time. But if the *kwoxot* could hear the scalp cry a little, he knew that "the time is good for war."[29]

Once a plan had been agreed upon, the war leader sent messengers to the Quechan villages. The warriors who gathered had had a "sporadic" training throughout their youth. They had all practiced as boys in difficult tests of endurance such as long cross country runs. They had learned to dodge arrows and to avoid other hurtful objects thrown at them. They had learned to persevere in such painful joint enterprises as destroying hornets' nests, staying with the job until all was finished no matter how many were hurt or how badly. Supervised by seasoned warriors, youths had made war in sham battle, in which some of them were injured badly enough to need a doctor's care.[30] As mature men, they would then carry the burden of battle as foot soldiers clashing face to face with the enemy. Behind their ranks would come a new generation of boys accompanying the expedition to gain experience, staying to the rear of shock troops but close enough to beat wounded enemies to death. Women might also accompany the expedition, armed to defend themselves if need be, and also to join in dispatching wounded enemies. So prepared, the Quechan war party filed quietly out of the village in single file, without public ceremony or song or exhortation.[31] In contrast, the Maricopa custom called for a war dance, songs, and ritual speeches to send the fighters on their way.[32]

The Quechan expedition thus constituted had been created by proper authority and was freighted with great importance in the feelings of the people at large. As Daryll Forde put it, "War expeditions are the one feature of their practical life which are considered worthy of remembrance or attention." He found, as we will have occasion to repeat (p. 158), that, to the Quechans, "success in warfare was indispensable to welfare . . . the concrete expression of spiritual strength. To be severely beaten by an enemy or to draw back sluggishly and avoid attacks would bring down scorn and shame, for Yuma mysticism was essentially directed at the acquisition and manifestation of great 'power,' power which should make them invincible before their enemies."[33]

An explanation of the Yumans' dreaming, and of the "power-bestowing" dream in particular, is in order because the Yumans themselves have used the word "dream" to stand for broadly different experiences. First of all, ordinary dreams such as anyone might have of a quiet night were indeed experienced by these Indians, and the individual recalling what he had dreamed might be guided by the specific events remembered or by symbols that had appeared to him while he slept. He would not necessarily report such a dream to anyone else, perhaps because it was understood to him alone.

Yumans also understood "dreaming" to be "learning." At least they used the word in that way part of the time. A clear case involves the memory work supervised and corrected by others, such as was carried on by a person in the process of learning the tribal song cycles in order to act as a clan or tribal singer. After hearing the songs from someone else and committing them to memory, the aspirant singer might finish by saying that all this had come to him in dreams. That was a perfectly proper statement because all knew that one "learned" these enduring, mythological songs and narratives by transporting oneself to the first moments of creation, to Mount Avikwame where the culture hero and creator Kumastamxo (Mastamho) was inventing people and instructing them in everything they would need to know. Being there and hearing it all said and done in that ancient "first time," the spirit of the modern person could then return to his body and repeat the historical epics, narratives, and songs that instructed the people in the ways of a proper life.

As the Quechan shaman Joe Homer explained his mastery of the long narrative that recounts the origins of the Quechan people, "It takes four days to tell all about Kikumat and Kumastamxo. . . . I was present from the beginning, and saw and heard it all. I dreamed a little of it at a time. I would tell it to my friends. The old men would say: 'That is right. I was there and heard it myself.' Or they would say: 'You have dreamed poorly. That is not right.' And they would tell me right. So at last I learned all of it right."[34]

The assumption was that there was a right way to be found. All warlike campaigns were foreseen and planned in this manner, and in some cases the dreaming continued until the night before the battle to be sure portents remained favorable.

"Dream" has also been used by Yuman peoples to refer to the personal skills that individuals develop—the work they are known to do especially well, the talents they possess, the career they prefer to follow through life. Yuman people talking with anthropologists or historians probably have this notion of personal ability and inclination in mind when they use the word "dream" for the everyday competence each person may develop—whether as a fisherman, a farmer, or a person skilled in the use of a bow and arrow—because he "dreamed" that skill. In Mohave all these senses are called *sumach ahot*, which virtually everyone who has written on the subject has translated as "good dreams." The broader understanding of those words, however, is whatever comes from the "good roots," that is, whatever is drawn from traditions, from the correct upbringing and lifeway of the Mohave person. One's *sumach ahot* was the path one's personal inclination took from the cultural core, from the origins of the people, that best mirrored the inclinations in the religious literature of the people. As Alfred L. Kroeber once expressed it: "Dreams . . . are the foundation of Mohave life; and dreams throughout are cast in mythological mold. There is no people whose activities are more shaped by this psychic state, or what they believe to be such, and none whose civilization is so completely, so deliberately, reflected in their myths."[35]

Mohaves whose *sumach ahot* inclined them toward a career as a warrior were not so systematically trained as were Quechan warriors. Little boys who obviously preferred rugged activity and who more easily withstood and endured physical pain were observed, encouraged, and tested as early as four years of age. Mature warriors continued to test these boys from time to time until they were ten years old or older in order to mold their reactions and teach them courage in painful situations.

As a boy proved himself, people began to suspect that this was a boy who at birth had "dreamed" of becoming a warrior. Such youths were seen to be hardening themselves physically and to be acquiring skills necessary for a battlefield fighter or scout.[36]

Some of the most precocious of these lads might accompany a war party from ages thirteen to fifteen;[37] the usual practice, however, was for them to go to war for the first time at nineteen or twenty. As George Fathauer interpreted it, a youth grew up hearing his elders comment on his performance until he had "gradually come to pattern his behavior according to cultural expectations and would actually experience the prescribed dreams."[38]

As for Mohave leadership and its role in launching tribal war parties, it is clear that the Mohaves' customs were much like those of the Quechans, Cocopas, and Maricopas.[39]

The underlying basis of Mohave leadership was different from that of the Quechan, however, in that the Mohave settlement or village had no particular significance. Habitat, as noted earlier, might change frequently. Individual Mohaves identified more with the tribe than the village. There were no ranchería leaders. Instead, there were six men of prestige, called *pipa tahone*, each of whom lived in a different part of Mohave territory and made his influence felt in that region. One of the six was a moral leader of the people as a whole and he was known as *pipa tahahone*. There was also a tribal war leader and there were the warriors, *kwanami*, perhaps some fifty, sixty, or more in the tribe at any one time.[40] Finally, there was a shaman, or *ahive sumach*, with particular skill in "dreaming" about enemy people or about any people who were not Mohaves.

No one has recorded in any detail how these leaders discussed a war expedition or how a decision to attack an enemy was reached. The Mohaves, like other Yumans, called a general council to persuade every man to favor a coming enterprise. It is not known, however, whether the council debated all ideas openly from the first or whether the large meeting was convened only after some of the leaders and other warriors had decided on a particular project.[41] Neither is it clear that the war leader accompanied all expeditions against enemies. What can safely be said is that major enterprises of war were as clearly tribal affairs for Mohaves as they were for Quechans, if not more so, and the likelihood is that much advance discussion in conference was involved before any major war expedition was agreed upon.[42]

During the last few days before an expedition was to depart, there were public preparations. A meeting was convened by the war leader, many people came, and a day and night of dancing ensued. Warriors were exhorted to join the expedition, which might muster to fifty, sixty, or even a hundred men.[43]

Some men in these battle expeditions were career warriors, the *kwanami*, but how many, or in what proportion to the total number of people bearing weapons, is not known.[44] Equally uncertain is whether these *kwanami* were the shock troops in battle, those who went into the

fight with the short mallet club as their weapon.[45] There were probably
more *kwanami* among the Mohaves and more who occupied leading roles
in the society than is evident from the published record. Present-day belief
is that *kwanamis* were the only ones who could aspire to moral leadership
of the tribe; only they could hope to become war leaders or one of the six
regional sub-chiefs. A Mohave could occupy dual or triple statuses: shaman and career warrior, or moral leader, shaman, and career warrior. It is
improbable, though, that many men choose to act in all these capacities
simultaneously.

Although it is not clear in historical sources that Mohave scouts were
kwanami, current tradition among Mohaves living at Fort Mojave insists
that men who appear in history books as "scout" or "spy" were simply
career warriors who specialized in this more constant and more active
form of a *kwanami's* calling.[46]

The battle expedition was made up of *kwanami*, additional armed men,
some boys, and perhaps a few women who went along prepared to take
part in the fighting.[47] Like the other tribes involved in the Gila-Colorado
wars, Mohaves took their medical practitioners with them. It is not known
how many different specialists traveled to battle, but it is reported that
there was an arrow-wound doctor, a doctor who treated massive abrasions
and breaks from clubbing, and persons with other curing specialties.[48]

The most important of these men was the *ahwe sumach*, who exhorted
the warriors during evening rest periods. He steadily consulted omens as
the party moved deeper into enemy territory. While traveling toward the
objective, the *ahwe sumach* also tried to work magic that would affect the
enemy in such a way that they would be less watchful and less prepared
when attacked. He also took possession of and cared for enemy scalps. He
might be a curer as well, intervening early in cases that cropped up on the
homeward trail when some warriors began to show weakness due to *ahwe*,
a serious and sometimes fatal affliction resulting from contact with non-
Mohave people.

Along with the medical specialists went an important practitioner who
could treat for soul loss. A warrior's soul—after he received a heavy blow
or any serious shock-inducing wound—could rise from his body and
either hover overhead or, in extreme cases, leave this world altogether. The
specialist—not thought of as a doctor or curer but as a "spirit dreamer,"
xelyetsxa'm cama'—could use his power to bring the soul back, show it
where the man was located, induce the soul to reenter, and thus save the
life of the fallen comrade.[49]

Even though Mohaves paid a great deal of attention to omens and tried to work magic while approaching the enemy's villages, they are reported never to have turned back even if omens portended disaster. It was a bad omen, for example, if an animal—often a deer—strayed within sight of their camp and died. Such an occurrence, given their ideals of courage, must have placed Mohaves in a difficult situation of personal stress. Omens, when read by a qualified specialist, were weighted with authority. To move ahead in the face of virtually assured disaster could only have raised the level of warriors' anxieties. It may be that such anxieties were the reason Mohave contingents sometimes left the field before the battle reached its climax. Something like this could have occurred in September 1857, when at least some Mohaves fled the Gila before the dénouement.

Maricopa war customs were similar enough to those of Quechans and Mohaves that not all of them need to be described. There were, however, differences which should be noted.

Leslie Spier has supplied broad outlines on the subject of Maricopa warfare.[50] Not available are details peculiar to each of the constituent "Maricopa" groups: Kaveltcadom, Halyikwamai, Kohuana, Halchidhoma, and Maricopa proper.

As mentioned above, by the 1850s remnants of all these peoples had come to occupy two villages on the Gila River near its confluence with the Salt just downstream from the more numerous Pimas.[51] This position provided a refuge—though not perfect in that their own downstream side remained unprotected—where they could farm and carry out activities essential to their survival. Their safety depended on remaining close to their Pima allies. This consolidated colony of Yuman peoples called "Maricopa" could expect raids by Yavapais, Apaches, Quechans, and Mohaves, not to mention occasional large battle expeditions in which these enemies might combine forces.

This is not to say Maricopas were poor fighters or were unprepared to defend themselves. By the 1830s and through the 1850s their numbers had fallen dangerously low. Without Pima help they could be badly outmanned in a very uneven competition. So they wisely remained at the edge of the much stronger Pima settlements, providing advance warning stations on the Pimas' otherwise unguarded western flank.

Precisely how this mixed two-village community governed itself is something of a mystery. Spier attempted to learn how many prestigious leaders, or "chiefs," resided in those Maricopa villages at any one time. The data offered Spier by his informants—who generally lacked interest in or knowledge of the subject—were confusing and equivocal. Whatever a former system of governance may have been with its input from five cultural groups, the Maricopas of Spier's day (1929–1932) felt themselves to have been a "single homogeneous people, all participating equally in their group life and all united against their enemies."[52] Beyond that, each of the fragments of peoples seemed to have hereditary "chiefs," one at a time, selected from among the nearest male relatives considered fit for the dignity and respect inherent in the position. As Spier found, it was difficult to be sure of specifics in these matters because "the groups were then impoverished in numbers and lived in scattered settlements interdigitated with the Pima."[53]

It also appeared from what people said that although men of prominence might be found in several villages, there was only one "chief," and he was chief of the whole tribe. In the mid-nineteenth century there were a Kohuana chief and a Halchidhoma chief, the latter possibly having been so appointed by Mexicans in the 1830s. Spier was able to discover which individuals had been moral leaders of these ex-tribal groupings during mid to late nineteenth century. He further learned that two of those individuals had been killed defending their villages against River Yuman attacks, evidently in the 1840s and 1850s.[54]

The sketch of Maricopa leadership drawn by Spier looks much like that of the Mohave and Quechan. Maricopa leaders were first of all exemplars and teachers who moved among their people in good spirit, reminding them of what they should be doing and how to live properly. They also presided over councils—which among the Maricopa were poorly remembered and their functions unclear. What is clear is that the prestigious leader acted as host for night-long meetings of the mature men at which all kinds of important matters were discussed. Warfare was one such topic, but decisions were not made nor were war expeditions planned there.

As with all Yumans of the Gila and Colorado rivers, proposals and plans for war had to come from someone reporting a "power-bestowing" dream.[55] In Maricopa understanding, this experience was somewhat different than that among Quechans, Cocopas, or Mohaves. As best as Spier could understand it—and he found this hard to do because his Maricopa and Halchidhoma friends felt no need to make these matters specific— "the dream is not as we would say a phantasy based on a particular physiological state, but it is a state in which some spiritual quality of the dreamer goes out to meet the spirit: in other words, it is the dream experience which is at once the dream and the spirit."[56] These spirits appearing to the Maricopas included a large number of potent beings, many of them in the form of birds and other animals, each of which stood as a symbol for some kind of activity or problem.

The power dream came involuntarily. And from Spier's careful gathering of statements, he was convinced that all the dreams conveying whatever varieties of power could come to only about twenty or fewer people—only to those who were shamans, singers, orators, the tribal war leader, or the one prestigious moral leader of the tribe, more customarily called the "chief." These persons had their respective powers, and the knowledge necessary to enact their roles, bestowed by different spirits identified with the different skills and careers. For example, it was Mocking Bird who in the dream experience taught those who were seeking to become orators, and taught them progressively in each dreamed experience from childhood onward.[57] Of all the persons who experienced these dreams, it may have been that the war leader was the only one to propose warlike enterprises. As one of the Maricopas said to Spier, "There is one war leader, the only man who dreams of going after the enemy."[58]

However they may have decided on a plan for war, Maricopas staged a tribal dance the night before the war party was to leave the villages. Everyone took part in it. The singers presented a wide variety of traditional melodies, and people danced to some of the music, either when they chose to do so or when tradition required it. One of the orators spoke that night, addressing himself to the warriors and encouraging them to go with the war party. Each night while on the march another oration would be recited to members of the expedition, each speech appropriate to the unfolding stages of the enterprise.

Medical shamans went with the fighters to cure various kinds of war wounds. This strained tribal resources inasmuch as there probably were only six or seven medical practitioners among the Maricopa at any one time. Of greatest importance to the war party was one of these shamans whom Spier called the "clairvoyant," a man who could dream the location of the nearby enemy and lead the warriors to the place, even if the search was for a small Yavapai camp concealed somewhere in the mountainous terrain.[59]

Maricopa expeditions, whether small raiding parties or larger groups that made war by ritual battle, had a particular problem in arranging their arrival at a time of day favorable to them. This problem arose because

Yavapai and Apache settlements moved frequently and might be found almost anywhere; Quechan rancherías also moved with the seasons and in terms of best prospects of planting here or there within their vast territory. There is no evidence Maricopas ever managed to arrange to strike the Quechans at the most favorable moment. When attacking the Yavapai, they reconnoitered carefully until locating a camp, then remained nearby in hiding until late afternoon when there was still enough light for their attack with bow and arrows.

Women did not accompany Maricopa war parties; boys may have been excluded as well. Maricopas did train boys for war, encouraging them to "be brave to stand anything."[60] When only four to six years of age these boys, like Mohaves of the same age, were tested from time to time by the men. "If they did not cry when struck, they were next placed on an ant hill to be bitten and finally pushed into a wasps' or bees' nest. It was taken as a sign that they would become brave warriors, if they did not cry."[61]

At ages sixteen to eighteen they underwent a more formal test wherein old warriors exhorted and instructed them, sang a certain song, and took a group of youths to seat them on a hive of bees, expecting them to kill the bees one by one.[62] This procedure represented going to war, the bees being the enemy. Boys also trained themselves by playing rough games that taught them to hold fast in the face of pain.[63] They were constantly using bows and arrows, shooting at targets even as they spent long hours guarding the growing crops against ravens and other predators.

In his conversations with Maricopas and Halchidhomas concerning war, Spier caught much more clearly than did other anthropologists the apprehensive feeling of warriors who went forward not merely into enemy country, but into a territory literally filled with magically malevolent enemies. The feeling of oppression of spirit was very strong. Spier recounts or discusses the almost overpowering feeling of the Maricopa warrior on coming into an utterly hostile environment from which he wished to be gone as soon as possible. Maricopa fighters knew names of mountains in their enemies' territories, and they knew those peaks could work them ill. They turned their faces so as not to see the looming enemy, and they averted their looks from the bodies of an enemy slain but a moment before. All of this may help to explain why they alone of all these peoples scalped a living enemy, tearing away the top half of the skin and hair from his head while he still struggled against them in mortal agony.[64]

Maricopas, like the Mohaves, worked magic while on an expedition through shamans or other specialists who accompanied the warriors. This was unlike the Quechans, whose *kwoxot,* the prestigious tribal leader, stayed at home to work his magic, producing dust storms or, if need be, a blinding cloudburst to shield the war party against early detection.[65]

The nature of leadership among Gila River Pimas in the years preceding 1857 can perhaps best be inferred from studies carried out in the 1930s among the neighboring Papago Indians by Ruth Underhill. Both Pimas and Papagos call themselves O'odham; they speak mutually intelligible dialects of the same language; and except for differences imposed upon them by environment and the specifics of history in their dealings with non-Indians as well as with other Indians, they are essentially of one culture. There is a good possibility, indeed, that Gila River Pimas—when first seen by Europeans in the late seventeenth century—were in reality one or more groups of O'odham who had only recently arrived on the river from the south, perhaps as late as sometime in the sixteenth century.[66]

If there is any reliability in taking a portrait of "aboriginal" Papago political organization drawn in the 1930s from the memories of elderly informants and projecting that onto Gila River Pimas as their "aboriginal" situation, the picture that emerges is somewhat as follows:

Pima settlements were made up of a group of kinsmen, people related through blood or marriage. According to anthropologist Underhill:

A village was a settlement of kin and others entered it only by invitation or by marriage. . . . In the course of time, the villages . . . proliferated, sending out one group after another to look for more land. The new settlement thus made might be only a suburb of the home village, obeying its officials and coming home for ceremonies. But sometimes the daughter village was so large or far away that it needed a leader of its own. Then it appointed one, but considered him always subsidiary to the leader of the parent village. . . . If intervillage games were held, it was understood that all played and bet on the same side. If one went on the warpath, the others were notified and asked to join. Modern interpreters speak of these related villages as "partners."

But we know that during the eighteenth and most of the nineteenth century there could be no daughter villages. That was the time of Apache attacks, when the people were obliged to concentrate and, no matter how far away their fields were: "They could not live far apart. They were afraid."[67]

Traditionally, government operated at the level of the village or village unit in the classic manner of all ranchería settlements. The moral leader of a Piman village had several jobs to perform, many of them reflected in the various terms by which he was known: Wise Speaker, One Above, One Ahead, One Made Big, Fire Maker, Keeper of the Plaited Basket (which contained the village fetish), Keeper of the Smoke, and Keeper of the Meeting. He presided over meetings held in the village's only unit of public architecture, the large brush and mesquite structure known variously as the round house, rain house, or big house. It had to be large enough to accommodate all the men in the village.[68]

When it was time for a meeting, either the moral leader or others appointed by him would enter the public house, start the fire (as Fire Maker or Keeper of the Smoke), and climb to the roof to shout to summon other men. According to Underhill, "He called meetings to decide on the dates of ceremonies and whenever the other officials, the war, hunt and game leaders, had communications to make. When the men assembled, he . . . opened the meeting with a moral talk bidding them pay attention to what was to be said and to use their best judgement."[69]

He acted as religious leader in all ceremonies to bring rain and to promote the growth and health of crops and recited the proper Wise Speeches. He was also a patriarchal advisor to the village. He could name his own successor when he retired, but it is likely the council of elders had to approve the choice.

The moral leader had a young man as his messenger, a status position known as The Leg. Sometimes there was also a man with an exceptionally strong voice who served as village crier. Additionally, there were a hunt leader, a game leader, and a war leader. The hunt leader was in charge of communal hunts for deer and rabbits. He "set the day, chose the locality, called the people together at dawn, appointed the beaters and made the required speech. . . .He passed his office down, as did the others, by instructing a younger man, usually a kinsman, and finally asking the council to ratify his appointment as the new leader."[70]

The game leader made arrangements for inter-village games. His duty was to "see that the runners were properly trained, take charge of the party on the march to the challenged village, lead the cheering, argue for his side in the matter of fouls, appoint the referees, see that the relay runners got off in the proper order. His ceremonial duty was the recitation of a speech before the contest began."[71]

The best description of a war leader is also that given by Underhill:

The war leader was, in ancient times, like the [moral leader], a ceremonial official whose first duty was to know the war ritual and to recite it on the proper occasions. He received his office from his predecessor . . . and held it up to old age. It was he who directed a war party and planned its strategy even if he was too old to do much fighting himself.

But there was often a younger man to head the actual fighting . . . . It would appear that the practice differed in different villages. In San Xavier and Komarik he was a different man each time. In Komarik he was chosen by the elders as the most capable young warrior, in San Xavier, he volunteered and got up a war party in the Plains fashion to take vengeance on the Apache for slain relatives. Archie had a more or less permanent field leader chosen for his prowess and known as the Bitter Man, "because he would not give in to the Apache." Kuhatk also had such a leader and it was understood that when Kuhatk and Archie went on the warpath together, Kuhatk should lead "because it had been given them by Elder Brother to be the best fighters."[72]

Finally, the real governing authority of any village was vested in the council, all the mature males. They met each night and they made all decisions concerning community activities: the dates of ceremonies, inter-village games, farming, hunting, and warfare. The council approved the installation of leaders of any kind, including that of the moral leader, and their approval had to be earned by would-be new village residents.

Although all adult males attended the council meetings, only those who were either wise or "ripe" took part in actual deliberations. "Ripe" men had been through purification of the sacred journey to the Gulf of California to get salt or through the purification ceremony required of those who had killed an enemy. Wise men had proven their worth by showing good judgment, a practical sense, and a knowledge of traditions. Men who were neither "ripe" nor regarded as being wise attended as listeners.[73]

During much of the eighteenth and nineteenth centuries the northern Pimans, and especially the Gila River Pimas, lived in almost constant fear of attack by Apache Indians. Because of the friendship with Maricopas, they were further subjected to the possibility of attack by Yavapais, Mohaves, and Quechans, although Western Apaches seemed always to be their worst nemesis. A speech of admonition told in a Papago council house and recorded by Underhill might just as well have been a speech told in the council house of a Gila River Pima village in August 1857 on the eve of the great attack on the Maricopas:

> Well then! Will you not be ready? Will you not take care! Already I have said thus to you: that you shall make arrows, that you shall make bows, that you shall be watchful. When the enemy will arrive, you do not know. It may be at night that he will come—at night, or in the morning, or when the sun stands almost anywhere. Beside you do you place your bow that you may snatch it up and fight. Early in the morning do you eat, that you may be able to fight. Always I say this. Every morning I shall say it to you at the meeting, that you shall keep near you your bow, your hunting arrows, your war arrows, your quiver.
>
> Your women, very early let them cook. Let them feed the youths that they may fight the enemy, wherever the sun stands. Let them fetch water, let them search for firewood, that they may cook something. Early in the morning let them practise running, then when the enemy arrives they may run far down yonder and save themselves.
>
> This I recite and this I say to you. Do you listen and let it enter your ears and your head.[74]

While they were perfectly capable of taking the offensive, Pimas and Papagos seem to have done so only when revenge was called for or as a counter-offensive to protect lives and property. There is little to suggest that northern Pimans ever made raids for the sole purpose of obtaining booty, although it is well documented that Gila River Pimas, as well as Papagos, took captives, selling some of them as slaves.[75] Neither does it appear that northern Pimans engaged in ritualized, formal battles with their Apache and Yavapai enemies during most of the eighteenth and nineteenth centuries, although one such formal battle was recorded for 1698.[76]

In 1695 and again in 1751 there were major uprisings of northern Pimans against the Spaniards. In 1840 they rebelled against the Mexicans, recalling that Mexico gained her independence from Spain in 1821. In all cases there appears to have been a perception on the part of Pimas and Papagos that their lands and water sources were being threatened by expropriation and their liberties were being constrained. Individual Pimans suffered indignities as well, enough to inspire them to armed revolt.[77]

All three of these rebellions were successfully quelled by the power of Spain and of Mexico and northern Pimans thereafter resigned themselves to the presence of non-Indians in their territory. By the time the United States acquired all the lands south of the Gila River to the present international boundary as a result of the Gadsden Purchase of June 1854, the rebellious spirit of the area's native peoples had been suppressed. To Anglo Americans the Pimas and Papagos were the "peaceful" people, a designation which ignored their history and which failed to recognize the ongoing record of bravery and skill being compiled by northern Pimans in their fights with Apaches.

Be that as it may, it is perhaps fair to characterize northern Piman warfare, especially after the start of the eighteenth century, as having been essentially defensive in nature. Even the Piman myth concerning the origins of warfare places responsibility on a young man who seeks vengeance among Apaches for the death of his father.[78]

Once again, it is Ruth Underhill's account of Papago warfare that probably best describes the situation for all northern Pimans:

War . . . was not an occasion for prestige as with the Plains tribes [and as with the River Yumans] nor of booty as with the Apache. It was a disagreeable necessity. The enemy . . . was regarded as a shaman. His person, or anything that had touched him, was taboo. Therefore all booty was burned and the man who had killed an enemy or been wounded by him had to go through a long ordeal of purification.

War was enveloped in a mass of ritual but none of it was glorification of combat. . . . The reward of victory for the individual was the acquisition of power, not for war, but for curing. For the community as a whole it was that summum bonum of an agricultural people, rain and a good harvest.

Nevertheless, because of the Apache menace, the Papago were forced to train their youths to war; the respected men in the community had to be Enemy Slayers and a man who had no taste for fighting at all was practically forced to declare himself a berdache. Training began when boys were about fourteen.

In leisure periods, like the time after harvest, boys would be gathered daily at the house of the Keeper of the Meeting and he or the war leader would tell them war stories and explain fighting methods. Beginning with the age of twelve or so, they were given practice in using the shield, in shooting and dodging arrows. A row of boys holding shields would stand at one end of an open space and at the other a row with bows and blunt, wooden-tipped arrows. They were told to run toward each other and at a given distance the archers were to shoot, aiming at the legs so a wound would not be dangerous.

The business of the shield bearers was not to attack but to learn to dodge the arrows. They were told never to stand with their legs together, since this made a better target. They were to watch the arrows as they left the bow, to squat to avoid the high ones, leap to avoid the low ones, or throw the body from side to side. Boys practised in this way alone whenever they had a chance. They also practised shooting, by throwing a bundle of rags in the air and trying to shoot it before it fell. Before a war party all the fighters practised in this way under the direction of the war leader or the retired warriors. [79]

Just as Yumans were accompanied on the war trail by shamans, so did northern Pimans look to shamans to aid them in battle. Although it is not clear shamans served in that capacity in defensive situations, such as the times in which a Piman village might be under attack, they clearly functioned in helpful ways when Pimans were seeking out the enemy. Each village's group of warriors ideally took with them a shaman whose job it was to "see" the enemy and to cast spells which would disable him. These shamans were of a special class, so-called "owl-meeters" whose guardian spirits were owls. Piman belief had it that the spirits of the dead, which live in the east, are embodied in owls. Dead Papago warriors haunted enemy territory as owls, and it was with these owl "spies" that Piman shamans communed. [80]

In his discussion of native leaders among Gila River Pima Indians, Paul Ezell is generally unwilling to project information gathered from informants living in the twentieth century backward into "aboriginal" times. He instead regards as trustworthy only data gleaned from the documentary records of Spaniards, Mexicans, and Anglo Americans. His reading of these documents convinces him that "in each village there was at least one individual looked upon as a leader," and that additionally "one man [in the late seventeenth and early eighteenth centuries] was accepted to some extent as having influence extending beyond his village. Perhaps this influence was not tribal in scope . . ."[81]

In general, tentative conclusions reached by Ezell about native leadership based on his search of the literature conform with the outlines suggested by Underhill in her 1930s ethnographic and oral historical research. For example, Ezell writes:

> . . . leading men decided important questions in deliberation with an informal council composed of older men, on both the village and supra-village levels.
>
> Although leadership of war parties was one of the primary functions of both the village and tribal leaders, frequently that role was played instead by a separate individual. The construction and maintenance of dams and ditches, the decision on the subjugation of new land, and the distribution of water were often the specific responsibility of individuals. Evidently these were decided by separate men.
>
> Finally, there was a public figure whose role and function can only be partially perceived from the data, the . . . "much talks person" [probably the Wise Speaker, or moral leader]. . . . [A]pparently he functioned almost as a "preacher" in so far as he harangued the people, exhorting them to conform to certain ideal behavior patterns.
>
> Officials and council members occupied their positions as a result of recognition by most, if not all, of the adult men in the village and nation of their status as being men of outstanding ability in some field or fields. Initiative and willingness to assume responsibility were also factors in the choice of men for office. . . . Age, i.e., maturity, evidently was a requisite and a concomitant of the prestige and status necessary for leadership and council membership . . .
>
> Offices were not hereditary . . . A son or nephew of the incumbent, however, was in a favored position to acquire the standing necessary for election . . .
>
> The Gila Pima official in aboriginal times evidently was a leader in the narrow sense, rather than a commander with means for enforcing his decisions.
>
> . . . [M]ost courses of action probably represented the decision of at least a majority of that group rather than of one man, and government was by agreement rather than by fiat.[82]

By the mid-nineteenth century, leadership patterns in northern Piman villages had been variously altered as a result of Spanish and, subsequently, Mexican influence. In some riverine villages in the southern part of northern Piman territory, Spaniards succeeded in superimposing a whole layer of Spanish governmental offices and institutions on what were the native counterparts. Eighteenth-century documents speak of native "governors," "mayors" (*alcaldes*), "judges" (*regidores*), "policemen" (*topiles*), "sheriffs" (*alguaciles*), and of both superior and minor church officers (*fiscales mayores* and *fiscales ordinarios*).[83]

Among the Gila River Pimas, however, Hispanic influence was more indirect than direct. There was never a full time Hispanic presence among the Gileños; there were no Spanish or Mexican towns, mines, ranches, forts, or missions ever established in their territory. Even so, Spaniards or, after 1821, Mexicans may have had at least a partial effect on Gila River Pima government. In January 1860 Indian agent Silas St. John reported on his seven months' full-time residence among the Pimas:

> I find their internal government superior to any other tribe I ever met. The hereditary chiefs are men of but little influence. Their government consists of a council made up by delegates, two or more being chosen from each pueblo or community. This council controls the affairs of the nation. Separately their functions are somewhat similar to those of the Mexican Alcalde [mayor]. These delegates or alcaldes are generally men of intelligence and the ones whom it is the policy of an agent to cultivate, and influence gained over a majority of these alcaldes would render any measure intended to benefit the nation comparatively easy of accomplishment. . . . [W]hen cases of theft are reported to them, they are jealous in their efforts to make restitution of the property, and are almost invariably successfull [sic], beside never asking or expecting reward for the same.[84]

Four months earlier, in September 1859, St. John forwarded a list of Pima and Maricopa villages and various leaders to the Commissioner of Indian Affairs. He showed Antonio Azul as "chief" of all 3,770 Pimas and their ten villages; Francisco Dukes was "chief" of the 472 Maricopas and their two villages. "Captains" of individual Pima settlements were Malarco, Ojo de Burro, Xavier, Candela, DeGuerra, Jose, Cuchillo del Mundo, Ortiz, Ignacio, and Francisco. The two Maricopa "captains" were Juan Cheveriah and Juan Jose.[85]

In 1858, Lieut. A. B. Chapman listed Juan Chevereah as "head chief" of the Maricopas and Juan Jose as "chief" of both Maricopa villages. Antonio Soule [Azul] was "head chief" of the Pimas while "chiefs" of the nine Pima settlements listed by Chapman were Ojo del Buro, Yiela del Arispe, Miguel, Xavier, Cabeza de Aquila, Chelan, Tabacaro, Cadrillo del Mundo, Ariza Aqua Bolando, Francisco, La Mano del Mundo, and Boca Dulce. The discrepancies between this list and that of St. John are probably the result of Chapman's short visit among the Pimas and his obvious lack of command of Spanish rather than of wholesale changes in personnel in the year between the two reports. Of these "chiefs" and "captains," or, if one prefers, of these "head chiefs" and "chiefs," it is clear that Antonio Azul was the principal political officer among the Gila River Pimas at the time of the 1857 battle. He was probably the war chief as well, although St. John said that because of his youth (about 25 years old in 1857), command during the fight was taken over by "subchiefs" who were older and more experienced.[86]

Antonio Azul had been preceded as principal political officer and war chief by a man known to outsiders as Culo Azul ("Blue Asshole"), but known to his fellow Pimans as Ti'ahiatam ("Piss"). Culo Azul shows up as a Piman head man in Mexican accounts of the 1830s; he was, according to a Forty Niner who saw him in June 1849, "the captain general, a very dignified looking old fellow"; and it was he who was regarded as "head chief" by John Russell Bartlett when they met in July 1852. Bartlett said he "appeared in a large blanket overcoat, pantaloons, and a green felt hat, while his attendants were either naked, or wore around their loins the white cotton blanket of their own manufacture." Culo Azul was still looked upon as "the Gileño general" in November 1853, when Captain Andrés Zenteno of Tubac's Mexican garrison sent messengers to ask that the two of them meet in Tucson to discuss mutual problems with Apaches.[87]

Antonio, Culo's son, succeeded his father as the principal Pima leader sometime between November 1853 and "early" 1855 when a delegation of Pimans visited the Mexican Ayudante Inspector in Santa Cruz, Sonora, asking in behalf of "General Antonio Azul" and the rest of the tribe what their status would be should they come under jurisdiction of the United States.[88] And in June of that year, "Capt. Antonio Azul, head chief" of the Pimas, as well as Francisco Luke and Malai,[89] Maricopa chiefs; chiefs Shalan, Ojo de Burro, Tabaquero, and La Boca de Queja of the Pimas; and chiefs Jose Victoriano Lucas and Jose Antonio of the San Xavier Papagos paid a personal visit to boundary surveyor William H. Emory when the latter was at Rancho Los Nogales near the United States and Mexican border created under terms of the Gadsden Purchase in June 1854.[90]

In 1902–03, ethnographer Frank Russell referred to Antonio Azul as "the present head chief, . . . known among his people as Uva-a'tuka, Spread Leg, from a peculiarity in his gait; also as Ma'vit Ka'wutam, Puma Shield, and by other names less elegant."[91] Emory gave his Pima name as Che-t-a-ca-moose (*Ce:dag̃ Mus*, "Blue Cunt").[92]

Although it is not altogether clear who the principal leader among the

Maricopas was in 1857, it would appear that Juan Chevereah (also Chivaria, Cheveriah, and Echevaria) and Francisco Luke (or Dukes) are likely candidates. An earlier Maricopa head chief, Juan Antonio Llunas, was described in January 1852 by Amiel W. Whipple as having been "commander-in-chief of the confederate [Maricopa and Pima] tribes," but he had been killed by Quechans or Apaches "within the last year."[93]

Aside from their influence on Piman and Maricopa social structure, Hispanics in both the colonial and Mexican periods had an even greater impact in the forms of items introduced into the native cultures: wheat, livestock and poultry, and—in all probability—canal irrigation. Hispanics, moreover, became a market for goods such as slaves and scalps and for foodstuffs surplus to the needs of Pima subsistence. There is little doubt that Pima agricultural products made their way south to Tucson and even farther south to other Hispanic settlements.[94]

From the Spanish and Mexican points of view, the Gileños were not only producers of needed goods, they were the first line of northern defense against the relentless raids and military attacks of Western Apaches.

With respect to Hispanic influence on Pima leadership, Ezell offers an excellent summary:

> The principal effect of Hispanic contact on the governmental structure of Gila Pima society was to formalize, to regularize, offices, functions, and procedures. The aboriginal organization of a headman and a council in each village, with one of the headmen occupying a (slightly) paramount position in some affairs, and some kind of intervillage council representation, was one which could be fitted easily into Spanish colonial government policy. Thus there was an existing culture pattern which could be integrated into the form of elective government provided by Spanish policy. Men who already had sufficient status to have made them acceptable to the Indians as leaders were, at Spanish instigation, so designated by the Indians. This choice was then formally confirmed by the local Spaniards. Because of the transient nature of the contacts between the two societies, a uniform and elaborate hierarchy of officialdom, such as came into existence in the south where contact was close and continuous, apparently was not achieved on the Gila River. The only real addition may have been that of choosing specific persons to represent the village in the intervillage council.[95]

A system of irrigation canals requires that there be persons who are responsible for their construction, operation, and maintenance. Frederick E. Grossmann, who was agent among the Pimas in 1870–71, wrote that "each Pima village elected two or three old men who decided everything pertaining to the digging of canals and construction of dams and regulated the distribution of water for irrigation. Landholders were responsible individually for the lateral which irrigated their fields."[96]

To be a Piman leader—which is to say, to occupy a status position within the society acknowledged by its members to qualify for that title as it is conceived by non-Indians—was first of all to be a mature male. Within the family setting, individual women may have been more infl uential than the men. And among groups of women, there were doubtless adult females who exerted more personal influence over their fellow females than others. There were female shamans, but there is no record of there having been such women who accompanied war expeditions into the field. Their powers seem to have been wholly curative.[97]

Women were systematically excluded from having a formal voice in council deliberations. The hunt, war, and game leaders were men; the owl-meeter shamans seem exclusively to have been men; those in charge of major decisions concerning activities related to agriculture were men. The community's moral leader was always a man.

It is clear from mid-nineteenth century accounts by non-Indians that each of the ten Pima villages had its own moral leader when the great battle occurred in 1857, and there was one leader, Antonio Azul, whose influence extended over all ten settlements.

THE WARPATH: BY FOOT AND HORSEBACK

All River Yuman war parties traveled on foot, although by the middle of the 1800s some men are known to have gone on horseback. Why the Quechans, Mohaves, and their allies chose to attack the Maricopa on foot requires some explanation.

First of all, the Colorado River Yumans did not integrate the horse into their cultures in the same thoroughgoing way as was being done on the Gila. For them, the supply of horses was intermittent and difficult to come by.[98] Even after the Quechans, Mohaves, and Cocopas began to value them highly they were unable to trade for them easily or amply, probably because they had so little to offer in commerce with northern Mexican settlements. We suspect also that the Quechans' and Mohaves' relations with the obvious middlemen in such transactions, the Papagos living south of the Gila, tended to deteriorate by the late eighteenth and early nineteenth centuries.

In any case, members of all three of these tribes loved to eat horsemeat. One of these animals coming into their possession would have been lucky to last the day. Harvey Wood, who crossed the Colorado River at Yuma in June 1849 made the point in his reminiscences:

> . . . [W]e got the [Quechan] Indians to swim our animals, the river being high and some four hundred feet in width, we thought it best to hire the Indians to get the animals over. The Indians were very unfortunate with every animal that was in good condition, and, what was singular, they would drown close by the opposite shore, and on watching, found the way it was done. Mr. Indian having the end of the rope attached to the mule or horse and swimming along side of the animal, when near the shore would jerk the animal's head under the water by using his foot on the slack of the rope, then the carcass would be drawn out on the shore, cut up and devoured by hungry Indians. They drowned six before we discovered the plan; after that a rifle drawn and aimed at the Indian attempting the trick again prevented any more accidents. [99]

They also slaughtered horses at funerals and in the annual Mourning Ceremony. [100] No evidence exists to show that they bred horses at any time up through the 1850s. [101] Thus it was that even though opportunities both for theft and for purchase increased remarkably beginning in the late 1840s with the great flow of horse-borne travelers passing down the Gila trail to California these tribes never built up large herds. Nor do many of the River Yumans seem to have taken to horseback for the wide-ranging travels for which they were so well known in the region.

Cocopas are known to have raided herds that were passing through to California in the 1850s, difficult as that must have been in the very heart of Quechan country a few miles south of Yuma Crossing. [102] Quechans first attempted large-scale horse theft in the late eighteenth century, and by one point in 1830 had built up two large herds for themselves. [103] Hunger will out, however, and they tided themselves over during lean periods by continuing to enjoy horseflesh. [104]

Mohaves were even less inclined to accumulate large numbers of horses, and this in spite of the fact they of all Colorado River peoples were those given most to long-range travel and trade with Indians living far from the Mohave Valley. We find no record through the first half of the nineteenth century of their having even a small herd of horses.[105] Neither are they known to have raised livestock of any sort.

Yavapais stole any horses that came their way and ate them, usually at once.[106]

One result of the appearance of the horse in the Gila-Colorado country was a new emphasis on taking captives in war so they could be traded for horses. It is probable that all these tribes had taken captives even in aboriginal times, but captives were merely symbolic or token objectives. By the early nineteenth century, however, captives—thanks to their marketability among Spaniards—assumed an enhanced value.

Evidence for Spanish-encouraged exchange of horses for captive Indians is more suggestive than ample.[107] Information is scanty for several predictable reasons. Wherever there was a legal requirement to record such transactions for purposes of taxation or purchases of licenses, it would have been to the advantage of those involved not to leave any record. Furthermore, a large part of the trade was conducted among Indian tribes and even within the same tribe,[108] meaning many transactions must have escaped the white man's attention. Finally, from time to time the Spanish government frowned on this practice.[109] Even so, it is documented that numbers of women and children were being taken and sold during the early and middle nineteenth century. The item often offered in trade was the horse.

Although they were said to have 153 horses in September 1859,[110] Maricopas seem never to have learned how best to use them in battle nor how to make their mounted contingents an effective weapon in raids into Quechan territory. It is clear that by the 1840s and 1850s they were trying to support their formations of clubmen with mounted warriors, perhaps by more than twenty in a given expedition.[111] But the Maricopas' own battle narratives suggest they never had enough riders to produce a real shock effect against massed club wielders. Perhaps their cavalry and infantry never learned to coordinate an attack against an enemy much more numerous than they. Also, the Maricopas may have put their least effective fighters on horseback in some of those engagements, with meager results.[112] More likely is that Maricopas simply lacked sufficient manpower to provide large enough contingents both on horse and on foot.

In spite of their penchant for supplementing their diets with horsemeat, and despite problems of keeping livestock in a period of intense hostilities among tribes, Cocopa, Quechans, and Mohaves began to make at least some use of horses as steeds as the nineteenth century wore on. Quechans used sizeable mounted units in attacking Cocopas on two occasions in 1849.[113] Given the fluctuating and uncertain supply of horses, however, such a strategy was a rare luxury. The Quechan supply of horses fell sharply in the 1850s when their hostilities with Cocopas, Maricopas, and U.S. soldiers reached a peak. They had to eat some of their animals during a time of famine in 1851–52; then the Cocopas attacked, killing fourteen of their remaining twenty-three mounts. Even early in 1851 Major Heintzelman, passing through Quechan territory from south to north along the river toward Fort Yuma, had difficulty finding a horse to buy.[114]

The Mohaves are supposed to have taken from two to five horses on war parties.[115] They used a few at home, probably not more than four at a time, to mount those *kwanami* who moved constantly about as watchmen in Mohave Valley and as sentinels beyond its boundaries to warn of approaching foreigners.[116] They never had enough horses for all their scouts to use, nor did they think it important to keep that many. This is a reasonable assumption because of several U.S. government expeditions that reached Mohave country in the 1840s and 1850s, not all saw horsemen.

It follows that it was after the unexpected hostilities brought on them in the 1820s by heavily armed fur traders that Mohaves initially concerned themselves seriously with defense of their valley. They already knew of horses, having acquired some in southern Alta California after 1819, and they pounced on others that came to hand in later years. They probably used horsemen as one means of providing early warning of attack and of quickly rallying defenders from widely scattered farmlands.

But the Mohaves had no regular source of supply for livestock, and they seem never to have expanded their trade into southern California in an effort to obtain horses in large numbers there. Neither did they make any noticeable attempt to equip large mounted contingents for war.

All this appears to indicate that the availability of the horse occasioned only a limited response among these tribes in the conduct of their mutual warfare and raiding.

If by mid-century the Quechans had finally begun to use sizeable detachments of mounted men in their war parties, they had already lost the opportunity that had lain before them in the 1830s, as Jack Forbes has pointed out, when the tribe might have played a major role in Indian-white conflicts in southern California.[117] To have done so would have required them to make many important changes in their culture, only two of which would have been a program of animal husbandry and the use of horses in long-range travel and communications. As it turned out, rather than expanding the limits of their trade and travel, Quechans withdrew into their riverine world beginning in the late eighteenth century and continuing to that fateful day in September 1857 when many warriors might well have traded a kingdom for a horse.

Mohaves, too, remained singularly unaffected by the potential offered by horses. They showed no signs of changing their military practices; neither did they launch expansionist enterprises. This was the case even though Mohaves were ideally situated both culturally and geographically to have taken advantage of the horse. They traditionally visited people who lived great distances away; they were well acquainted with leaders of many other peoples in present-day California and Arizona; they carried on a trade that could readily have been expanded into a major enterprise. They had plenty of well-watered grazing land far from the range of enemy depredations and they themselves were safe at home from attack by Indian neighbors. They were visited only occasionally by white people, none of whom settled nearby. It would have been easy enough for Mohaves to have put their whole tribe on horseback, but the thought seems never seriously to have occurred to them.

The Gila River Pimas became exposed to horses and livestock at least as early as the late seventeenth century in the time of Father Eusebio Kino, the pioneer Jesuit missionary who visited the region. In 1795 it was said of them that "they raise some horses and some kine, both large and small, although in small numbers. Under better guidance, however, these may increase so far as land will permit."[118]

One observer, describing Pimas as he saw them in May 1855 wrote, "They are owners of fine horses and milch cows, pigs and poultry, and are a wealthy class of Indians."[119] And Silas St. John counted 850 Pima horses and 799 Pima horned cattle in 1859.[120] The Gileños obviously took the horse unto themselves, even adding a myth to their oral literature to account for its origin.[121] They did not, however, look on the horse as providing the means by which to mount a campaign of annihilation against Yavapais and Apaches. They were far more interested in becoming equipped with rifles as a method for eliminating the Apache menace once and for all at a single stroke.[122]

In defense, it was another matter. Pimas were alone among the 1857 combatants in keeping large herds of horses on hand and in knowing how to use them effectively in pitched battle. By having sizeable mounted contingents, Pimas held a great advantage in defending their own territory.[123] They had a veritable cavalry. We do not know precisely how they managed their mounted forces in battle, but there is no doubt that they produced confusion and disarray among enemy forces while simultaneously large numbers of Pima foot soldiers entered the ranks against Mohave and Quechan club wielders.

Both Pimas and Maricopas took a few mounted men on raids against Yavapais and Apaches, the likelihood being that such small and middle-sized raiding parties had both horsemen and foot-fighters.[124]

Frank Russell, the ethnographer who worked among Gila River Pimas in 1901—02, asserted that Pimas had "very few" horses until about 1875, only enough to mount a small number of warriors going against the Apaches.[125] He cites no particular sources for his information, however, and, as noted above, by the time of his visit Pimas had even accounted for the mythical origin of the horse in their own territory. It is true that the sizes of Pima horse herds may have fluctuated as a result of Apache raiding and as a result of opportunistic sales of horses by Pimas to emigrants passing through their territory. It is certainly the case that after 1875 these two principal sources of fluctuation were greatly diminished.

What is clear is that Pimas have remained farmers throughout their history. Livestock, including horses, have always been peripheral to their central cultural and economic interests. There was surely a mounted Pima cavalry, but as in most armed conflicts, it was the foot soldier who carried the brunt of attack.

THE WARPATH: STRATEGY AND DREAMS ON THE TRAIL

Warriors in Yuman expeditions went lightly clothed and little encumbered by equipment or food. The only noticeable weight was in their weapons and in the small gourd canteen of water. These warriors took no more than a few handfuls of dried food whether the trip were to last for a day or two or for as long as eight to ten days. The people knew the local water resources by heart. They refused to raid into lands whose reliable sources of water were unknown to them.[126]

Warriors had consciously accustomed themselves to long periods of time without water and with short rations of food.

Charles Wilson, a Quechan Indian, told ethnomusicologist Frances Densmore that no songs were sung by a war party before its departure. When the party drew near enemy territory, warriors disguised themselves by rolling in mud and then in sand. "This caused their bodies to resemble the ground so closely that they could either work themselves forward without being seen or could lie motionless without attracting attention."[127]

As Mohaves neared their objective, the warriors reversed their travel routine, sleeping in concealment by day and moving forward only at night. Their interest was in drawing near the enemy's villages to launch an attack at dawn to kill as many residents as they could. Whether they often had it in mind to remain on the scene for a ritual battle is not known, although they did so on several occasions. One Mohave born too late to have seen any battles himself reported that a major engagement would ensue if—and probably only if—an enemy should escape the first attack and bring reinforcements down upon the raiding party.[128]

Anything so potentially dangerous as a war expedition was bound to heighten personal anxieties, inspire dreams, and cloak the warpath experience in supernatural overtones. That such was the case among Quechans is clearly seen in the vivid account related by Joe Homer to E. W. Gifford. It is a classic warpath narrative:

> Certain of the Yuma were living at Algodones. Some were also living on the Arizona side of the river opposite Algodones. Others were living at Fort Yuma. An Algodones man dreamt that they were going to have good luck in killing the Maricopa. Then the Algodones people called upon the Yuma people on the east side of the river to interpret the man's dream for them. The dreamer said, "I dreamed that I had all kinds of animals and birds around me on the mountain. I laid hold of all these things and killed them. I call upon you to ask you the meaning of this dream." The Yuma on the east side of the river said: "That means that you will be a good warrior and kill many people." Then the Algodones man said: "Ten days from now I am going into the desert to attack the Maricopa." The allied Yuma and Mohave forces were to meet at Parker.

After ten days had elapsed the Algodones people went to Fort Yuma to ask permission of the Yuma chief Pasqual to go upon the war party. They told him they intended to meet the Mohave at Parker and then to proceed into the desert to go against the Maricopa. The chief Pasqual said: "I do not think you are good fighters. You are worthless. I will not allow you to take my people over there." Then the Algodones man told his dream in the same way to the chief. When he had finished relating it, the chief said: "That dream is nothing. I can tell you what your dream means in a minute. It means that you are going to die, and that all kinds of birds and animals are going to come and eat you. That is what the dream means. I do not want you to take my people [of Fort Yuma]. You can take your own people."

The Algodones man was undeterred and he said: "I will have to go and hunt deer and rabbits and have a good time at Parker." The chief Pasqual and many of the people did not go, but others went with the Algodones man. They camped at Picacho, Eclipse, and Sibolio on three respective nights. At Sibolio a deer came from the mountains toward the people. It fell down and died. The Algodones man interpreted the omen as follows: "I am lucky. You will not be starving to death on the desert, for the birds and animals will come and die for us to eat. I think we will have a good time all the way through." Then the people cooked the deer meat on the coals.

The warriors started for Ehrensburg [Ehrenberg]. They passed through it and saw a jackrabbit running by the road. The jackrabbit fell dead.

When the warriors were a little beyond Ehrensburg a messenger from the chief at Fort Yuma overtook them. The chief besought them not to proceed against the Maricopa. The following is the message sent by the chief: "I am sorry that my people are going on a war party. I dreamt that all of the Algodones people stood on the north side, and all of the Fort Yuma people on the south side. A storm and darkness came. It drove all of the Algodones people away, but did not bother the Fort Yuma people. I wish you would come right back. Do not go."

The Algodones leader made fun of the message and said the Fort Yuma chief was a woman and loved one of the young men whom he wished to marry, and that he feared that the young man might be killed. He said to the messenger: "You tell him all that I say." There were some great warriors with the party. Four or five Yumas gave heed to the chief's wishes and returned with the messenger.

The party went on and reached Parker seven days after having left Fort Yuma. There they joined the Mohave whom they informed that they had the permission of their chief. The assembled allies then thought that they were ready to proceed against the Maricopa. The night before their intended start against the Maricopa another messenger related another ominous dream which the chief had: "I was asleep one night and dreamt that a big whirlwind came and carried all you people far away. Then there was darkness all over the place. I could not find any of you. Now I want you to come back. My dream is a very bad sign. I wish you would mind me." The Algodones leader sent back the following taunting message: "Why don't you keep quiet and stay away? When I come back you will be my wife."

Next morning the expedition started out on the desert. An eagle appeared in the air and fell dead in front of the troops. The Algodones man interpreted the omen as indicating that his dream was right and they should go on. "We are great warriors," he said, "and everything favors us."[129]

The events of 1 September 1857 would prove him wrong. This was one time the warpath should have been abandoned and the advice of Pasqual of Fort Yuma taken to heart. His dreams were the most powerful.

FOUR

Armed Conflict:
Tools, Techniques, Victory, and Defeat

I f armed conflict has its methodology, which is to say its relationship to aspects of culture such as political organization, economics, social structure, and religious beliefs, so does it have its methods: military paraphernalia, costume, and techniques of combat. So does it have its almost inevitable conclusion: withdrawal from engagement and those various acts of exaltation or lamentation. Those, too, differed among participants of the 1857 affair on the Gila.

TO OUTFIT FOR BATTLE

Warriors of all the Yuman tribes used almost identical weapons. Important variations were in the numbers in a war party carrying each kind of weapon. Another difference lay in tribal preferences for various weapons on the battlefield.

The most important weapon, the one that decided many hand-to-hand fights and that was most useful in dawn raids against small settlements, was the short, very heavy club made of mesquite or ironwood and shaped like a potato masher or a mason's or woodcarver's mallet. This club had an enlarged knob at one end; the shaft of the handle was sharpened to a point. This weapon was designed for fighting at close proximity. It needed to be heavy, yet light enough for rapid and powerful arm motions. These weapons—the Quechans' *ke'lyaxwai,* the Mohaves' *kălyá'hwai,* the Northeastern Yavapais' *baavi,* the Cocopas' *i·š*—were never more than two feet long and many were shorter than twelve inches. Some of the tribes slightly indented the top of the knob so that a sharpened cutting edge ran around the outer circumference.[1] The Northeastern Yavapai club, carved of mesquite or acacia, had a rounded or ball head with no sharp edges. The Western Yavapai, however, used the potato-masher shaped club, while the Southeastern Yavapai followed Western Apache custom in using a war club made of a stone encased in rawhide attached to the end of a stick partially or wholly covered with rawhide.[2]

An almost equally useful club was the *to'kyet,* also made of mesquite and used in slashing and beating. These tapering staves or truncheons were used by both Cocopas and Quechans. It is "astonishing," said Spier, that the Maricopa failed to adopt this weapon, some two to four feet long and giving its wielder a considerable reach advantage over an opponent carrying a potato masher.[3]

Many raiders or fighters went armed with the bow, which was made of willow, cottonwood, or even mesquite. Arrows used by Yumans varied in construction more than is reflected in the anthropological literature,[4] but most shafts were made of arrowweed with a few being fashioned from the less satisfactory cane (*Phragmites communis*) found in stream courses. Most were of a single shaft. Many were pointed merely by sharpening and subsequent hardening in fire. The weapon was not useful for long-range killing because of the weak pull of the bow. The three-foot long arrows hardly penetrated at ranges beyond a few dozen yards. Some of the tribes poisoned the arrow tips and claimed that they could kill people from the effects of the poison alone. Yavapais pulverized a mixture of rattlesnake venom, spiders, centipedes, a variety of long-winged bee, and walnut leaves. They bagged this mixture in deerskin and buried it in hot ashes for a day, thus rotting some of the ingredients. Then they hung the mixture up to dry until it was smeared on the arrowpoints.[5]

Many Quechan arrows were marked with messages. "Such an arrow could be shot over the heads of an enemy and its message would summon help to a war party that was hard pressed."[6]

Almost all these warriors carried some sort of knife or dagger. The Quechan knife was eighteen inches long,[7] and while most were of stone or fire-hardened sticks, by the middle nineteenth century some of the knives were of metal.

Some warriors carried shields into battle.[8] Yavapai shields were often a mere curtain of buckskin rigged to hang from the bow when held across the body. Southeastern Yavapais carried a foot-wide disc of mountain sheepskin that would turn arrows.[9] Mohave clubmen bore shields made of the toughest part of deerhide, with a wooden handle at the center as a one-handed grip. These shields could be hung in front to free both hands.[10] The Maricopa shield could be worn either in front or back.

Only one tribe, Southeastern Yavapai, wore anything resembling body armor. They discovered that cooked mescal (*Agave* spp.), if pounded, molded, and dried into plates, could be shaped into such pieces and worn to protect the area from the neck to the upper leg. Bigger plates worn on the back shielded a man's head as well.[11] The amount of clothing worn by warriors in battle was normally so little that it afforded no protection. The exception was the Yavapais' buckskin shirts and leggings, but when Yavapais raided in the south they wore only the leggings and not the shirt.[12]

The Quechan war leader was black from head to toe and wore two eagle feathers in his hair. He might also wear the distinctive helmet of feathers with a roach of horsehair running from back to front with more feathers trailing all around the lower edges at sides and back.[13] The men with him painted their faces "black, with a red streak down the center" from forehead to chin. "Their hair they also colored, red, for the battle, weaving it into a sort of helmet or turban, which renders them fearful to behold."[14]

The Mohave, like the rest, went into battle wearing only breechclouts. This gave a full view of their body painting of "rows of white lines, zigzags, circles, or spirals on the chest, and . . . red paint on their hair."[15] The hair was bound back, held by a rawhide band, partly to keep it out of the enemy's grasp. Some of them brought long braids of vines from the black-eyed pea plant to wrap around their stomachs for protection during battle. Some wore eagle feathers, or eagle down, worked into their hair. One or more of the Mohave leaders wore the battle cap, a high fan of feathers standing up and sideways from a central point on the head. Like the Quechans', the Mohaves' pike-bearer was covered with black paint, and the war leader appeared with black paint banded with red across his forehead.[16] The warriors had a black stripe running horizontally across the face at eye level.

Maricopa warriors came into battle togged and painted very much like their Colorado River enemies. The Maricopa stavebearer painted himself jet black and like the warriors wore breechclouts and sandals as did the Quechan and Mohave men when they came across the desert to attack Maricopa villages. The warriors of the Gila sometimes coiled their hair in long strands atop the head or joined the long hair down the back in braids held together. They came painted as if for one of their fiestas, with a "mask-like black stripe across the eyes and horizontal lines in white across the long back hair."[17]

To demonstrate their bravery, a few fighters wore an eagle feather cap with the plumes projecting sideways and up, very much like the Mohave cap. Other Maricopas worked a feather, or more than one, down into their back hair.

Opposing forces could be arrayed so much alike that individual warriors sometimes added decoration to be sure they would be identified by their own men in battle. The most vivid such device was used by Quechans, who mudded hair and face, then drew striations in the wet mud with their fingers thereby making themselves unmistakably and immediately known to each other.[18]

Fighting men among the Gila River Pimas were divided into two groups: those who fought with club and shield and those who were bowmen.[19] The bow used in warfare, as distinct from the hunting bow, was made of mulberry wood gathered from the Superstition or Pinal mountains. Willow served as a substitute. The Pima hunting bow was a simple arc. Bows were undecorated and, according to Frank Russell, who collected a double-curved compound bow, they were not very carefully made. "Those which exhibit weakness through splitting or otherwise are bound with fresh sinew in bands which shrink around the arms at the point where reinforcement is needed."[20]

In 1696 or 1697 Father Eusebio Kino, the pioneer Jesuit priest among the northern Piman Indians, drew a picture showing two Pimans assassinating Father Francisco Javier Saeta. This sketch, drawn by Kino to illuminate a map drafted to accompany a biography of his martyred Jesuit missionary companion, shows both Pimans using compound bows.[21] They are surprisingly similar to the war bow collected by Russell in the early twentieth century.[22]

Pima war arrows were fashioned from the straight stem of the arrowweed (*Pluchea sericea*). The nocked end was fitted with three feathers, each less than a hand's breadth in length and slightly curved.[23] According to

Castetter and Underhill, Papagos preferred eagle feathers or feathers from three species of hawk. Buzzard, turkey, and crow feathers were not used because "the buzzard is stupid and does not kill and the other two birds are timid." Papagos kept chicken hawks in cages for their tail feathers.[24] Russell notes that Pimas also kept hawks, as well as eagles, but he says their feathers were plucked "for the paraphernalia of the medicine-men."[25] Owl feathers were never used for fletching since owls were an ill omen.[26]

Most Pima arrowheads, according to Russell, were those made by the prehistoric Hohokam. These were subsequently found and reused by Pimas. "However, the Pimas always had a few arrowhead makers who worked in obsidian, shale, or flint."[27] Captain Frederick E. Grossmann, who was the Pimas' Indian agent in 1870–71, published a report which said, "For hunting fishes and small game they use arrows without hard points, but the arrows used in battle have sharp, two-edged points made of flint, glass, or iron. When going on a scout against the Apache Indians, their bitter foes, the Pimas frequently dip the points of their arrows in putrid meat, and it is said that a wound caused by such an arrow will never heal, but fester for some days and finally produce death."[28]

Edward F. Castetter and Ruth Underhill wrote that Papagos usually made stone-tipped arrows for war and large game, and wooden-tipped arrows for small game. And Papagos, apparently unlike Pimas, set the stone arrowhead in a foreshaft of hardwood, usually creosote bush (*Larrea tridentata*). The foreshaft, once dried, was split at one end, dipped in a boiling secretion or gum that is collected from white brittlebush (*Encelia farinosa*), and fitted with the stone point. When the secretion cooled, the arrowhead was tied to the foreshaft with wet sinew where it was further held in place by the gummed split. Papago arrow shafts, contrasted to those of the Pima, were made of soft woods such as those of cane (*Phragmites communis*) or desert broom (*Baccharis sarothroides*).[29]

Russell says that "all [Pima] arrow shafts are measured and cut the length from tip of forefinger to nipple breast of the maker. Both bows and arrows are sometimes stained with the blood of the jack rabbit, and war arrows may be dyed at the ends with the cochineal which makes its home on the Opuntias. The quiver is made of wild-cat skin."[30]

Shields carried by the club-and-shield fighters were round and only about two feet in diameter. According to Grossmann, they were "made of rawhide, which, when thoroughly dry, becomes so hard that an arrow, even if sent by a powerful enemy at a short distance, cannot penetrate it."[31]

A Pima shield in the Smithsonian Institution's collections obtained in the nineteenth century is described by Russell:

> It is a rawhide disk 49 cm. in diameter, provided with a cottonwood handle of convenient size for grasping. The handle is slightly concave on the side next to the shield. It is attached by means of thongs, which pass through two holes for each end of the handle, at the center of the disk. When not in use, it was carried by a sling strap that passed through two holes at the border 24 cm. apart. It is ornamented by an ogee swastika in blue, red, and white.[32]

Pima war clubs were similar to those carried by various groups of Yumans. Again, shaped like old-fashioned potato mashers, these were carved out of mesquite or ironwood. The ends of the handles were brought to a point to make them effective weapons in a back-handed blow. Four such clubs reported by Russell ranged in length from 38.4 to 48 centimeters, with heads about 9 centimeters in diameter. Russell also said that the lance was another Pima battle implement. "A short sharpened stick was sometimes used by the Pimas, who adopted it from the Yumas and Maricopas after the Spaniards supplied steel heads for the weapon. The sticks were covered with red mineral paint."[33]

At least some, if not all, Pima warriors donned a feather headdress in battle. The Reverend Isaac T. Whittemore, who worked as a Protestant missionary among the Pimas in the late nineteenth century, wrote that when the Indians agreed on a time for an offensive campaign against their enemies, "all the war chiefs and warriors then got ready, with feathers in their hair, faces and hair painted, and clubs and shields or bows and arrows and sometimes lances, and some food."[34]

Russell collected a Pima war headdress at Gila Crossing in the early twentieth century. He described it as follows:

> . . . an old Pima headdress made from the hair of an Apache and the wing feathers of three species of large raptorial birds. The hair is about 45 cm. long and is gathered in strands 1 cm. in thickness, which are held by two strips of cotton that are twisted or twined on each other a half turn between each pair of hair strands. Viewing the headdress from the rear there are on the left four owl feathers, symbolizing keenness of vision by night; next are three hawk, then

one owl, and again hawk feathers to the number of five, symbolizing keenness of vision by day; on the right are two eagle feathers, the symbol of swiftness. Thus the wearer of this headdress possessed the courage and cunning of the hated enemy, the keen sight by day and by night of the birds that have great magic power, according to Pima belief, and the swiftness as a trailer of the king of birds, which occupied a prominent place in Piman mythology.[35]

Father Kino's sketch of the two bowmen assassinating Father Saeta in 1695 depicts them wearing headdresses of some kind, possibly headbands with three feathers protruding from each at the rear.[36]

Body and face painting among Gila River Pima warriors is less clearly described. Waterman L. Ormsby, who in October 1858 saw two or three Pima men who had just returned to their Gila River home after a fruitless search for Apaches, wrote, "Their faces were painted an ebony black and their lips of a deep red color, so that at first I thought they were blacks."[37] Reverend Whittemore, quoted above, speaks of "faces and hair painted," and Russell writes of men dressed "in feather headdress and battle colors."[38] Unfortunately, he does not say what the colors were. Grossmann notes that a Pima who had killed an enemy had to undergo a purification rite that involved sixteen days of seclusion. During the second four days of this seclusion he plastered his hair with a mixture of black clay and mesquite gum. This was allowed to dry hard before being washed out on the night of the eighth day. "On the ninth morning he again besmears his head with black clay without the gum."[39]

Thanks to Ruth Underhill, we do have a fairly good description of the well-painted Papago warrior:

> The warrior's hair was clubbed in a knot at the back of his neck. He wore one of several sorts of headdresses or possibly none at all. His face according to some informants, was painted black from the start, and after killing an enemy, the lower part was white. According to others, it was not painted at all until he had killed an enemy and then all black. Black paint was considered symbolic of dizziness and drunkenness and therefore of war. One of the chants says:
>
> > My desire was the black madness of war.
> > I ground it to powder and therewith I painted my face.
> > My desire was the black dizziness of war.
> > I tore it to shreds and therewith tied my hair
> > in a war knot.[40]

It is also Underhill who gives us the best description of the properly out fitted northern Piman warrior embarking on a raiding expedition. Although her informants were Papagos, it is likely that a Gila River Pima going would have been similarly equipped and attired:

> They carried shield and club or bow and arrows as they chose. Specialization in one or another form of fighting was a permanent arrangement, only a few of the bravest using shield and club, which meant close-in fighting. Archers put a new string on the bow and carried another string in the quiver. They carried three hundred arrows, stone-tipped if possible, but a few wooden ones might be used to fill out the number. Every man took two pairs of sandals. Many wore headdresses in any form that suited them and these were repaired and made by the warrior himself.
>
> When equipped, the warrior had his quiver slung over the right shoulder, so that it hung with the opening at the left, just at the waist. His bow he carried in his left hand and while fighting he would have several more arrows in this hand also. His other baggage hung from the thong around his waist that held the breechclout. Even if he were not a club fighter, he might carry a club to finish the enemy. This was hung directly at the back. At the right he had a pouch, containing cornmeal which, mixed with water, would be his only food. In the same pouch might be a smaller one for tobacco and cornhusks or reed tubes for cigarettes. Another small pouch contained black and white paints. A half gourd, to serve as mixing bowl and drinking cup was slung from his belt by a thong. Some warriors distributed these various possessions in several pouches, elaborately made of fox or other animal skin with the fur on.[41]

Differences in appearance and equipage of warriors depended on whether fighting was offensive or defensive. The Yumans of the Colorado River and their allies arrived on the Gila in 1857 in full battle regalia, the men dressed according to their various elaborate cultural prescriptions. For the Maricopas and Pimas, however, it was more likely their warriors grabbed whatever fighting tools were at hand and joined the fight with bows, arrows, clubs, shields, and perhaps a few lances. Contemporary accounts mention no firearms. Joe Homer, the Quechan who spoke to E. W. Gifford in 1921, asserted Pimas used rifles. And George Devereux, writing in the 1950s, spoke of the Mohaves' "contempt for the Maricopa, who refused to play fair and allied themselves with mounted Pima Indians armed with rifles."[42] No Yumans making these claims, however, had been alive in 1857.

BATTLE

All attacks, whether by Yumans or Pimans, aimed at initial surprise. Among the Yumans, most attacks were made at dawn. If the objective was a small settlement with only a few families, and if the attackers were numerous and determined enough, they could surround the place and kill or capture everybody. Sometimes they were content to catch one person outside the settlement, to kill or carry that person off, and to steal a few horses or anything else that came easily to hand. Raids such as these must have been by far the most frequent of all inter-tribal hostilities.

One gets the strong impression these raids were aimed at damaging the enemy without losing attackers. Tribesmen seem to have tried to plan the kind of attack that would not develop into a major encounter resulting in heavy loss of life. The reasons for this were surely many, but among them might have been the fact that Yuman men feared the thought of dying in enemy country. To be abandoned there meant the dead warrior's soul could never be laid to rest. To make the journey from this world to the next, the warrior must be dispatched via a four-day funeral and mourning cere-mony, one progressing in proper stages accompanied by songs and culminating in cremation. Without that ritual, the warrior's soul would wander forever, without hope of finding a final resting place.[43]

Of all the kinds of hostilities in which these tribes engaged, ritual battle was the only type of warfare in which one might expect there would be casualties on both sides. The record makes it clear that those on the offen-sive in a warfare expedition repeatedly left dead fighters on the field. Only one of the battles on record resulted in victory for those who launched the assault (see Table 1, p. 107). In all the rest, the attacking party was forced to flee to save lives.

The element of surprise was equally important to Pima Indians who went on a raid. "They usually surround the Apache rancheria at night," wrote Grossmann, "some warriors placing themselves near the doors of all huts; then the terrible war-cry is sounded, and when surprised Apaches crawl through the low doors of their huts the war-clubs of the Pimas descend upon their heads with crushing force."[44]

Unlike the Yumans and Apaches, Pimas raided primarily for vengeance rather than for booty. Their offensive engagements could even be viewed as ultimately defensive in nature—raids staged to signal Apaches that Pimas could not themselves be attacked with impunity. Any captives or captured horses were simply a bonus, a by-product of Pimas' attempts to settle scores.

When a Pima warrior was killed in battle his bow and arrows were broken and left on the spot. "Oftentimes," noted Russell, "the body of a man killed in battle was burned, though this method of disposal of the body was never employed at the villages."[45] And writing about Papagos, Underhill says, "Cremation was definitely for the purpose of destroying enemy magic, for it did not take place after accidental shooting at the hunt, nor after murder by a fellow Papago. Only enemy wounds made it necessary."[46]

The record is silent on what occurred should a Pima die in battle and his comrades not be able to retrieve his body for cremation. Chances are that when Pimas were unable to retrieve their warriors' bodies from the battlefield, it was looked upon as a calamity.

For Yumans, the first act in a ritual battle was confrontation, with warriors often drawn up facing each other in lines while defenders were still taking arms and hurrying in from distant villages. Meanwhile, the attackers showed their bravery by waiting until anyone who wished to oppose them could be found and brought forward.

Time was usually allowed before battle for well-known fighters and orators to roar out their defiance at the enemy, fully expressing their disdain for his little courage and doubtful manhood. Accounts of this prelude to battle make it sound as if the leading warriors were working themselves up to a pitch of anger. One of Leslie Spier's informants told him such a verbal interchange had occurred before the 1857 fight:

> The Yuma boasted they had been to the Cocopa three days before and killed everyone there. They said they had come to stay a few weeks and marry [to trifle with?] some girls. The Halchidhoma champion replied, "When a girl wants to marry, she goes somewhere to stay a few weeks. So I think you came here because we are handsome men. We will keep you three or four weeks, and if we do not like you, we will turn you away." Each side was implying that their opponents were women. When the Maricopa champion marched up and down, he said he had always been successful in battle; he would annihilate the whole Yuma tribe even though he die in the attempt. He was actually killed in the fight.[47]

Kutox, who was Spier's principal Halchidhoma informant, added details to his version of the 1857 battle (recounted earlier on pages 23–24):

Soon after [the Maricopas attacked the Quechan villages on the Colorado River] the Yuma came to our village near Sacate to fight. They had about the same number of men as we had at this village, and about one hundred Mohave came to help them. Our bravest warriors had been killed but we had some left, so the Yuma decided to come here to exterminate the whole tribe. The enemy and our people lined up a short distance apart. A Yuma walked up and down in front of their line, saying that he had come to live with the Maricopa, to be friends; that he had brought his men to take care of [rape] all the widows [they would create]. Then our man said that he had thought of going to the Yuma villages to take care of all the widows there, but thought he had better wait for some childish people to come play with him. He might play for a day or two, then he would start for the Colorado.

After the talk was ended, both sides shot at each other. Then the Maricopa sent word to the Halchidhoma, who lived [to the east] near Sacate, and to the Pima. Shortly after the fighting began, the Mohave deserted. When the Yuma saw the Halchidhoma and Pima horsemen arriving by the hundreds, they felt afraid and fled. The Maricopa drove the Yuma toward the Gila, but killed nearly all before they had gone far. Only a few men escaped: some count five, some six.[48]

At other times, the champions on each side may have come forward for single combat, or for small encounters of four against four. The impression one gets is that the formal battle always began with one or another of these small demonstrations among a few of the most notable fighters.[49] Before long, however, everyone was eager to take part and the formations of warriors surged forward. In the forefront would be a very few men who were especially brave and famous as fighters who bore the symbolic feathered stave.

Each of these Colorado River and Gila River Yuman tribes used the feathered battle stave or pike, a mesquite pole about five feet long with a cord looping around the stick so as to provide tying points for many pairs of long feathers that would wave beautifully in the breeze when the pole was held overhead.[50] The stave served as a rallying point and an inspiration to all of one's own warriors. It was carried to the front of the lines, probably just as the warriors surged forward toward each other, and sometimes it was planted in the ground to be defended at all costs by its bearer so long as he could keep his feet and stay alive.

The stavebearers had slightly different parts to play during the battle. Two such warriors entered the fight for the Quechans. Neither could use his stave as a weapon, and only one of the two bore a short club with which he tried to defend himself and his companion. The Maricopa battle stave likewise was not to be used as a weapon; but the man carrying it, who was supposed to be the tribe's best fighter, had a mallet club for his own defense and for attacking enemies. The Mohave staveman used his pole as a weapon, making jabs with either of its sharpened points. None of these champions was expected to retreat from the field once he had made his appearance in the front of battle, even if his fellow fighters were driven away.[51]

Most often the stavebearers were quickly surrounded by a dense mass of warriors at the center of the lines, men who wielded the short club against each other and who endeavored to force their way through the enemy phalanx to break his line into fragments and to drive the warriors individually from the field. This would enable them to kill their enemies one by one or in small fugitive groups. Warriors advanced on each other holding the short club near its knobbed end, thrusting or jabbing the point at the enemy's body until he doubled over in pain. Then, with a twist of the arm that brought the heavy end uppermost, he banged it upward against his opponent's face, knocking him down severely wounded, perhaps dying.[52]

Maricopas and Mohaves used the club in a different way from the Quechans, seizing the opponent's long hair to pull his head down, then delivering a smashing blow from above or slamming the weapon upward into his face.[53] The Mohave were also known to seize an enemy and heave him over the shoulder, holding him suspended down his back with the enemy's head exposed to the blows of other Mohaves coming up from the rear.[54]

It is no longer possible to know exactly how the different tribes arranged their warriors into formations. Some accounts have the warriors spread out laterally with the best fighters at the center with mallet clubs and flanked by less effective fighters who carried either the long club or bows and arrows. At the very outside edge of a formation might be a few horsemen. Other reports have the River Yuman force arranged with mallet wielders in front, those with longer clubs just behind, and archers in the rear, sometimes also with horsemen following behind and then charging through the people who were on foot.[55]

As fighting shifted slowly across the battleground, those who had been hard hit and knocked off their feet were in danger of being killed by other enemies who followed, lashing tremendous blows with the longer mesquite club, the *tokyeta*. At that stage, any boys, older men, or women on the scene would make their presence felt. And it is likely that in each of these formalized encounters there came a moment when one side or both could see victory at hand. The enemy, reduced drastically in numbers, was in danger of annihilation. Some encounters did not progress this far. Sometimes, however, remaining warriors on the losing side chose to die rather than return home in defeat or be killed while retreating.

Both sides enjoyed advantages. Quechans fighting defensively at their own villages could take good advantage of the longer club. Maricopas with shorter mallets were beaten down in numbers before they could strike.[56] On the other hand, the Maricopas' advantage over the Quechans was in the ready support they had from hundreds of rugged Pima warriors who fought equally well on foot or on horseback. The Pimas' cavalry often turned the tide when the horsemen broke through the massed Quechan club wielders and rode down individuals, sometimes totally destroying the Colorado River force. So, at least, says tradition.

But these strengths on either side actually bespeak something simpler, the advantage of numbers when fighting on one's own ground. No matter how effective Quechans were with the long clubs, they are not known to have used them effectively against Pima horsemen in fighting at the Maricopa villages. The successful use of the *tokyeta* by Quechans against Maricopas was the result of arming every available defender, young and old, male and female, with clubs. Such defenders far outnumbered the attackers.

The same was true in Maricopa country, where the sheer numbers of Pimas and Maricopas wore down attackers from the Colorado River. In an effort to balance the disadvantage of numbers they would face in Maricopa lands, Quechans brought allies with them—Mohaves and, occasionally, Yavapais and a few Western Apaches.

It becomes obvious that to launch an attack with a battle as the intended culmination was to invite disaster. In most of the battles involving Yumans of which we know, the attackers died on the field with only a few survivors.

Although the Gila River Pimas were perfectly capable of organizing and carrying out successful vengeance raids on their enemies—especially the Apaches—they were far more concerned with defensive than with offensive strategy. They were successful sedentary farmers and their major interest along military lines was in finding means to protect themselves while they planted and harvested crops.

In July 1852, John R. Bartlett and his group of United States and Mexico boundary surveyors came into Pima country from the direction normally taken by Apache raiders. The reaction of the Pimas, lucidly described by Bartlett, was probably not unlike their reaction five years later when their Maricopa neighbors were attacked from the west by Quechans, Mohaves, and their allies:

> *July 5th.* At half-past four [in the morning], without waiting for breakfast (for the reason that we had none to cook), we resumed our journey, and in two miles reached the Gila, or rather its bed; for it was dry here. As we entered the first fields of the Pimos, the sentinels in the outskirts, seeing us approach in long single file, mistook us for Apaches and gave the alarm accordingly; a very natural mistake, as no party of emigrants or travellers had ever entered their country from the north. We heard the alarm given, and echoed in all voices, from one tree or house-top to the other, until it reached their villages. "Apaches! Apaches!" was the cry from every mouth; and when it reached the first village it was borne onward to every part of the community, even to their allies the Maricopas. The two Indian guides who were with us, discovered the stampede we had so unintentionally caused among their Pimo brethren, and seemed to enjoy the joke much. In a few minutes we saw the Pimos mounted, bounding towards us in every direction, armed and ready for the contest; others, on foot with their bows and arrows, came streaming after them; and in a short time, the foremost horseman, who was doubtless striving to take the first Apache scalp and bear it as a trophy to his people, reigned [sic] his steed before us. As he and those about him perceived their mistake, they all burst into a hearty laugh, which was joined in by the rest as they came up. [57]

In September 1859, Silas St. John reported to the Commissioner of Indian Affairs there were 3,770 Pimas and 472 Maricopas. He estimated that of these, some 1,200 men and women were "working people," while there were a thousand men "who follow the war path." He said if U.S. military posts were to be established in the Apache country it would "relieve the necessity of the large war parties now kept in the field by these Indians." [58]

In a letter written to the Commissioner of Indian Affairs four months later, St. John asserted, "There are at least one thousand professed warriors in the nation, from three to four hundred who are constantly in the field against their hereditary enemy the Apache. Their weapons consist only of a short club and the bow and arrow, while their adversaries [Apaches] are quite well supplied with guns and ammunition. A few rifles—say one hundred—would be invaluable to the Pimos."[59]

Those "in the field" were in all probability lookouts on guard duty rather than warriors on attack. Columbus H. Gray, who arrived in southern Arizona in 1868, recalled an event which occurred some time during the following decade:

> While sojourning in Pima and Maricopa counties, I witnessed several incidents which are hard for me to forget. One that impressed me so much I will relate it. We turned our poor cattle loose to hunt forage. They were compelled to range out ten to fifteen miles. It was my custom to cut sign every morning, go outside of all cattle tracks among the sand hills. Occasionally the squaws would band together and go away out to procure mesquite wood. The first time I witnessed this sight I was out some ten or twelve miles. From the top of a sand hill, looking back toward the river, I saw a strange sight. I saw two hundred and fifty Indian women in a long line with their three-cornered baskets and long slick-sticks, that at first resembled a herd of cattle, their sticks looking like horns. The wood being reached, they began filling their baskets, and when filled they each had a good burro load. It was a sight to see them when loaded start back with their heavy burdens in a little trot peculiar to themselves. I noticed, too, what struck me so forcibly, a picket line being maintained along the crest of the sand hills by the Pima warriors. They were armed with bows and arrows, and each sentinel stood with his bow slung ready to fire on the first sight of an enemy. Thus was the frontier being maintained . . . .[60]

Paul Ezell speculates that the Pima system of sentinels probably postdates 1774 when Apaches were able to kill some sixty Pimas in a single village.[61] Be that as it may, by 1857 they had a well-developed military defense organization, one which involved not only sentinels and a rapid communication system, but one which included both mounted cavalry and armed warriors on foot. Says Russell: "The men may be forgiven for allowing the women to perform certain tasks in the cultivation of the crops

that are usually considered to be the portion of the stronger sex when it is
learned that this plan was necessary in order to maintain pickets constantly
for long periods, and that an armed guard was the sole guaranty of safety
to the villages."[62]

About all that is known about Pima battle tactics is that mounted Pima
fighters were most often the first to get into a fray, and that some men
wielded bow and arrows while others carried wooden clubs or lances.
Warriors on horseback were surely able to intimidate enemies who were on
foot, but it is likely that infantry rather than cavalry was responsible for
most of the actual killing.

As for Pima techniques of hand-to-hand combat, a detailed account is
available. Evanico, a seventy-year-old one-time Pima warrior in 1933 discussed the matter with historian Arthur Woodward:

> [Pima war clubs] were carried in the belt, head upward, when not
> in use. A Pima warrior was usually armed with a rawhide shield
> about two feet in diameter, a bow, a quiver of arrows, and a knife or
> lance.
>
> Desert fights were generally fought at close range, when the stub-
> by war clubs and knives were brought into play. Shields were held at
> arm's length by a wooden handle fastened to the inner side with
> rawhide thongs. Upon the face of the shield a design was painted, the
> pattern radiating from the center in a series of straight or wavy lines,
> scrolls, circles, or in the form of a swastika. These designs were
> painted in red, blue, yellow, white, etc. Usually the warriors armed
> with such a shield carried only knives or clubs. In a fight the shield
> carriers leaped nimbly about, twisting the shield constantly until,
> seen from the front, the disk presented an illusion of colors, making
> it a difficult target and a distraction to an opposing bowman . . .
>
> I asked Evanico as to the nature of the designs on the shields . . .
>
> Evanico insisted that the designs were intended only to baffle the
> enemy.
>
> "The sun shines on the face of the shield. We move it so, and so,
> and the colors deceive him. He can't see to hit the man carrying the
> shield."
>
> "But why carry it at arm's length?"
>
> Evanico's eyes sparkled with the memory of old fights waged
> against hereditary foemen, the fierce and cunning Apache.
>
> "Apache arrows are long, in two pieces [i.e., shaft and foreshaft].
> If I hold the shield here [he demonstrated, bringing an imaginary

shield close to his chest], maybe an arrow came through, just this far
[indicating about six inches], and I die. If I hold the shield out here
and shake it from side to side, I fool him, and if he does hit the
shield, the arrow come in this far, maybe farther; it sticks in the
shield and I don't get hurt."

I had heard among some of the tribes of the Colorado River,
whose warriors used clubs similar to those of the Pima, the blunt
end of the club was thrust violently into an enemy's face, crushing
the front of the skull. Perhaps the Pima did the same thing.

I asked Evanico.

"No, the Pima never fought that way."

"Then," I persisted, "did they strike thus?" To illustrate my
query I brought my right arm forward in a sweeping overhand blow.

Then it was that Evanico laughed outright.

"Evanico wants to know," [said the interpreter], "if you are a
woman. Only an old woman strikes like that; a man never uses his
club in that manner. He says that if you ever asked an old Pima
warrior if he struck like that, it would be an insult. He says you
must be an old woman."

Then Evanico explained.

"A warrior fighting with a knife or club at close quarters would
never have struck an overhand blow; it would have been too easy to
block with the shield. A man always struck sideways and upward.
Such a blow would have come under the enemy's shield and hit the
wrist or arm that carried the knife or club. That is a man's way of
striking."[63]

Russell also gives a colorful account of the fighting of the shield bearers,
one that does not agree with the information supplied to Woodward by
Evanico concerning symbols on shields:

Their appeal to the God of War was expressed by the sun symbols
that decorated the shields, and the latter were kept swiftly rotating
upon the supple forearms of their bearers as the advance was made
for hand-to-hand conflict. The frequent use of the figure, "like
predatory animals or birds of prey," in the ceremonial speeches
imbued all with the spirit of agility and fierceness that manifested
itself in the leaps from side to side and the speed of their onward
rush. Crouching low, springing quickly with whirling shield that
concealed the body, in feather headdress and battle colors, they must
have presented a terrifying spectacle."[64]

AFTERMATH: SCALPING, VICTORY, AND MOURNING

To take an enemy scalp was an important part of ritual warfare of the formal kind, both in the large raids conducted for revenge by Yavapais, or in battles between the Gila and Colorado river tribes, and most of all, in the intermittent fights and ambushes conducted between Cocopas and Quechans. To bring back a scalp was a sign of success. The trophy was saved and exhibited at opportune times. The Mohave probably took but one scalp in any single encounter; other tribes brought back more; and the Cocopa probably took as many as they could because they alone among these tribes had no fear of the enemy scalp.

Most of the scalps were the whole skin of a warrior's head, including the particularly prized long hair. The only bit missing was a small section from the nose to the chin. All the tribes save for the Cocopa entrusted the taking, care, and handling of the scalp to one of the shamans who had "dreamed" this role and who would be safe from the otherwise inevitable contamination from such close contact with the enemy's person.[65] The scalp itself was treated and worked during the trip home from the expedition. It would be in reasonably good condition for exhibit by the time the warriors reached their villages.

A rigorous set of rituals was observed by warriors on their return from battle, designed to keep them safe from the sickness that might otherwise befall anyone who had exposed himself to the "enemy sickness." The procedures varied from one tribe to another. Maricopa warriors on their way home segregated those who had killed, who had taken part in scalping, or who had helped to take a prisoner. All the men ate very moderately. At a distance from the village, all of them stopped over for a time to induce themselves to vomit and also to bathe thoroughly. Once home, they went directly to special huts constructed for them as soon as a messenger had brought news of the fight back to the villages. Isolated in the huts, they spent twenty days in various stages of ritual purification. The earlier part of the period was spent in fasting, with a tapering off of all such observances in the final four days.[66]

As with the other tribes, Maricopas' captives were sent through the same kind of purification, presumably to avoid any later contamination of people in the tribe. The scalps, too, were purified by the old man who had custody of these grisly objects, and kept them in an earthenware jar in his home. After sixteen days of intensive purification for warriors, captives, and scalps, the whole tribe held a dance that lasted an entire day. The scalp was now "safe" enough to display on that occasion. Warriors did not take part in dancing, however, which was carried on, for the most part, by old people. Women, painted to resemble the fighters going into battle, came forward to imitate the warriors. They threw dirt at the scalp and uttered degrading remarks to it as they danced. That night the scalp was moved to a short pole within the tribal meeting house and singers intoned traditional song cycles the night through.

At some point during that period of almost three weeks, warriors who had returned badly wounded and had subsequently died at home were cremated. A Maricopa man's house was burned and all his possessions were buried when the ceremony was in his behalf. Four days of mourning ensued, including the proper rituals, and routines of purification *(mataRáě'k)* enacted by his relatives. The man's name would probably not be mentioned again until a year later when a formal mourning ceremony was held in his honor. Eight days' preparation included carving a wooden image of the man. Four days' *mataRáě'k* followed this anniversary ceremony as well.[67]

Quechan customs closely resembled those of the Maricopa. When the battle ended and remnants of the war party made good their escape, one messenger preceded the group to carry the news home. Like Maricopas, they took special care with those warriors who had killed enemies. They had to undergo eight days of full-scale denial and purification rites. Unlike the Maricopas, Quechans staged a tribal fiesta managed by their *kwoxot* soon after the war party's return. The scalps were placed in the care of the *kwoxot* who consulted them when it was time to prepare for another war expedition against the same enemy. Some Quechan warriors also brought back long hanks of the enemies' hair as trophies which, so far as we know, lacked religious significance.[68]

Mohave customs were similar. As the party started home after a battle, a messenger went ahead of the group.[69] Even before leaving the field the *ahwe sumach* began to work the scalp, rubbing it with adobe soil. He continued to clean and prepare it en route; only he could handle the object until entrusting it to the *kwoxot* who already had as many as a dozen other scalps in an earthenware vessel in his house. The two men went through purification procedures after lodging the new scalp in its proper place, and they carried out another four-day *mataRáě'k* each time they had to exhibit scalps. No one else dared have anything whatever to do with these important relics.[70]

Acting upon the messenger's news, the *kwoxot* invited people to a huge victory dance and celebration which began with the arrival of the war party and continued for four days and nights. While everyone rejoiced, the "owners of the songs," the tribal and clan singers, ran through some of their almost endless cycles of music and narration.

For Mohaves this occasion was a major social meeting, which may account both for the long duration of the party and for the fact that it was carried on with such expansive joy. That is, the *kwoxot* was here discharging one of his main duties, which was to bring together all young people in the tribe who wished to become acquainted with a view toward possible matrimony. This kind of mass social gathering was necessary among Mohaves, who were prohibited from marrying within the mother's clan and whose life partnerships typically took them a distance from home to live elsewhere within the tribal territory.[71]

The victory party was a remarkable display, with the warriors represented by women painted as if for combat dancing about the display of scalps. Armed with bows, they shot arrows at these trophies, mimicking the harangues delivered by warriors at the inception of battle, and narrating exploits of great Mohave fighters.[72]

Warriors themselves were not present for the feasting and dancing, having gone straight into their houses to begin the four or eight days of ritual purification. They remained at home, taking very moderate amounts of bland food and drinking water, avoiding meat and salt,[73] and bathing each morning in the river. So also with captives: they had to be purified to inhibit transmission of fatal illness to Mohaves. Likewise, families who were headed by warriors observed a somewhat reduced scale of *mataRăĕ'k* during the period of the warriors' confinement.[74]

The scalp of an enemy was of remarkable importance for the Cocopa warrior. He brought the object back with him and soon retired to a place isolated from other people where he spent several nights and days in communion with the scalp. During that time it talked to him, "especially at night, telling him how to be a great warrior and giving him special powers." To these tribesmen, "the war scalp was one of the primary rationalizations for fighting."[75]

Many times the war party met with terrible defeat. Funeral ceremonies could be held for those warriors whose bodies had had to be abandoned on the battlefield. Their houses were burned, and their horses killed.[76]

Notwithstanding Captain Grossmann's assertion that "The Pimas never scalp their dead enemies,"[77] there is abundant evidence that they did so.[78] The war headdress collected by Russell and already described (pages 77 – 78) contained ample strands of Apache hair.[79]

Scalping is especially well documented for the related Papagos.[80] If it can be assumed that Papago traditions with regard to scalps were similar to those of Pimas in the mid-nineteenth century, then Frances Densmore's discussion in this regard is to the point:

> While the wounded warriors and those who had killed Apache were in seclusion the remainder of the war party were leading a victory dance. The scalps of the Apache were placed on poles that were stuck in the ground and the people danced around them. Any member of the tribe might take one of the poles, dance with it, and return it to its place.
>
> [The end of the victory celebration was called] the Limo, which lasted four days and was characterized by the final disposal of the Apache scalps . . .
>
> In the early morning of the [first] day an Apache scalp and an effigy of an Apache were placed in a "spirit basket," to be kept and respected by each warrior who had killed an Apache. He assumed the care of this scalp as a serious responsibility, believing that sickness and evil would follow any neglect of his obligation to it . . . Thus the preparation for the Limo included the providing of the spirit baskets, the making of the effigies, and the count of the scalps (or portions of scalps), so there was one for each warrior who had shared in the killing of an Apache. The dividing of the scalps made it possible to provide for the spirit baskets and also have scalps for carrying in the victory dances.
>
> An old medicine man had charge of the ceremony of placing the Apache effigies and scalps in the baskets. At the time of the ceremony he sat facing the warriors, holding the effigies and a corresponding number of Apache scalps or pieces of scalp. The warriors who had taken the scalps were seated in a row. Each had his spirit basket open before him on the ground, the cover being laid at one side of the basket with the ties spread underneath, ready to be quickly fastened. The medicine man took up a scalp and held it toward the Apache country. When an Apache spirit passed by he was aware of its presence and at once wrapped the scalp around the head of the effigy. He handed this to one of the warriors, who received it in both his hands and laid it very carefully, with both hands, in the spirit basket

. . . When all the effigies had thus been placed the medicine man made a speech about the bravery of the warriors. At the conclusion of this speech he told them to take hold of the baskets, and they put on the cover simultaneously. Then the medicine man said, "I wrap one wrapping," and the men passed the cord once around the basket, all acting together. This was repeated four times and the fourth time he said, "I tie and finish it," then they tied the last tie in the cord. Each man put his basket under his arm except the head warrior, who stood up, pointed the basket toward the sunrise, and remained standing until the sun was fully risen. It was said, "They tie the sun stripes together," referring to the streaks of light at dawn.

The men who had taken care of the warriors then conducted them to a clear cold pond, breaking the ice if necessary. The men took a cold plunge, after which each man went to his own lodge, taking his spirit basket with him. It was kept in a safe place and frequently was placed in an olla . . . The scalps that had been carried in the victory dances were taken to other villages and carried in one dance after another. Finally they were given to the warriors [Enemy Slayers], who kept them.[81]

This "scalp basket" or "spirit basket" was kept with great care and offerings of food were given it. So long as this was done the spirit of the dead Apache was said to be satisfied, but if it were not "properly treated and fed" it escaped from the basket and "put poison in the food," causing disease. If the basket was carelessly treated by its owner he would fall ill, and if one of his children disturbed it the child would be seized with illness at a later time.

When a person was "troubled by an Apache spirit" it was customary to use, in the treatment, certain songs given by Apache spirits for that purpose . . . If these were not effective the diagnostician was recalled. He would "look inside," say the sickness was still there, and tell the family they must send for a *siákum*—i.e., a man who has killed and scalped an Apache. This man would bring his "spirit basket" which contained the Apache scalp fastened to a wooden effigy. He would take out the effigy and press it against the man's body, saying, "Cure this man."[82]

It should be pointed out that the Piman word for "Apache" is *ó:b*, which more literally translates as "enemy." Insofar as Gila River Pimas were concerned, Quechans, Mohaves, and Yavapais fit that classification equally well. Ezell asserts that E. W. Gifford's recounting of Yavapai and Pima versions of battles with each other present a picture "devoid of any

supernatural overtones." He uses this as an argument that Pima purification ceremonies followed only on the heels of Pima contact with Apaches.
A close reading of Gifford, however, shows that the Pimas about to fight
Yavapais had a pre-battle divination ceremony, and so there is mention of
the Yavapais' having forsaken the taking of Pima scalps—clearly a supernatural act—for purely practical reasons. [83]

Ruth Underhills says that the trophy taken from his victim by a Papago
Enemy Slaver "was originally the scalp and so it appears in the tales of
Elder Brothers' campaign. Later it was only a lock of hair or four hairs
from each temple . . . Some men did not take scalps at all but brought one
article of clothing, such as a moccasin or belts."[84] Whatever the nature of
the trophy, at the conclusion of the victory celebration the Enemy Slayer
could touch this dangerous object.

> . . . and he took it in his arms and addressed it as "my child!" His
> wife called it by the name a woman uses to her children, and each of
> his children in turn called it "younger brother."
>
> The warrior might now take it home. He kept it wrapped in
> many layers of buckskin or in a jar, often not in the house "because
> of the danger of its power," but in a crevice in the rocks some miles
> away. The enemy slayer must visit it regularly, must supply it with
> offerings and eagle down, tobacco, deer tails, if he were a hunter, and
> sometimes with food. He must speak to it affectionately, reciting the
> ritual over it. This treatment made the trophy his servant and added
> the dead Apache's power to his own, but if he were lax in his
> attentions, he and his whole family would be open to misfortune.
>
> He could, now, touch a dead enemy or an enemy's possessions
> without fear . . . He would expect to sit in the council, to have the
> right to speak, and to be generally regarded as a "ripe man."[85]

A further analysis of the supernatural significance of scalps to Pimans is
in the study of Donald Bahr and his colleagues of Piman shamanism and
sickness. [86]

The Pima victory celebration, like those of the Yumans described
above, consisted of purification of the enemy slayers and of those wounded
by enemies simultaneous with a victory dance held by the other warriors
and everyone else in the village or groups of related villages.

The Pimas regarded the killing of an enemy to be such a dangerous act
that according to some observers a Pima warrior withdrew from battle the
moment he killed his opponent to begin his rites of purification. To

United States Army officers, this meant Pimas could not be relied upon in battle to stay in the fight beyond killing a single enemy. John Bourke, who campaigned with General George Crook in Arizona in the 1870s, observed:

> All savages have to undergo certain ceremonies of lustration after returning from the war-path where any of the enemy have been killed. With the Apaches these are baths in the sweat-lodge, accompanied by singing and other rites. With the Pimas and Maricopas these ceremonies are more elaborate, and necessitate a seclusion from the rest of the tribe for many days, fasting, bathing, and singing. The Apache "bunches" all his religious duties at these times, and defers his bathing until he gets home, but the Pima and Maricopa are more punctilious, and resort to the rites of religion the moment a single one, either of their own numbers or of the enemy, has been laid low. For this reason [Major William] Brown started out from [Fort] McDowell with Apaches only. [87]

Although it is obvious Bourke exaggerates the situation, there is no question that ceremonial purification, or lustration, was important to Gila River Pimas. Russell writes:

> There was no law among the Pimas observed with any greater strictness than that which required purification and expiation for the deed that was at the same time the most lauded—the killing of an enemy. For sixteen days the warrior fasted in seclusion and observed meanwhile a number of tabus . . .
>
> Attended by an old man, the warrior who had to expiate the crime of blood guilt retired to the groves along the river bottom at some distance from the villages or wandered about the adjoining hills. During the period of sixteen days he was not allowed to touch his head with his fingers or his hair would turn white. If he touched his face it would become wrinkled. He kept a stick to scratch his head with, and at the end of every four days this stick was buried at the root and on the west side of a cat's claw tree and a new stick was made of greasewood, arrow bush, or any other convenient shrub. He then bathed in the river, no matter how cold the temperature. The feast of victory which his friends were observing in the meantime at the villages lasted eight days. At the end of that time, or when his period of retirement was half completed, the warrior might go to his home to get a fetish made from the hair of the Apache whom he had

killed. The hair was wrapped in eagle down and tied with a cotton string and kept in a long medicine basket. He drank no water for the first two days and fasted for the first four. After that time he was supplied with pinole by his attendant, who also instructed him as to his future conduct, telling him that he must henceforth stand back until all others were served when partaking of food and drink. If he was a married man his wife was not allowed to eat salt during his retirement, else she would suffer from the owl disease which causes stiff limbs. The explanation offered for the observance of this law of lustration is that if it is not obeyed the warrior's limbs will become stiffened or paralyzed.[88]

An earlier description of Pima lustration is that given by Captain Grossmann:

Even the act of killing an Apache by means of an arrow is believed to make the Pima unclean whose bow discharged that fatal arrow. They firmly believe that all Apaches are possessed of an evil spirit, and that all who kill them become unclean and remain so until again cleansed by peculiar process of purification. The Pima warrior who has killed an Apache at once separates himself from all his companions, (who are not even permitted to speak to him,) and returns to the vicinity of his home. Here he hides himself in the bushes near the river-bank, where he remains secluded for sixteen days, conversing with no one, and only seeing during the whole period of the cleansing process an old woman of his tribe who has been appointed to carry food to him, but who never speaks. During the twenty-four hours immediately following the killing the Pima neither eats nor drinks; after this he partakes of food and water sparingly, but for the whole sixteen days he cannot eat meat of any kind nor salt, nor must he drink anything but river-water . . . On the evening of the sixteenth day he returns to his village, is met by one of the old men of his tribe who, after the warrior has placed himself at full length upon the ground, bends down, passes some of the saliva in his mouth into that of the warrior, and blows his breath into the nostrils of the latter. The warrior then rises, and now, and not until now, he is again considered clean; his friends approach him and joyfully congratulate him on his victory.[89]

Ezell comments concerning these two versions that "the really essential difference between the two accounts is that Russell saw the ceremony as an expiation 'of the crime of blood guilt,' which seems more likely to have been a projection of a Euro-American concept as the meaning of the ceremony, whereas Grossmann's statement of the meaning as one of cleansing after contact with inimical supernatural forces is more congruent with the rest of Gila Pima concepts." Bahr and his Papago colleagues would doubtless agree.[90]

Papago lustration, virtually identical to that of the Pima, is described in considerable detail by Densmore, Underhill, and others. In fact, the description for the Papagos' rites of purification are far more detailed than those published concerning the Pima.[91] Densmore notes, moreover, that warriors who had been wounded were "taken to a quiet place at some distance from the camp, where they remained four days. By the end of that time it was known whether they would recover." In the meantime, a medicine man had already treated their wounds with a poultice prepared from a powdered root and had given the victims an herbal tea to drink.[92]

While the Enemy Slayers and the wounded were being secluded and purified, a dance in celebration of the victory was being carried on by everyone else. John Cremony, who was with the United States and Mexican boundary survey party in the early 1850s, witnessed such a victory celebration near the westernmost Maricopa village. He said that "from four to five thousand Indians were present," both Maricopas and Pimas, dancing around the "horrid spectacle." This consisted of "a human head, and the forearms with hands attached, . . . placed upon the ground—the head standing on the stump of the neck, which was supported by a stick driven into the ground and thrust up through the throat, and the arms and hands crossed, one over the other, immediately in front of the face." The head was that of Antonio, a hapless Quechan warrior who had made the mistake of accompanying the Mexican boundary survey party to the Pima and Maricopa villages.[93]

Russell gives the fullest description of the Pima victory celebration:

Upon the return of a victorious war party the emotions of those who had remained at home in anxious waiting and those who had returned rejoicing were given vent in vigorous shouting and dancing. It is interesting to observe that the abandonment of these occasions was not wholly approved by the leaders, as is shown by the invariable formula that closed every war speech that was delivered while the party was on campaign: "You may think this over, my relatives. The taking of life brings serious thoughts of waste; the celebration of victory may become unpleasantly riotous." Throughout the ceremonies the women of the tribe play a prominent part, particularly in mourning for relatives if any have fallen victims to the attacks of the Apaches.

The dance was held on the low rounded hill near the Double Buttes, or on a hill near the railway siding called Sacaton, or upon some alkali flat which the deposits of the rainy season leave as level and the sun bakes nearly as hard as a floor. Sometimes the dance was held on any open ground about the villages. Four basket drums were beaten in the center, while either four or ten singers formed a close circle around them. Within a larger circle numerous appointed dancers stamped and swayed their bodies, moving ever in a sinistral circuit. Sometimes the crowd danced within the circle of selected dancers, in which case they danced as individuals without holding hands; but usually they remained outside the circle. Outside the circle of spectators twenty men and two or more young women, according to the number of female relatives of those killed in battle kept running. In addition to these forty horsemen also circled from left to right about the whole gathering.[94]

As described by Underhill, the victory celebration of the Papagos lasted sixteen days to coincide with the period of seclusion prescribed for Enemy Slayers.[95] Anthropologist Marie Gunst and Papago warrior Baptisto Lopez have both said the victory dance lasted four nights rather than sixteen.[96] Densmore writes of the four-day observance called *Limo* [*limhu*] which began on the sixteenth day of their seclusion when warriors "went to the victory dance." She also says this victory dance began on the first evening of the warriors' return from battle, which, if correct, would add up to a twenty-day celebration.[97] Neither Russell nor anyone else indicates how long the celebration of the Gila River Pimas lasted.

Although the Yumans uniformly cremated their dead, Pimans interred their dead except under special circumstances. The most special of those circumstances appears to have been death at the hands of an enemy, usually an Apache. When this occurred, cremation of the corpse was in order. Ezell speculates that "Pima cremation represented not simply a means of disposing of the dead, but also a technique for warding off harm to the living. Pimas dead as a result of contact with the Apaches were cremated out of fear of the Apache power which had mastered and slain the body— by cremation, handling the corpse and hence exposure to this grave danger was minimized."[98]

Pimas' mourning for a warrior fallen in battle was possibly not unlike their mourning for a warrior who died a natural death, except that in the first case the corpse was cremated—probably *in situ* or, at least, as soon as possible after the person's demise—whereas normally the body was buried. In 1864, seven years after the battle on the Gila, the Pimas were visited by Judge Joseph Pratt Allyn. Either based on his own observations or on information given him by trader Ammi White, he penned an excellent description of a Pima funeral:

> . . . A man's personal property is all burned at his death, even to his house, in the belief that it enriches the deceased in the next world.
>
> When a warrior dies, the nation mourns, and imposing obsequies are performed. After his death, his family takes possession of the body, and with a *reata* or hide rope, tie up the body, passing the reata under the knees, around the neck, drawing the legs up to the chin. It is then buried with the head toward the east, and the grave covered with brush to keep the coyotes off. Four days after, processions are formed at each end of the chain of villages in this order: first, women clad simply in the tapa, or cloth wrapped about the loins; second, warriors in the full panoply of war; lastly, men on horseback, i.e., old men, farmers, etc.
>
> The two processions met near Casa Blanca, the women part to the right and left, the warriors advance to the front and halt; an old man now grasps a tattered banner attached to a long staff which assists his tottering steps as he advances to the open space, and in trembling accents recounts the virtues of the departed. As he proceeds, a prolonged wail goes up from the assembled Nation. Afterwards they proceed to the grave, near which a Ramada is erected (a ramada is a brush shed resting on poles), under which baskets of wheat are placed. The circle completed around the grave, the women sow the wheat over it, and sprinkle it over the heads of those present. This is that he may have bread in the next world. Then an old man advances, pulls off his blankets, or some other valuable thing, and throws it down for the beginning of the funeral pile, others follow, and soon the rush becomes general, everyone throws on something: beads, blankets, saddles, and every description of personal property. Sometimes the women strip off their tapa, and throw that on the blazing pile, which oftens reaches thousands of dollars in value. This consumed, the ceremony is over. Beads, in some way, are sacred:

those unconsumed in the funeral pile are carefully gathered, and buried with the deceased.[99]

As soon as word of the 1857 disaster reached the Quechans on the Colorado River they began to mourn. "The whole country there was howling with Indians mourning for their dead" when John Hinton arrived at Fort Yuma about mid-September.[100] And the San Diego *Herald* of September 26 reported:

> The Indians for some weeks have been mourning and making sacrifices for the warriors slain in the recent expedition. They have been killing their horses, burning their cornfields, and houses, arms, beads, cloth, and trinkets, all of which to them is valuable property. The commanding officer at the Fort deemed it his duty to interfere and endeavor to prevent the destruction of their means of subsistence, the absence of which is sure to make them pensioners upon the Government until their next crop. Last winter they were supplied with bread and blankets, to some extent, by the commanding officer at the Fort.[101]

So ended the battle, we may guess from the slim historical record that survives. But it was not remembered in that way when the details were recounted for scholars half a century and more beyond the time of battles. By that time the bravery and glory and rejoicing had become the history; the terror, deprivation, and the horror had all passed away.

FIVE

Yuman Antagonists: Maricopas, Quechans, and Mohaves to 1857

J ust before the white man arrived in the sixteenth century, more than a dozen Indian peoples lived in western Arizona north of the Gila River. They occupied the region west of Apache country to the Colorado River and beyond. Almost all of these people spoke Yuman languages. They earned their livelihoods by gathering, hunting, and most of them, by raising a sizeable proportion of their food. [1]

The Pai—divided in the Anglo-American period into the Walapai and Havasupai—lived in a large area along the upper Colorado. The Yavapai occupied huge zones of north central Arizona. On the Colorado between its great bend and the delta there lived the Numic-speaking Paiute, then Mohave, Halchidhoma, Quechan, Kamia, Alakwisa, Halyikwamai, and finally the Cocopa. West of the river there dwelt those Southern Paiutes called Chemehuevis. They lived opposite the Mohaves and Halchidhomas. On the lower Gila River, upstream from its junction with the Colorado and distant from Quechan settlements, were the Kaveltcadom ("Cocomaricopa" in Spanish documents) and the Maricopa ("Opa" in Spanish documents). Farthest south, and west of the Colorado delta, were more Kamia, Paipai (Akwa'ala), and Kiliwa. [2] None of these peoples were numerous, the largest populations counting five or six thousand at most.

In the absence of comprehensive archaeological data we cannot be altogether certain of the identity of the forebears of these groups. By far the best summary of the problem to date is that of Randall McGuire,[3] a discussion further supported by a recent analysis of prehistoric ceramics of the region by Michael Waters.[4] Both McGuire and Waters use the label "Lowland Patayan" to refer to the pottery-making prehistoric peoples of the Lower Colorado, whereas Albert Schroeder, another archaeologist, conceptualizes a larger and more geographically widespread group he calls "Hakataya."[5] Whatever the case, it is clear that the cultures of these riverine peoples were in many respects quite similar by the middle of the sixteenth century when white men first began to visit the region.[6]

As already pointed out, most of these tribes lacked a central government. The institutions which unified them and gave them a sense of historical and continuing identity were their family and clan organizations, their habits of reciprocal visiting and dealing peacefully with each other, and, in some cases, intermarriage with families living some distance away. Enmity with other tribesmen may also have promoted in-group unity, a sense of "we" versus "they." So far as we know, only the Mohave achieved a unified political system that recognized one head man, a council of subordinate leaders, and specific groups of people for whom those subordinates spoke in council.[7] By the middle of the 1500s the Quechans may not yet have come to the custom of recognizing leadership as being vested in a single person. They were probably still being "governed" only by headmen, one to each ranchería.

The neighboring Cocopas had no unifying leadership then or later. As for the Walapai and Yavapai, they lived in numerous small bands, each with a recognized "leader." It was probably true for all these peoples, however, that common decisions were possible only after the mature men had come together formally for lengthy discussion and ultimate agreement. And one of these people, the Chemehuevi, never acted in concord because they lived too dispersed in small groups scattered over a very large expanse of desert. Extended families were their only units of settlement, and they often traveled from one place to another.[8]

None of these peoples developed complex religious practices in the sense that there were neither temples nor priesthoods. Each recognized its own body of basic teachings steadily handed down to everyone by singers or narrators. These teachings contained elements to be found in any living religion. They explained the origin of the people and relationships between people and the land with its living creatures, both plant and animal. They also explained the society itself and prescribed proper personal conduct for each stage of life from childhood through old age. Thus, with grandparents to help instruct the children in necessary beliefs and skills, with frequent repetition of the teachings by tribal singers and in community gatherings, and with regular demonstrations of the healing arts as practiced by a variety of medical specialists, young people steadily absorbed the viewpoints, beliefs, and behaviors which led them to become mature members of their tribe. They became aware of how to act according to the canons of tribal life.

One of the origin stories was shared in similar versions by a number of tribes on and near the Colorado River. In that account, many Arizona and southeastern California peoples had been created in one place, Avikwame, designated on modern maps as Mount Newberry. Everyone had been created there by a single being—Mastamho, Mustamxo, or Kumastamxo, as he was variously known. He brought forth the different peoples and sent them off to live in the regions they still occupied when Spaniards first came. He also created the Colorado River and every living thing in the whole territory. He taught people about all of his accomplishments as well as all they needed to know to make their living, to defend themselves against all kinds of dangers, and to live with each other.

Some of the teachings clearly delineated a tribe's boundaries. In many cases it was further made manifest which tribes were to be regarded as friends and which as enemies. For example, Cocopas could depend on their friends the Maricopas, who lived many days' travel away on the Gila River, for help against their mutual Quechan enemy. However, these quasi-historical, quasi-religious narratives[9] do not tell us all we would wish to know about the achievement of tribal unities, incipient national identities, or the building of relationships among Arizona and southeastern California peoples. Some of these stories are doubtless a mixture of episodes, some of which date from remote past time and others of more recent date—all fused together in the form of a charter for the contemporary status quo.[10] Such mixing of old and new becomes clear when we find mention in some origin stories of white men, horses, guns, and even steamboats. It may be, though, that elements in the stories concerning tribal identities, territories, amities, and enmities are in general of greater antiquity.

Growing up in any of these tribes, members of each generation came to understand how deeply planted in the land were the roots of their personal beings. "These roots were implanted and fixed by higher beings than men. They had existed from the beginning and could not be conceived as alterable by men, since gods had decreed them."[11]

For a Mohave, good and proper life began with birth as a full-blooded Mohave child into a family of properly married parents, thus emerging from what was thought of as the "good roots" of family, clan, and tribal identity. The child, taught carefully in a loving spirit by parents, grandparents, and respected elder men who held the few public positions of honor and moral authority, grew to adulthood to embody the virtues of a respectable Mohave person. Ideally, one always followed the teachings, always respected the land and everything that lived upon the land. A person thus reared need not be reminded to avoid marrying a member of some other tribe, since to do so would be to invite a serious illness, one of the forms of *ahwe,* which was potentially fatal. Such a person also knew better than to kill rattlesnakes or to hunt beaver, both forbidden by tribal custom. One could kill a deer if in serious need of food, but beavers were to remain unmolested under any circumstances.[12]

As for conflict among these Colorado and Gila river tribes, some wars were occurring by 1540 when Hernando de Alarcón's party became the first white men to visit the country. One scene of armed conflict was along the lower Colorado where at least six peoples lived close to one another. There was war between the Cocopas, who lived near the mouth of the river, and the Quechans whose settlements were near the junction of the Gila and Colorado. It is not known whether the Mohaves, who lived north of the Quechans, were as yet involved in these troubles. So far as we know, no other Colorado River tribes were yet taking part.[13]

Some of the tribes on or near the Colorado were isolated enough from potentially powerful enemies to avoid a threat to their survival. Thus it was with the Kamia, who lived well to the west of the Colorado and safely beyond the range of Cocopa territory. From time to time Kamias visited and lived among Quechan villagers on the Colorado. They occasionally intermarried with Quechans. So also with the relationship between the Paipai *(Akwa'ala)* and the Cocopa. The Paipai generally resided west and south of the Colorado delta, out of the way of Quechan raids. They were, however, close enough to their friends the Cocopa to render aid once in a while against Quechan attack.

By the sixteenth century, many small tribes in the vicinity were in the process of losing their struggles for independence as well as being forced off the Colorado River. The Alakwisa had disappeared from the scene before white men ever saw them; in fact, we are not sure such a tribe ever existed.[14] The Kaveltcadom, living on the lower Gila, were already finding it hard to withstand Quechan hostility. Indeed, they may have been forced off of the Colorado and up the Gila in prehistoric times. The hapless Halchidhoma, Kohuana, and Halyikwamai seem never to have forged permanent alliances. These three peoples were buffeted back and forth during the seventeenth and eighteenth centuries, siding at times with the Cocopas and at other times with Quechans—always losing too many people in warfare. Their farmlands on the Colorado were hopelessly open to attack from both upriver and downriver enemies.[15]

Meantime, in the late seventeenth and throughout the eighteenth centuries, Pimas and Papagos—essentially of one history and culture despite the two names known to us—were feeling Spanish pressure from the south. They also felt the first shocks of serious Apache raids against them. Apaches forced the Sobaipuri Pima to desert their lands along the San Pedro River.[16] Farther west, and just north of the course of the middle and lower Gila, various Yavapai bands and some Apaches lived close to the Pima-Maricopa settlements and raided them frequently. As we've already pointed out, some Western Apaches, particularly the Tontos, were close friends of their Yavapai neighbors. They sometimes intermarried, and Yavapais and Tonto Apaches occasionally joined in raids against Pimas, Papagos, and Maricopas.[17] Thus Pimas and Papagos were pressed from the east (Apaches), the south (Spaniards), and from the north (Yavapais and Apaches); and during the eighteenth century they retreated until on the northeast their villages lay no farther in that direction on the Gila than near where it is joined by the Salt River.

Spanish influence brought about marked changes in the cultures of all the people living in the Gila-Colorado region. Spanish and, subsequently, Mexican frontier settlers encouraged a slave trade. Pimas, Papagos, Maricopas, and Quechans sold Indians of other tribes in Spanish colonial or Mexican towns. This practice began in the late seventeenth century and continued until the middle of the nineteenth century.[18] This trafficking in people may have helped to embitter and even to terminate what had once been reasonably friendly relationships among some of these Indian peoples. It may, for example, have weakened earlier friendships between Quechans and many of the Papagos living in the desert south of the Gila and east of the Colorado.

We assume these new conditions, which were making themselves strongly felt by the eighteenth century, signaled a major change in the patterns of hostility and warfare among the Indians concerned. Until then, war had been neither constant nor intensive enough to bring about the disappearance or displacement of whole tribes—unless the enigmatic Alakwisa had been such an earlier casualty.[19]

It is clear that by the late eighteenth century some of the fighting among Indians was on a large scale and was carried out with deep hostility.[20] We believe the time was ending in that part of the world when natives could think of prolonged periods of peace or could consider safely trading with enemies during periods of "armistice."

One of the episodes fully described by Spanish chroniclers was the Spanish attempt between 1779 and 1781 to place a combined Roman Catholic mission, Spanish town, and army post in the Quechan homeland near the junction of the Gila and Colorado rivers. The Quechans annihilated this settlement, including two churches and four Franciscan missionaries, in July 1781. Gila River Pimas, Papagos, other Northern Pimans, as well as Halchidhomas, Cocomaricopas, and Kohuanas accompanied Spanish troops on largely unsuccessful punitive expeditions carried out during 1782, and their presence among Spaniards certainly did nothing to enhance their good standing in the eyes of Quechans. In fact, these 1782 punitive expeditions almost certainly heightened the bitterness between Quechans and the Gila River villagers, a precursor of events in 1857.[21]

During the 1780s and through the first third of the nineteenth century, Quechans and Mohaves collaborated in defeating the three neighboring tribes who had never found secure lodgment in either of the two local alliances along the Colorado. From the early years of the nineteenth century to about 1830, first the Halyikwamai and Kohuana and then the Halchidhoma were driven out. Most of the Halyikwamai may have ended up in the villages along the middle Gila, alongside the Pimas. The Kohuana were dispersed, some going to live among the Cocopa, some to the middle Gila, and others traveling west to mountainous retreats where they remained thereafter. The Halchidhoma first moved from their position south ʾof the Quechans up the Colorado to an unoccupied stretch of bottomland north of the Quechan villages but still well south of Mohave farming areas. There, however, they were finally attacked by Mohaves. Some of them began to leave the area in the late 1820s. The remainder departed together for Sonora, and at last, by about 1840, the survivors moved north again to join the Pima-Maricopa villagers on the Gila River.[22] Mid-nineteenth century records make it appear that Halchidhomas predominated in the second of two "Maricopa" villages, the one farther upstream and nearer the Pimas. In the twentieth century

Table 1. **Battle Expedition**[24]

NO.	YEAR	ATTACKERS	DEFENDERS	REFERENCES
1.	1832	Quechans, Yavapais (?)[2]	Maricopas[1]	Suárez (1832)
2.	1833	Quechans[2]	Maricopas[1]	Hall (1907:415) Russell (1975:38) Smith (1942:23)
3.	1838 (?)	Maricopas[2]	Quechans, Yavapais[1]	Spier (1978:172–73)
4.	1839–40	Quechans, Mohaves[2]	Maricopas, Pimas, Halchidhomas[1]	Spier (1978:173)
5.	1841–42	Maricopas, one Pima[4]	Quechans[4]	Russell (1975:40–41)
6.	1842–43	Quechans, Yavapais[4]	Maricopas[4]	Russell (1975:41)
7.	1843–44	Quechans[3]	Maricopas[3]	Russell (1975:42)
8.	1844–45	Quechans, Mohaves[3]	Maricopas[3]	Russell (1975:42)
9.	1845	Maricopas[2]	Quechans[1]	Hall (1907:418)
10.	1846	Quechans[2]	Maricopas, Pimas[1]	Hall (1907:418)
11.	1846	Quechans[3]	Maricopas[3]	Hall (1907:418)
12.	1847–48	Maricopas[2]	Quechans[1]	Spier (1978:173) Southworth (1931:13)
13.	1848	Maricopas[2]	Quechans[1]	Couts (1961:64–65, 73)
14.	1848–49	Maricopas[2]	Quechans[1]	Spier (1978:245–46) Gifford (1933:301)
15.	1849 (?)	Maricopas[1]	Quechans[2]	Sweeny (1956:63)
16.	1850–51	Quechans[2]	Maricopas, Pimas[1]	Russell (1975:44–45)
17.	1851	Maricopas[2]	Quechans[1]	Bartlett (1859(II):221)
18.	1851	Quechans[3]	Maricopas, at Gila Bend[3]	Cremony (1969:111–12)
19.	1852	Quechans[2]	Maricopas, Pimas[1]	Hall (1907:420)
20.	1855–56	Quechans[2]	Maricopas, Pimas[1]	Southworth (1931:13)
21.	1857	Quechans, Mohaves, Yavapais, Apaches (?)[2]	Maricopas, Pimas[1]	see this volume

[1]winners; [2]losers; [3]outcome not known; [4]bloody losses on both sides.

they are the "Maricopas" living near Lehi on the Salt River Indian Reservation in southern Arizona.[23]

After driving the other three groups away, the Quechans and Mohaves expanded along the Colorado, occupying or reoccupying lands formerly held by others. Mohaves took up lands inhabited by the Halchidhoma for nearly a century in the region now known as Chemehuevi Valley. Their ultimate victory left the Mohaves with no enemies within eighty miles of their homes. As for Quechans, the Cocopas, at most a few days' travel south of the southernmost Quechan settlement, remained their only nearby enemies. The distance between them varied as Quechans moved south to farm or to gather or as Cocopas moved north for the same reason.

And now, too, a real no man's land opened along the lower Gila, a long stretch of country no longer occupied by Kaveltcadoms, Quechans, or anyone else. Passersby became vulnerable to raiding by Yavapais and Apaches.

Quechan-Cocopa hostility continued in the nineteenth century. So did reciprocal raiding between Pima-Maricopa and Yavapai-Apache. The only additional hostile alignment in the Gila-Colorado country pitted Quechans, with their friends among Mohaves and Yavapais, against Maricopas who, when attacked, could count on support of the Pimas.

The fighting between Quechans and Cocopas became increasingly dangerous to both tribes.[25] Their numbers gradually diminished and the presence of the U.S. Army on the Colorado after 1850 raised the threat that one tribe might ally itself with the whites to drive the other out of its homelands. Members of both groups were particularly vulnerable in this armed conflict because they often lived in small, isolated settlements open to attack by an enemy who had only to march one or two days to reach them.

If Cocopa and Quechan enmity dated back at least to 1540, we know that as early as the 1740s Quechans and Maricopas fought each other and sold each other to Spaniards as captives.[26] Some Spanish visitors to the region believed the root of the trouble among these tribes was the slave trade. Whether or not this is so, by the 1830s and 1840s hard feelings had crystallized to a point that it was no longer thinkable for a prominent man of any of these groups to make a peaceful call at the home villages of any of his enemies.

Amities and enmities within the region remained roughly constant from about 1830 until the 1860s when the United States Army aggressively involved itself in western Arizona and eastern Southern California affairs.

The Army fostered new hostilities, new alienations of one tribe from another, and without mitigating the ill feelings of long standing. Also between 1830 and the 1860s, trade, where it existed among these groups—even if in an atmosphere of mutual mistrust—seems to have continued.

Aside from military alliances, real and potential, within the region, there were what might be thought of as "friendly associations." Thus the Mohaves and neighboring Chemehuevis got along amicably, as did Maricopas and Pimas with their Papago neighbors to the south. Some of the Kamia bands were involved on friendly terms with some Cahuilla lineages as well as with some closely related Diegueño groups.

As for cooler and somewhat suspicious relationships which nonetheless permitted regular visits and trade, there is the example of Mohaves and Walapais. Their lands adjoined, they traded between them, but they never became fast friends. Some Western Apache groups mistrusted the more westerly Yavapai bands, although there seem to have been no open hostilities. We assume that by the second third of the nineteenth century Quechans probably had little to do with any of the Papagos. Likewise, there is a tradition of Cahuilla resentment toward Quechans, and the nature of whatever relationship may have existed between them is no longer clear.[27]

What seems remarkable to us in the whole story of Gila-Colorado warfare is that peoples failed to form master alliances. Mohaves did not accompany Yavapai-initiated raids against Pimas and Maricopas. Apaches did not visit the Colorado to help Mohaves or Quechans against Cocopas. Pimas did not routinely accompany Maricopa raiders to the Quechan settlements. Within the whole zone, and probably over a period of two centuries or more, traditional pairings and patterns of friendship and confrontation remained very much the same. There was no tendency for weaker or smaller peoples gradually to be forced into hostilities brought on by their powerful friends.

So it was also at the outer edges of these zones of war. The zones were not expanded to draw in other nearby bands or tribes or peoples. The Cupeño and Cahuilla of Southern California did not come to fight along the Colorado. Papagos did not combine their efforts with those of Pimas and Maricopas against Apaches. Chemehuevis did not involve themselves in the Colorado River wars, nor did the Paipai (Akwa'ala) take more than a marginal part in those same hostilities. Walapais did not, so far as we know, try to involve the Mohaves against their deadly enemies, the Yavapais.

The lack of outward expansion of hostilities through the forging of grand alliances may reflect a lack of interest in further expansion on the part of the most powerful combatants in the zone: the Pimas, Quechans, Mohaves, and Cocopas. None of these people seem to have tried to alienate nearby tribes with whom they had never before fought.

During the decades between the 1830s and 1860s there were peril and instability for some of the warring peoples and relative security and peace for others. The most intense hostilities were carried on, as one might suspect, among near neighbors: Yavapai and Apache against Pima and Maricopa; Cocopa against Quechan. These were the most vulnerable and frequently threatened groups, including those among the Yavapai who in summer moved within easy range of Pimas and Maricopas to be just north of the Gila River. Other peoples had little to worry about unless they chose: some of the Kamia; the Mohave, who before 1865 were never attacked by other Indians so far as we know; and the Chemehuevi.

Surprising as it may now appear, the basic relationships remained the same even when so many shifts took place among non-Indians in the nineteenth century Southwest: as Texas became a republic and then a state of the American Union; as the War of 1847 was fought between Mexicans and their Yankee neighbors to the north; and as the news of gold in California drew thousands of American and Mexican citizens down the Gila Trail and across the Colorado River. The white man's presence became steadily more powerful, but in the meantime Indians continued in their traditional ways.

By the early 1850s the U.S. Army had subjugated the Cocopas, Kamias, and Quechans, but armed conflict among these tribes continued, sometimes within sight and sound of the Army's post known as Fort Yuma. United States officers several times made "peace" between the Quechans and Cocopas. However, as was so often then the case in that part of the country, neither the Army nor the reluctant Indians seem to have had anything more durable in mind than a "truce." In Arizona, such a holiday from war could last a few months or longer, depending on circumstances not accounted for by white "peacemakers."[28]

As for the Gila River people, by 1855 the leading men of the Pimas and Maricopas had discovered their villages now lay within the territory of the United States of America insofar as white men understood such matters.[29] In November of 1856 the United States finally got around to placing a detachment of troops in what was then southern New Mexico Territory— later to become southern Arizona—near the newly created boundary.[30]

That did nothing, however, to reduce hostilities between Gila River peoples and those to their north. Nor were there yet any white settlers north of the Gila to demand protection against Apache and Yavapai raiders.

Anglo Americans were delighted to discover the Pimas and Maricopas. Not only were they friendly to the newcomers, supplying emigrants and military trains alike with food and other supplies (for a price), but they were staunch allies of the Americans in the case of Apache warfare. Indeed, Pimas and Maricopas were the strong northern line of defense.

The federal government wasted little time in recognizing the importance of the Pimas and Maricopas. Their Gila River Indian Reservation became the first to be established in what became Arizona Territory. It was created by an Act of Congress dated February 28, 1859. And by September of that year, Indian agent Silas St. John had made the Pimas and Maricopas a gift of a blacksmith shop, carpenter shop, plows, mills, and all kinds of metal farming implements.[31]

Indians showed no signs of making new alignments among themselves and the United States government was not yet interested in injecting itself further into the picture by co-opting some tribes as allies while directing military campaigns against others. That process would not be felt in this region, especially on the Colorado, until the period from 1863 to about 1875.[32] In the meantime, the battle of 1857 would be fought in an aboriginal setting among traditional enemies, even though a white man's stage station was already in operation at the very edge of that fatal plain.

By now it should be clear that the 1857 battle marked the culmination of a long and complicated series of raids and of similar battles. We are fortunate in having at least a partial record of the immediate precursors, a record which commences in 1832. By that time, some groups comprising the "Maricopa" had been forced off the Colorado River and many of them had amalgamated themselves into settlements just downstream of the Pimas on the Gila River. Raids and battle expeditions of the Colorado River peoples against dwellers on the Gila could no longer be construed as attempts to gain further territory; other motives were clearly paramount. To understand the 1857 battle requires that we examine similar events of which this happened simply to be the last in a series.

To review the history of such expeditions is to show they occurred in a very uneven frequency and not in simple tit-for-tat sequence. The record we have is admittedly incomplete, based as it is largely on the calendar stick annals kept by Pima and Maricopa Indians. Such records are not by any means complete. Here and there, however, an episode is corroborated

by white man's written records. And some of the latter contain notice of
hostile events the keeper of the calendar stick failed to note. We hope that
the listing arrived at by combining Pima, Maricopa, and white men's
accounts is complete enough to make clear the variety of circumstances and
styles embodied in large-scale "battle expeditions."

Speaking solely of Quechan versus Maricopa, there is a record of what
may have been a total of twenty-one expeditions between 1832 and the final
engagement in 1857 (see Table 1, p. 107, and note 24). Of these, only
three or four can be said from the first to have been planned as formal
battles. Eleven attacks are alluded to so briefly that it is impossible to
know whether they were battle expeditions, raids that turned into battles,
raids that broke off just short of being formal battles, or raids that effected
damage and were then terminated to avoid losses to the raiders. For that
matter, some of these fifteen incidents could be in the calendar stick annals
simply because the keeper of the stick recalled their unusual success or
their unusually bad luck and heavy losses.[33]

The earliest record for the 1830s is an especially interesting one, partly
because it may document the beginning of the use of wooden sticks by
Pimans for record keeping. Previously unpublished, it comes in the form
of a letter written by Francisco Suárez to Sonoran Vice-Governor José
Ignacio Bustamente on behalf of the council of the District of Altar. It
reads as follows in translation:

Town Council of Guadalupe del Altar
October 1, 1832

To the Most Excellent Vice-Governor of the State of Sonora at
Arizpe.

With date of September 25, the Captain of the 6th Company of
Infantry, Citizen Enrique Tejeda[34] communicates to this corporation
what he copied:

"Last night I received intelligence by way of an Indian of Cubó
[the modern Kerwo or Gu Vo on the Papago Indian Reservation in
Arizona], a report for me from the Gileño [Gila River Pima]
bands concerning what happened this month (September) between
themselves and those Apaches and Yumas who were together. While
the Gileños were in fiesta, the Apaches and Yumas found some
families of Cocomaricopas by themselves, captured them, and killed
two of their women. One Cocomaricopa managed to escape and bear

the news to the Gileños. These gathered together, left, and fell upon the Apaches and Yumas who were careless. According to the marks sent me on a stick, of the three trails they were able to follow counting the dead, these amounted to 13 Apaches dead and among them some Yumas. And they took from them 23 animals and the families they had captured. Being thirsty, they could not count the dead along the fourth trail, [a number] they assure me was plenty. Considering the manner in which they give me this report, I feel no doubt of the truth of this happy fact. They also say they noticed that three Apaches were bearing firearms. Of the Gileños many were wounded but only two died. It has seemed well to communicate this good news to your Governorship."

I transmit to Your Excellency for your official notice, recording at the same time the proposal made by this corporation April 1 regarding Citizen Enrique Tejeda and Francisco Carro—the former to be general of the Pápago and Río Gila nations, the latter to be his lieutenant, because through the prestige and influence these [two men] enjoy with the aforementioned [Indian] nations, and [considering] how much these respect them, this corporation believes the ills will be remedied which are being suffered from them [the Indian tribes].

Francisco Suárez [rubric]
Francisco Suástegui [rubric]
(Secretary)[35]

This and the other accounts taken together appear to indicate that the Quechans attacked the Maricopas in 1832, 1833, four times between 1839 and 1845, six between 1846 and 1856, and finally in 1857. The Maricopas went against the Quechans once in the middle or late 1830s, once in 1839, three times between 1841 and 1845, and twice between 1848 and 1849. Some of the Quechan attacks included Mohave, Yavapai, or Apache allies; Maricopa attacks would occasionally find Yavapai visitors helping the Quechans in defense. Save for a lone Pima who accompanied one such expedition, Maricopas went alone against Quechans. Maricopas are not recorded as having had Cocopa help on the field of battle, although Cocopas later told Edward Gifford that one such attack had been planned. The timing of the joint venture misfired because the Maricopas, as a matter of honor, decided to launch the raid by themselves.[36] On another occasion Quechans and Mohaves struck early to forestall a joint attack being planned against Quechan villages by Maricopas and Cocopas. First the Quechan-Mohave party defeated the Cocopa contingent on its way north; then they defeated the Maricopas.[37]

With so few facts at hand, it becomes sheer guesswork to try to say why these large raids and battle expeditions occurred at what seem to be such uneven intervals. And in spite of all the information we have about battle expeditions of Quechans, Mohaves, and Maricopas, we cannot pinpoint motivations for launching these very special, large attacks. It is clear that such an expedition could only be put together after a respected man managed to persuade enough others that his "dream" of success was indeed genuine and that it gave powerful indications of the desirability of engaging in such an expedition at that time. It may be, indeed, that ritualized expeditions can be accounted for only in this way: a respected adult male's powers of persuasion. His personal motives are another matter.

If this is the case, then the record of expeditions is in fact a list of the few successful attempts by strong individuals to convince fellow tribesmen a war expedition should be undertaken. There must have been unsuccessful attempts as well, but of these we have no documentation.

In attempting to account for the occurrence of the expeditions we find it worthwhile to look outside the direct relationship between Quechans and Maricopas and beyond the formalities by which a battle expedition was initiated to see if their frequency might be related to larger events in the region. It may be so. Recalling that Quechans made one battle expedition in 1833 but not another until the early 1840s, we are reminded that the years 1833—1840 were busy ones for both Quechans and Maricopas quite apart from plans they may have had for each other.

In the case of the Quechans, in some mysterious way they were to an extent involved in the upsets and hostilities that swept Mexican southern Alta California between 1833 and 1840.[38] Those events had something to do with the gradual departure of many Southern California Indians from the Roman Catholic missions which by then were in an almost final state of decay. Small groups of non-missionized Indians were standing out against Mexican authority, and there was an unknown amount of encouragement of Indian uprisings by factions within Mexican-Californian politics. To what extent Quechans were involved in hostilities against other Indians or against Mexicans in Southern California has never been clear. The suggestion is strong, however, that Quechans' attentions were bent westward in the years just before 1840.[39]

As for the Maricopas, the records indicate they were being attacked frequently by Apaches, Yavapais, or both during those same years up to 1840.

From 1840 to about 1845 Yavapai-Apache raiding along the Gila seems to have been somewhat reduced. Troubles in Southern California smoothed out. During this half decade, while the Quechans' other hostilities were apparently at a minimum, a number of large raids or battle expeditions went back and forth between the Gila River and Colorado River villages.

Because so few white men left accounts for the years 1845–1848, we have no significant detail concerning Quechan warfare for those three years. But 1848 marked the beginning of a long period of danger and privation for the Quechans. They were raided by Maricopas, probably twice in 1848–49, and they became increasingly involved in heavy warfare against the Cocopa. Beginning by the summer of 1849, the flow of United States and Mexican citizens headed for California gold fields consumed more and more of their time, despoiled their food resources, and brought about new hostilities that posed great problems for Quechans. By 1851 they were trying hard to rid themselves of the small detachment of United States troops who had located in the midst of their country in November 1850. By 1851–52, after a year of very little food and with American soldiers forcing them away from some of their villages, the Quechans were for a time in danger of being dispersed and overwhelmed. Such might well have happened had the U.S. Army elected to use Cocopas against Quechans.

During these same years of crises, however, the report is that Quechans launched at least three raids against Maricopas. One of those, in 1850, was a traditional battle expedition. It looks as if Quechans tried incessantly after 1848 to free themselves from what were direct and mortal threats to their independence and very existence. As they fought during the 1840s and 1850s, Quechans frequently had to renew their leadership; they lost their most prestigious warriors and tribal leaders.[40]

Our guess is that as decisions for war or peace came to depend more and more upon the influence of two men, Pasqual and Caballo en Pelo, as well as upon such surviving village leaders as Francisco and Vicente, the direction and intensity of Quechan warfare came to reflect the accumulated wisdom of these few persons. There is no indication of the slightest move toward a negotiated "peace" with the Cocopa, although Pasqual was willing to make and to respect a "truce." These Quechan leaders ceased to fight U.S. Army detachments after 1852; and we doubt that either Pasqual or Caballo en Pelo, whose bravery cannot be questioned, had any interest in attacking Maricopa villages in the wake of the serious challenges to Quechan survival which began about 1848. Pasqual is known to have shored up his alliance with the Mohaves, and the two nations fought together against the Cocopa in 1853 and 1854.[41]

What we are suggesting is that Pasqual, and other Quechan leaders who may have given him their support, was showing during the 1850s he could play the part of a traditional leader while simultaneously facing and dealing with new facts and problems beyond the scope of traditional experience. He accepted a certain degree of dependence upon whites and he turned away from customary hostilities against the Maricopa, the better to ward off a mortal threat from the Cocopa. The numbers of his people were rapidly diminishing. Pasqual could probably find only a few hundred warriors during the 1850s;[42] and beyond the shortage of fighting men for offense lay the difficulty of mustering enough fighters to meet the threat of attack.

In concluding this brief history of hostilities among Gila River and Colorado River tribes, it needs to be emphasized again how serious and threatening to survival such warfare had become. We suspect it was not always so. During the seventeenth and eighteenth centuries, for some of the tribes, at least, there seem to have been lesser hostilities. Moreover, there were times of peace as well as times of war. Even then, however, the wars on the Colorado River were too rigorous for small or weaker tribes to sustain. We have seen that at least three tribes had broken up and fled the Colorado, while another moved from its location on the lower Gila to a safer position far upstream near the Pima villages.

During the following generation warfare remained equally serious and probably became more dangerous for Cocopas and Quechans. Their numbers slowly decreased from the impact, not only of war, but of disease and loss of farmlands and property to non-Indians. As for the Gila River Pimas and Maricopas, their troubles with Apaches and Yavapais intensified from the early nineteenth century onward, although they seem never to have faced the danger of losing their homelands immediately along the south side of the river. Hostilities there were serious enough, however, to prompt the Pimas to take up a permanent posture of defense that would best shield their settlements against the hit-and-run raids by their enemies.[43]

In all, by the middle of the 1850s the Indians of western Arizona and of eastern Southern California had entered upon a time when the old ways of doing things were becoming more difficult, more risky, or both. The new situation presented different challenges and choices to each of the tribes. We cannot guess how many Indians, in such a new predicament, yet recognized that their traditional lifestyles were now constricted by limitations that were a potential threat to their future independent existence.

Some of their leaders sensed the problems and challenges rapidly mounting out of reach of both the scope of traditional tribal government and timeworn customs of intertribal relations. Over the next few years some of those leaders acted to neutralize the dangers and to take whatever new opportunities offered themselves. To a degree probably never understood by most of their own people, some of these men managed to combine the necessary status and behavior of traditional moral preeminence with a strong power that traditional leaders had neither sought nor possessed.

In taking this new power position, some of the leaders succeeded for a time in gaining safety and strength for their tribesmen, while some of them failed in the attempt. In varying degrees among the Pimas and Maricopas, Mohaves, Quechans, Chemehuevis, Yavapais, and Cocopas, and in the disparate band-and-lineage politics of the Cahuilla, Cupeño, Diegueño, and Luiseño of Southern California, we can see new leaders at mid-century using nontraditional techniques to protect their peoples.[44]

On this scene, where age-old ways were now more quickly being accommodated to the imperatives of new conditions, the battle of 1857 nonetheless unfolded as a purely traditional event.

SIX

Motives and Origins:
Warfare and Peace
on the Colorado and Gila

I n looking for an answer to the question of why men wage war against one another, it is necessary to distinguish between *motives* and *origins*. Motives are overt and are triggers for particular battles, series of battles, or even prolonged enmities. Origins are the covert and latent wellsprings of warfare. Motives are immediate causes; origins are ultimate causes.

Various ideas have been advanced to explain the prolonged warfare that characterized relations among peoples of the Lower Colorado and middle Gila rivers and the warlike natures of some of those tribes.

CONTEMPORARY EXPLANATIONS

Capt. H. S. Burton, 3rd U. S. Artillery, and commander of Fort Yuma in September 1857, wrote a letter to the California Superintendent of Indian Affairs. He outlined what seemed to him to be the match igniting the 1857 battle:

> The immediate cause of these difficulties appears to be this.—In the early part of May last Jose Maria, a Yuma Captain, with four of his men joined the Tonto Apaches in a foray upon the Maricopas.—In this four of the Maricopas were killed and several wounded. About the end of June the Maricopas retaliated upon the Tonto Apaches

killing 16 and taking three prisoners, one girl 12 or 13 years old, and two boys quite small.

The Maricopas sold the prisoners to Ignacio Rovelo who is now in Los Angeles with the children.—He passed this place just before my arrival here from San Diego.—

The moment the Yumas saw the prisoners they became very excited and sent information to the Apaches immediately.

Previous to this, however, in the last days of July, the Apaches notified their friends of an attack to be made in August by a large force upon the Pimos and Maricopas. About this time "Caballo en pelo" the war chief of all the Yumas died, and his dying words were a command to his people "never to make peace with the Maricopas."

This with the appearance of the Apache prisoners precipitated the movements of the River tribes, and the 2nd or 3rd of September an allied force of Yumas, Mohaves, Chima-way-wahs [Chemehuevis], Yumpis [Yavapais] and Tonto Apaches, between 6 & 700 strong attacked the Maricopas.[1]

Lieut. Joseph C. Ives, headed up the Colorado River on a surveying expedition in January 1858, took on board his ship a Quechan Indian named "Capitan" who represented himself as a survivor of the 1857 battle. It was possibly from Capitan that he heard details of the affair, noting in his published report:

The Pimas and the Maricopas live upon the Gila. . . . They are peaceable, quietly-disposed Indians, and subsist principally upon the products they derive from cultivating the soil. They have always been friendly to whites, but, from the time of the earliest records, bitter foes to the Yumas and Mojaves, who have been disposed to regard them with contempt, as an inferior race.

In the year 1856 the principal chief of the Yumas became mortally ill. Upon his death-bed he charged his tribe not to be remiss in hunting down their hated enemies, and prophesied that if they would, during the following year, organize an expedition against them, it would result in the latter's complete overthrow.

After the chief's death the Yumas, regarding with superstitious reverence his dying injunctions, prepared for a secret attack upon the Pimas and Maricopas villages.[2]

As valid as these explanations may be in describing events igniting the fuse leading to the 1857 explosion on the Gila, they represent the observations and opinions of non-Indians. It is unlikely that the "death bed" admonition of a single Quechan leader, as reported by Burton and Ives, had anything to do with the 1857 battle. Attention given to the last words of a dying person is more likely to be a European custom than a Yuman tradition. More plausible are the explanations given by Isaiah Woods, the eyewitness to the 1857 battle (see p. 9), and by Joe Homer, the Quechan who told E. W. Gifford that an Algodones man simply dreamed such a war expedition would have success and that he persuaded others to follow him (see pp. 69–71).

MODERN EXPLANATIONS

Many motives have been adduced to explain the centuries-long hostilities among peoples of the middle Gila and Lower Colorado. The temptation to speculate will remain because we have no thoroughgoing knowledge of the history before the 1820s, and little enough from the 1820s until after the mid-nineteenth century when warfare among Indians in that region came to an end. Even indirect approaches to aboriginal history may not tell us what we want to know. A. L. Kroeber, for instance, who collected some of the most important historico-religious texts of the Mohave, found no clue: "Where fighting is involved, motivation becomes particularly elusive. The main thing seems to be that there should be war and the happenings that go with war. . . . [T]here is often a sense of foreboding or of the inevitability of what will happen."[3]

No European saw these peoples before the 1540s, and from then until the 1820s the sum of European observations of Gila-Colorado culture embodied but a few pages left by Spanish soldiers and priests who only briefly visited some parts of the region.[4]

Frederic Hicks highlights our basic ignorance concerning the native situation: "We actually know very little about the nature and function of aboriginal warfare, since nearly all descriptive accounts deal with inter-tribal warfare under the circumstances of European presence or penetration in the area. . . ."[5]

Indeed, other theoreticians have given no explanation for the origin of this warfare. Their suppositions begin late in the history of the Quechans, Halchidhomas, and Mohaves, when nationalistic identities were well established and when enmity/amity relationships were already part of the fabric of regional life. Explanations take as starting points the social organizations and the intertribal relationships glimpsed by Spanish visitors in the

1540s and that remained firm until past the mid-nineteenth century. Where most recent theories differ markedly is in their reliance on either environmental or on acculturative factors and in their stance on the degree of Spanish-Mexican influence on warfare. In reviewing the various theories we will consider three essays by Henry Dobyns, Greta and Paul Ezell, and Alden Jones; one by Edward Graham; and a fifth, the most recent on the subject, by Connie L. Stone.

WARFARE AND SCARCITY

We have already considered the possible relationship between hostilities and food scarcity among tribes of the Lower Colorado, but that discussion failed to take into account two important essays on the subject.[6]

Connie Stone asserts that the Indians' need for resources was pressing and that they turned to raiding and conquest because they could neither expand nor intensify their food resource activities while confined within their aboriginal lands and restricted to adjacent gathering zones. Thus, "economic incentives for engaging in warfare were stronger than incentives for increasing agricultural production."[7]

Stone argues that the River Yumans could not find sufficient labor to crop more land. Neither could they intensify farming in the choicest riverbank locations nor attain higher production by better use of water. Looking at the aboriginal situation in detail, she supposes that River Yumans had reached optimum production partly because aboriginal farmers are disinclined to farm more lands in risky circumstances. She says they "often chose security over productivity, reducing risk by employing subsistence strategies less vulnerable to natural catastrophes. Mesquite beans were a more reliable resource than agricultural crops."[8]

She further postulates that the labor of men and women was already stretched to the utmost by simultaneous chores of harvesting crops and gathering ripened mesquite pods. A second crop could not be added to their annual routine because along the stretches inhabited by Mohaves, Quechans, and Halchidhomas there was only one high-water stage of the river each year and, therefore, only one crop to be grown from seeds set into the mud as the flood waters receded during late summer.[9]

Because Stone believes that "subsistence stress would have been frequent" among these peoples, even as their warfare was "incessant," she concludes that "warfare was a response to frequent food shortages and subsistence stress."[10] In addition, although warfare was a "major response" to food shortages, the Indians' "possible minor response" to hunger or famine might be to migrate from the river.[11] This is what the Halchidhoma did gradually from the late 1820s to about 1835.

The major response was to recurring ecological emergencies, "defined here as hunger, starvation, and hardship associated with the increased time, effort, and travel in obtaining food." It was this which turned the peoples' desperation in upon their fellow tribesmen, as seen in Mohaves' struggles to dispossess each other of good farm land and gathering zones.[12]

Finally, Stone argues that the Indians never solved their resource problems, even when they resorted to incessant warfare.[13]

Edward E. Graham also casts the Indians' predicament as an environmental one to which they reacted by expanding into the lands of adjacent peoples.[14]

He, like Stone, believes that the resources available to aboriginal tribal territories were not sufficient: "[T]he land suitable for agriculture, primarily flood plain alluvium, was limited." The very utilization of that fund of land in farming and in gathering created a demand for still more productive land. Graham assumes that only certain peoples felt this outward pressure to acquire such additional territory. Those aggressors were to be found among the peoples who gained more of their food supply from farming, with fewer aggressors among gatherers. Thus, "those societies whose subsistence depended more upon food production exerted pressure, through warfare, on those societies less dependent on food production."[15]

The "more efficient" agriculturalists went in search of additional bottom lands when the proportion of their food supply from farming "had reached a crucial point, probably between 30 and 40 percent."[16] At this juncture such peoples embarked on territorial conquest, going after their neighbors' real estate. This is how Graham explains the hostilities resulting in the departure of the Halchidhoma from the Lower Colorado after the late 1820s. He also points out that his hypotheses fit the available facts concerning the victors in these hostilities, that is, the Quechans and Mohaves were at once the "more efficient in extracting energy from the flood plain alluviums," and "were also the most bellicose" of all those river peoples.[17]

To support his proposition, Graham draws on information from a Spanish visitor, Fr. Francisco Garcés, concerning the length of riverbank held by each people and concerning eighteenth-century population figures for the Cocopa, Quechan, Maricopa, Halchidhoma, and Mohave; and from Edward Castetter and Willis Bell concerning percentages of food each people acquired from farming and from gathering. He uses these data to derive figures for population density, food production, and food collection. His analysis reveals Halchidhomas to have been too numerous for their territory in view of the fact that almost all their food was collected and very little farmed. Thus, in Graham's thinking the Halchidhoma were vulnerable to pressure exerted by other peoples whose reliance was much greater on farming. To repeat his major contention, he feels he proved that "the shift from food collection to food production with its concomitantly increased need for homogeneous farmlands expressed itself in terms of warfare," and it was this warfare which ejected from the river those people who had not come to depend as fully upon overflow farming for their food supply.[18]

PROBLEMS INHERENT IN THE ENVIRONMENTAL/ECOLOGICAL THEORIES

It can be said of both Stone's and Graham's theories that they are at once too elaborate for the thin layer of available evidence and too often oblivious of evidence at hand. Both theories assume a desperate insufficiency of food—an assertion highly controversial at best and one which we contend is not demonstrated by the sources or by careful studies done in this century. Likewise, Stone and Graham both offer theories which account for war which prove in each case too fragile to account also for peace—which we suspect was the ordinary situation in bilateral relationships among people. This is to say that Stone and Graham confine their attention to lands and peoples exclusively within the Gila and Colorado riverbank zone. The full picture of subsistence activities, and of war and peace, requires taking into account the lands and peoples just beyond the river's course. Finally, Stone, and perhaps Graham, assume a frequent state of war among the riverine tribes. This is something that cannot be proven. We can say that war may have been frequent, but we have no basis in records at hand for speaking of Gila-Colorado warfare as "incessant."

Against Stone's assumption that hungry or famine-struck people would "lead themselves into competition for available resources"[19] stands her assertion that none of these peoples had the number of workers available at times when they were most needed even to be able to use all the resources already available to them. To follow her argument a bit further, she is saying that people would drop their busy struggle for survival and go off to steal food or to occupy territory somewhere else. But to take more land would be of no help, following Stone's argument, because working against the people was the fact that harvesting and gathering activities reached their peak in the single month of July. As she sees it, the predicament was that Indians could not possibly harvest enough crops nor gather enough mesquite pods because both those tasks had to be done during a few weeks in July.

Stone does not concern herself with one of the more difficult questions; namely, whether Cocopas, Quechans, Halchidhomas, or Mohaves ever used nearly all the good bottom land locations available to them in aboriginal times. William Kelly struggled with this problem for the Cocopas, concluding that "it is impossible now to estimate either the probable acreage of land suitable for agriculture under aboriginal conditions or the actual number of acres cultivated by the native inhabitants prior to 1905."[20]

We have not solved this problem and can only point to the fact that no visitor to the river from the mid-sixteenth through the late-nineteenth centuries ever reported any people as fully occupying the arable locations within its own territory. In short, we know of no reason to believe that population pressures existed in aboriginal times along the Lower Colorado or on the Gila.

Stone also gives too limited and rigid an impression of the annual round of cultivation, semicultivation, and collecting and gathering that was the drudgery of life for Indian women and, to some extent, for the men as well. Her statement that River Yumans' harvest of planted crops occurred in July is too narrow a view, and her belief that mesquite-bean gathering must be done mostly at the same time—during two or three weeks of July—is also far too constricting. To examine the authorities upon whom Stone mainly relies, Castetter and Bell in their *Yuman Indian Agriculture*, show how varied were the Indians' food acquisition activities; how variable the occurrence of those activities from year to year; and how the Indians could resort to a number of less-favored foods when their major domestic and wild crops were disastrously scarce.

Stone is apparently not aware that the Mohaves, Quechans, and

Halchidhomas cultivated wheat in historic times; that mesquite bean gathering could often be done before and after the harvesting of field crops; or that the River Yumans could produce one or more minor crops in addition to the major one coming to fruition in June, July, or early August.[21]

Graham's thesis rests on assumptions which are unlikely to serve his purpose, especially when viewed together. For example, by virtue of Castetter and Bell's estimate of thirty percent for the agricultural component in Cocopa food supply, one would, following Graham, be forced to assume that Cocopas had a tenuous hold on their territory. That pattern—more food collection, less from crops—did not, in fact, spell weakness for these Indians' grip on their land. Partly because they relied so little on domestic crops in their semi-drowned habitat in and near the Colorado River delta, they lived in dispersed groups. They traveled widely and sporadically throughout the year. Thus they rarely, if ever, presented an easy target for would-be conquerors or raiders. More than any of the other river Yumans, they were able to drift away for a time and to remain with friendly peoples until danger had passed. Yet they could return to defend their tract along the Lower Colorado as evidenced by the fact that the Quechans, their bitter enemies and neighbors, are not known to have gained a single square inch of Cocopa territory.

It is difficult to assess Graham's basic figures for the size of territories supposedly owned by the several tribes as of 1776. Graham depends on estimates made by Father Garcés based on his visit to the Lower Colorado in the winter of 1775 − 76; but Garcés failed to mention other tribes now known to have been resident on the river at that period: the Kohuana, Halyikwamai, and Kamia. We cannot say what effect the reinsertion of factors for these missing tribes would have on Graham's computations. It is perhaps best to conclude that Graham's figures are useful in seeking rough approximations, but that the figures are not precise enough to help in making comparative estimations of population or of relative efficiency of various peoples in using their habitats for acquiring food.

What kinds of information would be a sufficient basis on which to estimate whether a particular River Yuman group would have had enough food in a given year? First, we would need to know whether during spring and early summer there were enough foods in storage, enough wheat in the spring crop, enough tubers to dig, and enough fish and small game to be gotten. If there were, people could survive the lean times before the mesquite bean crop became available.

We would also need to know about the flow of the river: volume, velocity, and periodicity. Were enough bottom lands watered to provide ample plantings of corn, beans, melons, and other crops? Were there devastating floods that may have washed crops away? And at planting time, were the people still well fed and strong enough to get seeds in the ground as well as gather mesquite beans coming to fruit from May through August? Or were they too weak from famine to labor in this busiest of all seasons? Were there disastrous episodes of war which drove people from their planting grounds?

How well did mesquites and screwbeans, as well as other wild crops, produce that year? Was there time for people to carry these harvests to their weatherproof storage granaries so that enough food would be reserved for late winter and spring?

We would also need to know if in late fall there were good crops of cultivated plants or whether flood, birds, insects, and plant diseases had taken a toll. Had there been an opportunity for double cropping? Had it been possible in January and February to plant wheat? Were the people able to plant small household plots in February? And, if supplies were short, had people widened the range of their food gathering trips?

Finally, we would need to know how many able-bodied people were available to do the work and the size of the population having to be fed.

The problem is that these are questions no one can answer with any serious degree of confidence, either for prehistoric and early historic times or for those turbulent years of the nineteenth century. None of the visitors left us with such estimates as, "They had about ten acres of good crop land for the mile of riverbank"; or, "failing their corn and beans, these folks could feed half their numbers from the grasses, and from catching rabbits and fishing." We are by no means certain concerning population figures. We are unable to say whether people farmed all, or even most, of the good farmlands in their territory. In short, it seems futile to attempt to arrive at a description of population pressures along the Lower Colorado, especially through the early nineteenth century.

Particularly troubling in the Stone and Graham analyses is their failure to come forward into later historic times for which there are better data. The ultimate tests for ecological theories would be found in those years between the departure of the Halchidhoma and the end of tribal wars, between about 1835 and 1875. For these years we have some factual information, and some of it seems to defy the proposed environmental theories.

Table 2. **Lower Colorado (Quechan, Halchidhoma, Mohave) Agricultural Year**

April	Harvest wheat; gather desert lily and cattail leaves
Late April—early May	Early bean, calabash, maize planting; harvest wheat
Late May, into June	Harvest household crop plot; dig arrowhead tubers; gather lotebush fruit; plant crops if possible
Late June, early July	Gather mesquite beans; plant crops and semicultivated grass; collect green cattail bloom spikes
Late July, August	Gather screwbeans; guard young cultivated crops; gather mesquite beans
September	Gather pigweed; last mesquite bean harvest; gather careless weed, barnyard grass, and other grasses; collect cattail pollen
Late October, early November	Harvest planted crops; plant wheat; gather quailbrush, desert saltbush, ironwood pods; plant curlydock
December—February	Plant household crops (maize, watermelons)

Sources: Castetter and Bell (1951) and Niethammer (1974)

At times, for example, a few peoples living away from the river's edge were permitted by permanent residents to farm there and to occupy stretches of bottom land. The Southwestern Yavapai farmed in Quechan territory and the Chemehuevi farmed lands considered by Mohaves to be theirs.[22] How are such overtly peaceful relationships to be accounted for? Why did the Mohaves and Quechans remain on good terms, as did the Maricopas and Pimas? A comprehensive theory of the motivations and origins of war must also account for the absence of war. The latter seems more often to have been the situation in the Lower Colorado and middle Gila area.

ACCULTURATION THEORIES OF GILA-COLORADO WARFARE

The best known of all explanations for Gila-Colorado warfare relies on the concepts of diffusion and acculturation to explain what its authors see as an

intensification of hostilities that resulted in "new power relationships between societies in the lower river basin."[23] This idea, propounded by
Henry Dobyns, Greta and Paul Ezell, and Alden Jones, attempts to
account for those bitter wars which resulted in the departure of at least
four peoples from the Lower Colorado at various times from the late
eighteenth century until about 1835.

These authors have been no better able than anyone else in discerning
the origins of Gila-Colorado warfare. Like other ethnohistorians and anthropologists, they begin by assuming there was a particular set of opera-
tional motives in effect before the arrival of the earliest Europeans in the
year 1540. In their view, those wars were recurring because of the desire
for revenge. Such hostilities were accompanied by ethnic insults which are
presumed to have taken the form of ritual cannibalism to express best the
top-lofty attitude of members of one tribe toward those of another.[24]

Based on the assumption that members of each tribe felt superior to
others, Greta and Paul Ezell write that all the River Yumans could be seen
as sharing "a strong sense of nationality and an enthusiasm for belligerence, whether in the form of raiding or more formal battle."[25] They also
believe that aboriginal warfare had among its motives those of sheer fun,
kudos to be won, and exercise. As for economic motives for aboriginal
warfare, however, they are unsure any existed.[26]

In the general theory, the aboriginal functions of warfare were forever
and radically altered by acculturative influences from Spaniards and, later,
from Mexicans. There were at least two historic periods of such change.
In the first of these the River Yumans became acquainted with the horse
and, perhaps, with European trade goods. In their desire to possess
horses, the riverine peoples succumbed to the temptation to capture Indians to be sold as servants in Spanish settlements in what is today northwestern Mexico. Simultaneously, European-introduced diseases were
making their way to the Gila and Colorado rivers and the tribes'
populations began to decrease even as their activities in trade and warfare
increased.[27]

The second period of this change was characterized by intensification of
inter-tribal hostilities occasioned by slave raiding and the acquisition of
horses. Not only had raiding and trading reached a heightened level, one
necessitating further expansion, but there were now—just before 1820 and
increasing throughout that decade—terrible disturbances in the region. A
contributing factor was a developing cooperative relationship between

Mexicans and Halchidhomas who were then living on the Colorado between the Mohaves and Quechans. Vengeance raids of Mohaves and Quechans against Halchidhomas intensified, probably because of the friendliness of the latter with Mexicans and perhaps also because of Mohaves' problems with Anglo-American fur trappers in 1826–27. Thus vengeance raiding "was reinforced by the economic raiding theme, and these two combined in causing an historic intensification of riverain [sic] Yuman warfare which ultimately resulted in forcing three tribes off the Colorado River."[28]

Dobyns, the Ezells, and Jones see the working together of aboriginal warfare themes with additional themes resulting from Spanish and Mexican influence as reinforcing "the basic postulate of ethnic superiority held by each tribe. [These various influences] helped maintain the tribal sense of ethnic mission—the feeling of being a chosen people. They prevented Indian definition of Spaniards or another tribe as a dominant group."[29]

More recently, Greta and Paul Ezell have written that this turbulent series of developments in Lower Colorado River affairs so intensified rivalries and so complicated existing fears as to raise inter-group tensions and to sustain "pressures" on the peoples who continued to reside there. Further exacerbating the situation were increasing numbers of incidents with Anglo-Americans. As they follow the history into the 1850s, the Ezells see further sources of oppression in such events as the siting of a U.S. army post near Yuma Crossing. "[T]he almost continuous presence of Americans from this time [ca. 1846] forward, was to apply unremitting pressures on the Yumas." And the Ezells see these pressures as the immediate cause of the 1857 battle: "Possibly the catalyst was a combination of the increase in the number of soldiers at Fort Yuma and the intelligence that the Maricopa and Pima warriors were fighting with the United States Army against the Apaches. . . ."[30]

Thus the large view of Dobyns, the Ezells, and Jones is that of an aboriginal region where only limited warfare occurred among peoples aligned in ancient and traditional groupings of amity and enmity. The coming of Spaniards and, subsequently, Mexicans induced changes in Indian warfare customs, including motivations, and made warfare far more serious than previously. Just before the end of the eighteenth century and developing into greater violence in the nineteenth century, warfare contributed to a loss in tribal populations and to heightened desperation on the part of Maricopas, Quechans, Cocopas, and Mohaves.

There is much to be said in favor of this broad-ranging hypothesis, one whose intent is to link events on the Gila and Colorado rivers with changing circumstances elsewhere. That historic-period Yuman warfare was somehow connected with affairs taking place south of the Gila and westward into Alta California seems undeniable. The notion is clearly corroborated by the work of Jack Forbes, as is the assertion of a decrease in Yuman population.[31]

Concerning population decrease, however, we cite a note of caution in connection with the Mohaves. Regardless of diseases and warfare elsewhere along the Colorado, it may be their numbers were affected little if at all. This is especially the case if we give credence to the 1860 report of Peter R. Brady (see pp. 132–36). A. L. Kroeber found Brady's report surprising in that it indicates a larger population than Kroeber's own estimate. Kroeber commented on Brady's figures as follows:

> This seems a heavy proportion to have been living in Parker Valley before the 1859 fighting. Four of Brady's Needles Valley bands run to 800 warriors. From these we can extrapolate to 1200 for the six upper Mohave bands in their old homeland. At Mooney's old ratio of 3½ population to 1 warrior, we should have 4,200, plus 2,100 lower, total 6,300. Even at a ratio of 3 to 1, there would be 5,400, which is higher than all reasonable figures. One factor needs to be considered. One-third of all Mohaves may have at one time or another lived at Parker or planted there, and this is what Homaratav may have had in mind. Yet the number there probably fluctuated, as when Areteva took his following there after the defeat of 1859, but soon returned. . . . Those permanently established at Parker in 1860 may have been nearer one-fifth than one-third of the total; which would make Brady's estimates yield around 4,500-5,000 altogether, according as fighting men constituted one-third or two-sevenths of the population.[32]

In addition to our caveat concerning Mohave population figures, we do not to agree that Dobyns, the Ezells, and Jones have properly accounted for the continuation and intensification of Gila-Colorado warfare. While we respect the historical reconstructions involved, the fact remains that presently there is no way of knowing how intense this warfare was during the sixteenth, seventeenth, and eighteenth centuries.[33] It is impossible to know whether warfare intensified toward the end of the eighteenth century as Forbes believes along with Dobyns and his coauthors.[34] It is possible wrongly to adduce the increase in numbers of historical documents at that time as indication of more warfare.

We further notice that no amount of enmity brought on by slave raiding, horse trading, or other influences changed traditional alignments of friends and foes, alignments which had existed for a long time and which were destined to last until after 1850. Only the coming of more numerous Anglo-American settlers, and particularly the U. S. Army's adoption of some peoples as allies, finally turned former Indian friends into enemies. Thus were Yavapais enlisted to fight Apaches and Mohaves to fight Yavapais, Walapais, and Chemehuevis. Simultaneously, the U. S. Army played its part in bringing about peace between such long-standing opponents as the allied Quechan and Mohave on one hand and allied Maricopa and Pima on the other. These realignments took place between 1863 and the middle 1870s.

The principal effect of Spanish and Mexican presence on Yuman warfare may have been the introduction of the horse for limited use in battle and the introduction of metal weapons such as knives.

It is possible, if not proveable, that Spanish and Mexican influences encouraged larger numbers of smaller surprise raids against enemy peoples. These might have been vengeance raids or raids for booty, including kidnapping of women and children. But we see no influence from Hispanic culture on the formal war expeditions launched at one another by Quechans and Maricopas.

Both the environmental/ecological and acculturation theories rely for their causal explanations upon aspects of Indian history and life that were indubitably important and that created crises in the lives of Gila-Colorado peoples. When all is said and done, however, these theories do not account for the incidence of warfare among those riverine peoples. It is true that hunger and want called for emergency measures by those peoples; but there is no evidence to show that warfare was one of those emergency measures. Likewise, it is quite true that impinging developments, both from Mexico and from settlements near the Pacific shore, influenced Lower Colorado and middle Gila River Indian affairs. But we see no proof that all those influences did anything significant to swerve, increase, or deaden the recurrent hostilities. Those hostilities continued much as they had been until the Anglo Americans' dominating presence finally shattered so many aspects of Indians' lives, including their long-standing custom of going to war.

THE P. R. BRADY REPORT

Peter Rainsford Brady, whose 1860 report on the Mohave Indians is published here for the first time, was born in Georgetown in the District of Columbia on August 4, 1825. He graduated from the U. S. Naval Academy at Annapolis in 1844. Two years later he became a member of the North Texas Rangers, and in 1853—54 he went with A. B. Gray to survey for a possible railroad route along the 32nd Parallel. It was this effort which brought him to Arizona, then New Mexico Territory. He settled in Tucson in 1854, was post interpreter at Fort Mohave in 1860, sheriff of Pima County for two terms after 1863, and became a resident of Florence, Arizona, in 1872. After having had a career as a miner and as Special Agent of the Department of the Interior for the U. S. Court of Private Land Claims, he moved back to Tucson in 1899, dying there on May 2, 1902.[35]

In introducing this report we should add to A. L. Kroeber's comments, above, that almost all estimates of Mohave population in aboriginal or early contact times set their numbers higher than those of other River Yumans, commonly at some number between 3,000 and 4,000. So it should be no surprise that Mohaves, whose home valley was not attacked by other Indians before 1865 and who lost very few people in hostilities with Anglo-Americans, are estimated by Brady at a figure approximating 4,000 people.

Herewith, then, is the Brady report, for what it tells us about population, food resources, and other aspects of Mohave life:

Fort Mojave N. M.
Octr 9th 1860

Major G. Haller 4th Infy
Comdg Post

Sir,

From enquiries that I have made, in regard to the Indians of the Rio Colorado of the West, and those inhabiting the country adjoining, I am enabled to make the following report.

Commencing with the Ho-mok-have-es, who are by far the most numerous of the different tribes living on the river, I have divided them into two bands, the upper and lower Ho-mok-hav-es. The upper, are those who live in the valley, at the head of which this Post is situated, and occupy an extent of country about forty-five miles long by ten broad. They subsist by cultivation of the soil, and what few fish the river affords. The soil is remarkably rich in the low bottom lands adjoining the river and affords them subsistence with very little labor. They plant two crops in the year, one of wheat in January and February, which they gather in the months of April and May, and which ripens from the dampness of the soil alone. The second crop which is the largest and by far the most important, is planted after the annual overflow, which generally takes place about the middle of June, at which time they plant considerable quantities of corn, pumpkins, beans, and melons. They also gather large quantities of the mezquite bean and grass seed, which affords them some support. There is no game whatever in their country and they know nothing of the chase, which compels them to subsist on a purely vegetable diet, notwithstanding which, they are a large well made athletic race but not at all warlike, as they have been represented but on the contrary peaceful. Their habits and manners are simple, and from the little intercourse they have had with the whites, they have as yet acquired none of their vices, drunkenness the great curse of all the other Indians being unknown amongst them. Their language is that of the Cuchan family pretty much the same as spoken on the Colorado river, from its mouth to this point, and differs entirely from the languages spoken by the Indians inhabiting the country adjoining.

They live in rancherias composed of four to six or eight families sometimes more. In the winter time they build themselves houses which are quite comfortable and warm, but during the summer they prefer living under a shelter composed of green boughs or beneath the shade of trees.

I estimate the number of upper Ho-mok-hav-es that is grown men to be about eight hundred probably a little more. At the treaty made with them by Col. M. [sic] Hoffman 6th Infy U.S.A. there were six chiefs presented themselves, since that time two of these have been killed.

Hom-sik-a-hote who lives on the opposite bank of the river from the post, has control of all the Indians living for some ten or twelve miles down the river, and his band I think contains about two-hundred warriors. He appears to be friendly and peaceable in his disposition.

Ha-chur-ni-ah who was killed in the fight with Major Armistead on the 5th of August 1859 lived next below on the West bank of the

Colorado. It is difficult to estimate the number of his people, as he
himself during his life time was hostile, and his people have remained so. To-pi-ko-na-ho who lives next below, and whose lands
extend to the foot of this valley on the West side, can muster about
one-hundred-fifty warriors. He seems to be a peaceable quiet old
man and friendly disposed.

Commencing on the East bank of the river and about four miles
below the Post lives Ko-pa-tam and his band whose planting grounds
extend down the river about ten miles. His people are quite
numerous and may probably reach to two-hundred warriors. He
himself is rather disposed to be unfriendly to the Americans, and
never came in to the treaty held here by Major Armistead, when all
the balance of them came in and surrendered.

Ir-ri-ta-wa lives next below, and his lands extend down the river
ten miles on the East bank. His band numbers about two-hundred and fifty warriors. He is by far the smartest Indian in the tribe,
and his influence over them is very great. He was unfriendly for a
long time, but I believe of late, his feelings have changed a little
towards us.

Next below and still on the East bank you come to the lands of Ki-
rook, who was killed in the outbreak upon the guard at Fort Yuma.
His people frequently visit the Post and seem friendly. His son who
was held as a hostage at the time of his Fathers death made his
escape, he visits us often and appears to be one of the most lively and
goodnatured youths in the tribe.

About thirty-five miles South East from this Post, below the
valley, and at the point known as the "Needles" the Colorado for
about sixty-five miles runs through a very broken and mountainous
country, with some few little strips of bottom land. This is the range
of the Chem-mi-gue-gua Indians. I am able to say but little in
regard to them as they very seldom visit the Post. Some few of them
cultivate little patches of the soil, but by far the greater part of them
live back in the mountains West of the Colorado, and subsist by
hunting and on roots and grass seed. They lead a wandering vaga-
bond life, the same as the Pah-utes whom they resemble very much
in appearance and manners and I expect in fact are a branch of the
Pah-ute family.

As-pan-ku-yah is the principal chief of those who live in on the
river and says he has three-hundred warriors. He came in at the
treaty made with Major Armistead, and has visited the Post once
since.

About one-hundred miles from here you arrive at the commencement of the "Great Cuchan Valley," which is the country of the lower Ho-mok-hav-es and the Cuchans. The lower Ho-mok-hav-es with the exception of some few in their tribe did not join this portion of the tribe in their hostilities against the troops here last summer. Their habits, mode of life manners, language and customs is precisely the same as that of these Indians. Their principal chief is named Ho-mar-rah-tao and seems to be a very intelligent Indian. He has twice visited the Post with numbers of his people. When here last about a month ago, in a conversation I had with him, he told me that the number of his people was about one half of what there were in this valley. When we passed through his country on our march up here, I saw much more wheat planted, than these Indians had, which I now attribute to their being more extensive planting lands in the lower valley than in this.

Adjoining these Indians on the South still lower down the Colorado, you come into the Cuchan country which extends to forty miles down below Fort Yuma.

To the Eastward of the lower portion of the lower Ho-mok-hav-es country is the range of the Ya-ve-pais of whom very little is known. They are a wild wandering race of savages and continually at war with their hereditary enemies the Pimas and Maricopas. They subsist entirely by the chase. One month ago when Ho-mar-rah-tav came in he brought one-hundred-and fifty warriors of this tribe in with him. I was unable [able] to ascertain very little in regard to them except that it was their first interview with the whites.

East of the Post and commencing in the range of mountains immediately in sight of us live the Gualpais, whose range extends as far North as the little Colorado, East of the San Francisco Mountains and South to the Ya-ve-pai country a distance of over five-hundred miles. They are a very numerous tribe and roam over a vast extent of country that has been as yet little explored. From their mode of life and appearance they resemble the Apaches very much, and I think are a branch of their family. They have only visited the Post a few times. In their last visit which was at the talk held here one month ago there were one-hundred of them present. They subsist entirely by the chase and say that the game is very abundant in their country. To the West of us and extending North to the Great Salt Lake and South to within fifty miles of the Southern boundary of California roam the Pai-utes a wandering, thieving tribe of vagabonds who live upon rabbits lizards snakes rats and in fact anything that will support life. They seldom come to the Post in numbers of more than six or eight and but upon one occasion have a larger number of them been here, it was over a month ago when they held a grand talk and at that time there were not over twenty or thirty. It is difficult to arrive at any estimate in regards to their numbers, but I believe their numbers would not amount to over one-hundred warriors who roam through the country West of us to the California settlements. There are some few families of these Indians who plant up in Cottonwood valley forty-two miles above the Post on the Colorado river, but their numbers are quite small.

The above is respectfully submitted
I have the honor to remain
Very respectfully
Your Obdt sevt

P.R. Brady Post Interpreter

To Brvt Major G.O. Haller 4th Infy
Comdg Post at Fort Mojave N.M.[36]

ALLIANCES AND WARFARE

Finally, the proposal that there were two great alliance systems in what is now most of Arizona, parts of Nevada, and Southern California requires some discussion. The notion has been proposed by A. L. Kroeber, by Jack Forbes, and still more strongly by Chris White,[37] and it has gained credence over the years. As the acculturation theorists have it, a case of aggression by a people against one in the other group "tended to generate general warfare . . . as the tribes primarily involved called upon their allies for assistance."[38]

Jack Forbes contends there were two great Leagues; the conclusion might easily be drawn that an aggressor member of one League provoked retaliation from members of the opposing League.[39]

As we have said earlier (p. 109), it is a misconception to imagine coordinated warfare throughout that large zone including most of Arizona and Southern California, with parts of Nevada and northwestern Mexico included. No evidence exists for two alliance systems in the European sense. A number of bilateral and even trilateral involvements persisted for centuries, and some of these have been discussed here. But such associations were exceptions and seldom evidenced themselves in warfare. Most importantly, such intertribal associations did not tend to develop into regional alliance groups, nor did those friendships of long standing tend to spread warfare throughout the region.

It is true that Quechans and Maricopas saw each other as enemies throughout the long history of which we have a record. However, the record is less clear as it relates to Quechans and their relationships with western Papagos. For long periods of time Papagos dealt with Quechans in trade. This kind of relationship may have obtained until 1830 or 1840. After that date there may have been a falling out, perhaps even minor hostilities. But we wrench the facts to cast Papagos and Quechans as perpetual enemies.

What was probably the generally less structured relationship among these various peoples has been best described by A. L. Kroeber:

> The international relations of the Chemehuevi were determined in general, and probably for a long time, by a series of interconnected amities and enmities that threw the tribes of southern California, southern Nevada, and western Arizona into two great alignments that ran counter to their origins as well as their mode of life. On one side were the Chemehuevi, Southern Paiute, Mohave, Yuma, Kamia, Yavapai, and Apache. These were generally friendly to the less enterprising and passive northern Serrano of the desert, and, so far as they knew them, to the Yokuts, the Tübatulabal, the Chumash, and perhaps the Gabrielino. On the other side were the Hopi; the Pima and most of the Papago; of Yuman tribes, the Havasupai, Walapai, Maricopa, Halchidhoma, Kohuana, Halyikwamai, Cocopa, Diegueño, and the Cuñeil or northernmost Baja Californians; of southern California Shoshoneans, the Serrano proper, the Cahuilla, and possibly the Luiseño. There was nothing like a confederation, or even formal alliance among the tribes of either party. Rather, each had its enemies of long standing, and therefore joined hands with their foes, until an irregular but far-stretching and interlocking line-up worked itself out. Often tribes here grouped as on the same side had their temporary conflicts, or even a traditional hatred. But, on the whole, they divided as here indicated, as Garcés pictured the situation in the eighteenth century, as later reports of narrower outlook confirm, and as the recollections of the modern Mohave

corroborate. Small, scattered, or timid tribes, like the Chemehuevi, the Hopi, the Havasupai, and the various Serrano divisions, were less involved in open war and more inclined to abiding suspicions and occasional conflicts than aggressive, enterprising, or tenacious nations of numbers or solidarity such as the Apache, Pima, and Mohave; but their outward relations were largely predetermined by the general scheme.[40]

BEGINNINGS

We turn now to our own interpretations of the causes, both immediate and ultimate, of those hostilities known to have existed among Lower Colorado River Yumans for more than four centuries. Like others before us, we necessarily indulge in considerable speculation. The early history of these peoples remains in shadow. For example, we have no idea where the Quechans were living until the late seventeenth century. Even by that time they may not yet have coalesced into the tribal group they became when settled along the Colorado. Nor can we be sure how long the Gila River Pimas had been living on that river, developing their intensive irrigation agriculture and the effective mechanism for defense which enabled them to hold their own against Apaches.

The battles peoples fought during the nineteenth century were surely only the last hot sparks thrown from the embers of what had been a prolonged fire. There may have been many decades of war on the Colorado in prehistoric times that saw Quechans and Mohaves conquering and seizing lands of various peoples who once lived both south and north of the Gila-Colorado junction. It is possible the historical rivalry of Quechans and Maricopas, already in course during the sixteenth century, may represent a mere remnant of some larger struggle undertaken long before and far to the south, even involving other people whose conflicts and history remain unknown.[41]

In their twentieth-century form recorded by anthropologists, Yuman oral narratives do not explain all the earlier movements of the peoples, nor do they give reasons why the hostilities began. Some show which other political communities, by the nineteenth century, were considered to be enemies and which were friends. They give hints of what may have been the earlier history, as in the case of several different Mohave accounts.

One of these locates their original homeland in the Verde Valley to the east, while another suggests that the people came from the west, from what is now California.[42]

From these accounts told by Indians in one form at one time and probably changing such that different accounts might be given at other times, we cannot construct a picture of early tribal locations, nor do we have hints of the origins of causes of intertribal conflict.

Neither can we be sure that the patterning of conflict that occurred after the early 1830s—the unvarying routes, objectives, and participating peoples in the battle expeditions—existed in anything like the same form before then. The assumption has been that the nineteenth-century shapes of warfare are the same as those recorded by visitors in the 1780s and are probably much older than that. But we have no way of being sure. We cannot even see the stages through which all those Yuman-speaking peoples may have passed on their way to becoming separately self-conscious entities known to us by such names as Halchidhoma, Quechan, and Kaveltcadom.

CHANGING MOTIVES

Warfare continued for at least three centuries and was apparently first directed at one set of objectives: conquest and seizure of territory. Such was the situation by the late eighteenth and early nineteenth centuries. After 1830, however, when a few political communities had been eliminated altogether and remnant Halchidhomas were finally ejected from their lands along the Colorado, intertribal wars assumed a new character with different objectives.

From the earliest records of Spanish visitors during the middle-sixteenth century down to the third quarter of the eighteenth century, the objectives of regional conflicts are only partially discernible. Enmities had arisen between some people on the middle Gila and others living along the Colorado, and there was also serious strife among peoples on the Lower Colorado. Beyond this the facts are obscured because various names were used by Spanish chroniclers for various peoples and locations.

The record improves toward the very end of the eighteenth century and increases in clarity to about 1830 when the present-day locations and numbers of tribes were finally established, at the time of the expulsion of

the Halchidhoma. What has been shown is that there was intensive warfare at very close quarters. The Quechans and sometimes the Mohaves,
probably with different groups siding with them from time to time,
battled other peoples to dispossess them of lands just south of the Gila-
Colorado confluence. As time went on it may be that one people, the
Alakwisa, were either driven away or annihilated, assuming these "shadow
people" ever existed. What is evident is that the Halchidhoma, who earlier
lived south of Yuma Crossing, were first driven north of the river confluence and then, during the years just before and after 1830, were driven
away in groups until all were gone from the Colorado. First, they wan-
dered for a time in what is now northwest Mexico, and then they joined
with the conglomeration of other peoples now known to us as "Maricopa,"
who had earlier established one or two villages side by side with the Pima
on the middle Gila.

The scanty acounts of conflicts among Indians of the Lower Colorado
hint strongly at the role played in them by impinging cultures, first of
Spain and subsequently of an independent Mexico. From the late eighteenth century through the 1820s, Quechans—and to some extent Cocopas
and Mohaves—were influenced by trade with northern Mexican settlements. Perhaps this small commerce across the deserts was mediated
through friendly Papagos living southeast of the Gila-Colorado junction.
Indians of the Lower Colorado were selling people into slavery and possibly trafficking in horses and mules. They certainly stole horses and mules
for their own consumption. Moreover, they learned to speak Spanish in
varying degrees of fluency even as they learned about trade goods. These
were the relationships that brought Cocopas, Quechans, and probably the
Maricopas and Mohaves to the occasional use of horses in warfare; to the
possession of a few metal knives; and perhaps to some of the later military
practices.

As noted earlier, it has been suggested that the principal reasons for
raiding by that time were to take captives to sell to Mexican markets and
to acquire horses.[43]

Gila-Colorado warfare entered an entirely different phase after
Quechans and Mohaves had forced everyone but Cocopas off the Lower
Colorado. Earlier, such hostilities had almost certainly been aimed at
seizing and holding lands. Those tribesmen who had engaged in the
struggle over land remained conscious of the limits of territory they
considered to be their own by ancient right. The two contenders still living

close to each other—Quechans and Cocopas—continued an embattled relationship. These tribes remained in a state of mutual war, one characterized by intermittent battles, until the middle 1850s when pressures by United States military authorities became an important factor in ending their recurrent strife. In the fights between Quechans and Cocopas from about 1830 until about 1855, however, we doubt that anyone was thinking of seizing lands. They reciprocated with battle expeditions and raids, but there is no recorded hint of attempts to occupy the enemy's territory.

Also after 1830, Quechans and Mohaves remained hostile toward the Maricopa settlers on the middle Gila. This enmity produced intermittent war expeditions until the final encounter in 1857.

ADDITIONAL MOTIVES

Turning now to some factors that may have contributed to the continuation of battle expeditions after 1830, it is clear the expeditions themselves were neither of such scale nor duration that they were likely to result in the annihilation of an enemy people. Those involved were living too thoroughly dispersed through territories too large for any of their enemies to be able to find and kill all of them in a single attack. Moreover, attackers were never numerous enough for a war of annihilation, nor did they come prepared to remain in enemy territory long enough to win a total victory. For these reasons, we have not used the term "campaign" in discussing Gila-Colorado warfare.

The Maricopas' situation may have been a little different. There were only a few hundred of them, and they lived relatively close to one another in what travelers described as two communities but which were, possibly, clusters of some sixteen seasonally shifting settlements.[44] Even so, Maricopas are not known to have lost any battles on their own ground on the middle Gila, nor did they show any tendency to quail before the enemy, fleeing for their lives for protection among the Pimas. There is no hint they feared their annihilation could result from the loss of a major battle. They outnumbered even the very large contingent that came against them in 1857.

So also for the attackers. Until the middle of the nineteenth century their losses in battle were not so heavy that they would later have difficulty in protecting their own homelands. There was risk of death, but odds of survival were deemed greater. In this sense the battle expedition itself need not be feared by its instigators.

As for other contributing influences that may have helped occasion battle expeditions, one of the most obvious is the feeling for revenge. It is often assumed that the earlier wars, those in ancient times, were simply motivated by vengeance. Daryll Forde, as well as George Fathauer, although looking to the cultural value system for the motive for war, felt that individual raids and battle expeditions could have been caused by the urging of a person or family demanding revenge for the death of a loved one in war.[45] Here and there in the records we have seen testimony to this personal motive that could become the occasion for tribal action. We think it very likely that Quechans, Maricopas, and Mohaves sought vengeance for the loss of their kinsmen by agitating for war. The only detailed account of the genesis of a battle expedition—the one related to Edward Gifford by a Quechan (pp. 69–71) does not reveal that expedition to have been brought about by the desire for revenge. Nor do we have evidence from Yumans who were mature men before 1857 to prove that vengeance triggered battle expeditions.

It has been asserted by latter-day investigators, people other than ethnologists who conducted field work among Yumans before 1950, that battle expeditions often had as their goal some form of plunder: food, horses, or human captives to sell as slaves. It is doubtful the 1857 battle had any such ends in view, however, and we suspect those who make this assertion fail to take seriously distinctions between raiding and warfare made by the people themselves. Raids were carried out for booty or hit-and-run revenge; battles fought within the context of warfare, especially after 1830, involved booty only incidentally if at all. As already noted, before 1830, it is probable that one of the immediate motives for warfare was the taking of lands.

Of fifteen battle expeditions for which we have reasonably good account, only two resulted in victories for the attackers, and in one of these cases the victors did not attempt to enter the nearby villages of their defeated enemies even after scoring a triumph. For the other thirteen engagements the indication is that the attackers either left the scene as fugitives or that the fight took place too far from the enemy settlements for property to have been seized even in the early stages of fighting.[46]

Idealized conceptualizations aside, there is reason to believe that large-scale raids sometimes turned into ritual battles when the raiders were discovered. There is also reason to believe that booty was occasionally taken in the wake of a formal fight. Two entries on a calendar stick kept by a Salt River Reservation Pima serve as illustrations. The first recounts:

> 1833—1834. During the moon preceding the meteoric shower the Yumas, armed with clubs, bows, and arrows, attacked the Maricopa village. The Yumas surprised the Maricopas and captured their women, whom they surrounded and tried to take away with them. They were about to cross the Gila with their captives when the Pima arrived and attacked them. The women took advantage of the confusion to escape into the chaparral. The Yumas fought bravely, but they were overpowered by numbers and few escaped to tell of their defeat.[47]

One possible interpretation of this account is that the Quechans were merely raiding and were caught in the act. But the statement is too brief, and the suggestion of a large war expedition too strong, to allow us to be certain it was a mere raid for booty. It seems more likely the Quechans had intended a battle and subsequently took the opportunity to capture women, whose possession would signify victory and endow the victors with prestige.

The second entry on the calendar stick is very different. In the autumn of 1842, ". . . the Yumas again came to attack the Maricopa village, but did not attempt to surprise it. They formed in line of battle opposite the line of Maricopas. . . ."[48]

It is clear this was a ritual battle with no thought on the part of the Quechans of capturing property. The fight ended indecisively, farther from the Maricopa villages than the spot at which fighting had begun and with significant numbers of casualties on both sides.

It is not always possible to draw an accurate distinction between large-scale raids and battle expeditions other than to say that in some battles there is no sign of any attempt to take captives or other plunder. Because we can identify major hostilities that seem not to have sought economic gain, we do not subscribe to the view that the warfare these tribes conducted in later years were motivated by economic motives. The records of hostilities are insufficient, for example, to prove that warfare could bring enough captives to support either a large-scale or continuous slave trade. Hostile attacks could not replenish horse herds among people who did not yet breed horses; they could not obtain enough food for the many hundreds of people who greeted the few returning warriors.

MOTIVES FOR PEACE

We know of no Indian testimony on the subject of why the battle expeditions along the Lower Colorado and the middle Gila rivers came to an end. Neither is there any evidence that Maricopas or Quechans initiated their own peace agreement after the 1857 debacle. This is not surprising. The long series of attacks had continued for decades and toward the end had been conducted in an atmosphere of total hostility. In spite of the intensity of warfare between these two peoples, however, there were never signs of a sudden conclusion leading to the "surrender" of one of the parties.

It is possible the battles did not cease so much as recess. Other clashes, hidden from the documentary record, may have occurred after 1857. One might expect this so long as warriors remained alive who had fought in one of the encounters; so long as people still heeded the shaman in such matters; and so long as people were educated from early childhood in the traditional way, awakening to the song of an elderly person singing one more of the sacred texts of wisdom which unfolded the values of aboriginal life. The wars might have resumed had there been men among the Maricopas and Quechan who had been trained to fight one another. For the years after 1857, it is unlikely anyone in those two tribes would have thought of their mutual conflict as over and done with had it not been for outside influences.

It must have been difficult to alter the warlike relationship. We know of no trade between these two tribes nor of intermarriage at that period of their history. We suspect that for a long time no Gila River Indian dared visit the territory of the Colorado River peoples, and no Yuman came from the Colorado to the middle Gila settlements. The likelihood is that members of the Maricopa and Quechan tribes met peaceably after the battle of 1857 only when Charles D. Poston, a new Arizona Superintendent of Indian Affairs, convened a peace meeting at Fort Yuma in 1863. And at that, although leaders of the Pimas and Maricopas attended, with a leading Mohave and others who spoke for the Chemehuevis and some of the Yavapais, there is no certainty that a Quechan sat in the council.[49]

We can only guess why no battles may have been fought after 1857. Losses in war had finally mounted to a point at which the cultural and psychic gains in such an enterprise may have been overbalanced by fear of a future in which the tribe would not have had enough warriors to defend itself. Moreover, considering the nearly total annihilation in 1857 of able-bodied men among the Quechan battle contingent from Algodones, it was the restraint imposed by Pasqual on his people at Fort Yuma that may have saved enough Quechan males to assure the future of Quechans as a viable political and ethnic community.

It should also be noted that during the 1840s the Maricopas had lost several of their engagements, with casualties likely on the order of thirty, then fifty, and finally a hundred warriors. It is noteworthy that following a number of such expeditions in the late 1840s, none were launched after 1849. Years later, a Halchidhoma born in 1847 spoke of a battle that had taken place before his birth (probably in the 1830s or 1840s): "Our bravest warriors had been killed but we had some left, so the Yuma decided to come here to exterminate the whole tribe."[50]

The plight of the Quechans and Cocopas was as bad or worse. The Quechans lost men steadily through the 1840s and 1850s. On one occasion in 1851 they left 134 dead warriors at the Maricopa villages. All but one man of a large war party were killed in Cocopa country, probably in 1848. Now the 1857 battle had cost them upwards of eighty men.

The mortality among their leaders had been even more pronounced. After 1857 Pasqual, the preeminent moral leader, seems to have been the only prominent person to have survived. He had used the good offices of the United States Army to seek a final peace with the Cocopas in 1854. He had adamantly opposed the 1857 expedition. We assume—fearless old warrior that he was—that he could see disaster coming should his people continue to go to war.[51]

As for the Mohaves, at least one of their influential subchiefs had made up his mind by the middle 1850s that it was no use to fight against the whites. He also accepted the fact that the U. S. Army was opposed to Yuman intertribal warfare. The emphatic actions of this famous warrior, Yara tav, quickly began to promote "peace" and "war" factions within the Mohave tribe, and Yara tav was unable to sway the entire group toward peace. The moral leader of the Mohaves, Homose quahotah, continued to insist on belligerence and resistance in dealing with the whites. Warfare was still a deeply respected and accepted part of national life, and Mohaves remained vulnerable to appeals to go to war as evidenced by the fact that they had a contingent in the 1857 battle.[52] They also followed their traditional moral leader into rising conflict with white people, an effort which culminated in their defeat by the U. S. Army in Mohave Valley in 1859.

Soon after the event Yara tav split the tribe by taking many Mohaves to a
site far south of the valley to live apart from the traditional moral leader.
He then conducted his own campaign of making peace with Gila River
Indians and with white people.[53]

It appears that between 1857 and 1863 the division of views among
Quechans, for or against war, began to tip steadily in favor of peace.
During the same period the Pimas and Maricopas drew closer to the U. S.
Army, first as potential allies and as suppliers of wheat and other goods
and then as active allies in war against Apaches. In 1862–63, the large
California Column of troops staying over in Arizona relied upon the Pima
and Maricopa villagers for food and forage. Soldiers were often seen at
Maricopa Wells, remaining for weeks at a time to purchase supplies for
the U. S. Army.[54] In 1863 the U. S. government gave the Pimas a
hundred stand of old arms as encouragement to fight Apaches. In the
spring of 1863 Pimas were accompanying U. S. Army probing expeditions
into Apache territory.[55] We doubt the significance of these developments
was lost on such Colorado River leaders as Pasqual or Yara tav.

During those years the two leaders applied their influence where it
would count most: in tribal councils. The likelihood is strong that at the
time all decisions favoring war or peace still had to be made in a
thoroughly traditional manner, that is, by talking it out in a general
assemblage of all the mature men. Increasingly, after 1857 among the
Quechans and after 1859 among the Mohaves, the peace factions in those
tribes seem to have been able to swing councils against any warlike
enterprises.

Our assumption is that from 1863 through the 1870s the larger decisions
involving peace or war were arrived at in a different manner. The traditional making of decisions probably still involved discussion accompanied
by long orations in tribal council,[56] but we suspect that the tribal chief,
without any public show of the fact, came to exercise real executive power
in some of these tribes. His additional power, in those groups in which the
chief became that important, sprang from his close association with U. S.
Army officers, with an occasional energetic Indian agent, and with other
whites. In other words, the status position of "chief" was further enhanced through sanctions bestowed by the militarily and economically
more powerful Anglo Americans.

Thus Pasqual and Yara tav and Homose quahotah managed tribal
affairs as before, but now they acted the part as leaders of dependent

nations. They turned to the local Army commandant whenever there arose a possible threat from other Indians even as the commandant turned to them for needed military support. In this new situation that still wore the veneer of tradition, U. S. Army officers dictated new alliances and new enmities while insisting on compliance with their desires. Former friend-ships, alliances, and enmities were no longer life and death concerns. The new relationships brought new uncertainties and dangers, but sometimes in different geopolitical alignments in which the main contenders were the U. S. Army with Pima and Maricopa allies fighting against Apaches, Walapais, and some of the Yavapais. The Yumans of the Lower Colorado were effectively neutralized, and it became the U. S. Army rather than its Indian allies who decided when victory had been achieved and who dic-tated terms of peace.

The bygone shapes of the older wars lived on, but only in the memories of aging warriors and, indeed, in the minds of all their age peers. From them to their children and to their children's children, images of that warlike past have changed slowly down the years, fading with successive generations. In our own times there are those who bear in tribal memory, however imperfectly, this long span of history when Gila and Colorado river peoples fought each other, and the last great battle at Maricopa Wells in 1857.

SEVEN

The Fourth Age:
On the Origins of War

And one man in his time plays many parts,
His acts begin seven ages. At first the infant,
Mewling and puking in the nurse's arms;
Then the whining school-boy, with his satchel
And shining morning face, creeping like snail
Unwilling to school. And then the lover,
Sighing like furnace, with a woeful ballad
Made to his Mistress' eyebrow. Then a soldier,
Full of strange oaths, and bearded like the pard,
Jealous in honor, sudden and quick in quarrel,
Seeking the bubble reputation
Even in the cannon's mouth. . . .

William Shakespeare
As You Like It, Act II, Scene VII

Henry David Thoreau jotted his musings in his journal: "Where a battle has been fought, you will find nothing but the bones of men and beasts; where a battle is being fought, there are hearts beating. . . . The *past* cannot be *presented;* we cannot know what we are not. But one veil hangs over past, present, and future, and it is the province of the historian to find out, not what was, but what is. . . . We forget that [antiquity] had any other future than our present. . . . The heavens stood over the heads of our ancestors as near as to us."[1]

However fascinating the 1857 battle on the Gila may be as an exercise in historical and anthropological sleuthing, it is only when we reflect on its possible larger meanings that the exercise becomes more than parochial antiquarianism. Lessons are to be learned from knowing the particulars of the battle, of its antecedents and of the cultures of those who were involved.

We bow to Thoreau's admonition and try to fathom what *was* that we might better understand what *is*.

One of the most important questions concerning war is what are its ultimate causes, its origins? Innumerable scholars of many persuasions have grappled with this problem over the centuries. Let us look briefly at some ideas on the subject expressed by those who have preceded us.

THE ANTHROPOLOGY OF WARFARE

Keith Otterbein, reviewing what anthropologists have had to say on the subject of warfare, feuding, armed conflict, or armed combat, notes they seldom attempt to define what they are describing.[2] He quotes Bronislaw Malinowski's definition that warfare is "an armed contest between two independent political units, by means of organized military force, in the pursuit of tribal or national policy."[3] He further alludes to Margaret Mead's definition of it as "recognized conflict between two groups *as groups*, in which each group puts an army (even if the army is only fifteen pygmies) into the field to fight and kill, if possible, some of the members of the army of the other group.[4]

Nearly three decades later, Mead wrote: "Warfare exists if the conflict is organized and socially sanctioned, and the killing is not regarded as murder," explaining her criteria as "organization for the purpose of combat involving the intention to kill and the willingness to die, social sanction for this behavior, which distinguishes it from murder of members of its own group, and the agreement between the groups involved on the legitimacy of the fighting with intent to kill."[5]

R. Brian Ferguson observes: "War, by any definition, is a *social* activity, carried out by *groups* of people." And beyond that, he argues, it is "organized, purposeful group action, directed against another group that may or may not be organized for similar action, involving the actual or potential application of lethal force."[6]

Otterbein says quite simply that warfare is "armed combat between political communities."[7]

Much of the anthropological literature speaks of "primitive warfare." W. W. Newcomb, Jr., writes that primitive warfare is best understood as a type of conflict transitional between a peaceful state of affairs and "serious, deadly, competitive strife. Societies that practice primitive warfare cannot long sustain fighting men in the field, since they do not have the supplies. Nor are they typified by well-organized, strong, or centralized governmental institutions, so that raising and controlling large numbers of fighting men is difficult."[8] He goes on to assert that "true" war is associated with cultures which have reached an animal husbandry or agricultural technology. "In a very real sense 'true' warfare may be viewed as one of the more important social consequences of the agricultural revolution."[9]

Ferguson notes the "chaotic state of the field" of anthropological research concerning war. "If anthropologists studying war," he writes, "could agree that certain statements of causal priorities and interactions of factors were valid cross-culturally, this consensus would provide an invaluable frame of reference for studying the particular case of modern war. Unfortunately, any such consensus remains a long way off." [10]

Robert Netting would probably agree: "The factual study of primitive warfare has never had a fighting chance in anthropology."[11] He observes that field workers only rarely have had the opportunity to bestride the field of battle while hostilities were still in progress and that investigators have had a serious bias in favor of more constructive and happy aspects of social life. With so few data, students of the subject have struggled and have lost the battle against their own unstudied assumptions. They have failed to arrive at realistic hypotheses. Investigators' "explanations have often foundered on the old dichotomy of economic versus psychological causes . . . or latent as opposed to manifest functions" of warfare. [12]

Netting advises a search for the relationships between "ecologic and material variables" within any cultural system, focusing on the variables involved in people's behavior in conflict. He then advises us that whatever we assume or believe we see as students of the culture of someone else, we must somehow integrate our assumptions and observations with what the people themselves have to say about it. "The connection between what measurably *is* and what it *means* to people is the heart of the anthropological enterprise."[13]

Netting's assessment of the case corresponds all too closely with what anyone is likely to find who examines the subject of warfare and the hypotheses its study has occasioned. Anthropologists, ethnohistorians, historians—all of us are floundering as badly as he suggests.

Our goal is to arrive at a high level of confidence in useful generalizations such as the one so assiduously sought for so long by investigators like Andrew Vayda and Marvin Harris,[14] to name but two. They have insisted that discovery of such generalizations is an urgent matter. We are as eager as they to arrive at hypotheses to bring enlightenment concerning the causes of war. The battle on the Gila has been our springboard. And whenever we have heard tribesmen speaking, however filtered through translation, we have made sure to listen, to give these voices the authority they may deserve. We have tried to see the past as it was, including the perspectives of Indians insofar as we are able to infer them.

What follows is our analysis of why the Gila and Colorado Yumans made war upon each other for so long and so seriously. We try to recognize the hypotheses of others whenever these seem to illuminate our somewhat fragmentary record.

RAIDING VS. WARFARE

Attacks by members of individual Yuman "political communities," to borrow Otterbein's term, against other peoples took two forms. One can be designated as "raiding" and the other as "warfare." We have already discussed these concepts in great detail on pp. 35–39, as they apply to the tribes under consideration.

Such concepts conform generally with what has been seen among many peoples at other times and in other parts of the world. Raids were not ordinarily intended to gain territory or to increase a tribe's political importance in its region.[15] Raids became military engagements only should raiders be discovered and pursued by their victims.

To point up the deeper difference between warfare and raiding, the latter was an enterprise of no particular complexity, calling neither upon all the people nor requiring any special ceremonies or elaborate religio-cultural preparations. War, on the other hand, engaged to some extent the feelings of all the people, and it brought into play at least some, if not all, of the figures who personified political and religious leadership. The enterprise of war was preceded, accompanied, and concluded by religious observances without which the very continuance of the warriors' lives would have been in peril. All of this preparation for an enterprise as serious as warfare is what Anthony Wallace has discussed in a preliminary way as "mobilization," the taking on of psychological attitudes and feel-ings as these become necessary in the particular culture.[16]

The discussion which follows is concerned primarily with warfare and only incidentally with raiding.

THEORIES OF THE CAUSES OF WARFARE

If seen as a facet of culture, the general character of Gila-Colorado war-fare reflects many of the same patterns and outlines as have been found in many other histories of non-literate peoples. The data tend to support the ideas of W. W. Newcomb, Jr., for example, who feels that "whether or not a culture is warlike, and the way in which it conducts warfare, are . . . dependent to a large extent upon the technological development of the culture." Moreover, the role and shape of warfare in any society "are determined by the nature of other aspects of that culture and the condi-tions of its relationships with other cultures."[17]

He eschews explanations for warfare based on the notion that people are "genetically predisposed to be pugnacious and warlike" or on the idea "that wars are caused by war-making forces." He also does not believe "that psychological conditions of individual men cause wars."[18]

Newcomb's "culturological view" of warfare, positing as it does a direct relationship between the ability to be warlike and the stage of technological development, is also an evolutionary view. In this, he sides with Quincy Wright, whose elaborate study places primitive war as the earliest and least complex among three stages of the history of war among human societies. In Wright's analysis, it is this kind of warfare which precedes the develop-ment of urban life. It exists only before the coming of strong, obligatory central government with its administration, judicial institutions, and ac-companying hierarchy of social classes. Even at that early stage there was always a "law of war . . . group customs or behavior patterns . . . acquired through education and discipline to which each generation is subjected. . . ."[19]

Primitive warfare, to Wright's way of thinking, showed slow develop-ment, paralleling gradual changes in other aspects of the cultures of which it was a part. Going through this long first stage of alterations, he notes that the size of fighting groups tended to increase; warrior classes tended to become specialized; and missile weapons "tended to be superseded by piercing and striking weapons." Discipline and morale tended to increase, "and the battle of pounce and retreat tends to give way to the battle of mass attack and maneuver." As such changes occurred, "casualties and destructiveness of war tended to become greater."[20]

Many of these statements apply to the role and scope of warfare among the Gila and Colorado River peoples. The known history of their hostilities up to the final battle in 1857 makes it appear likely that warfare retained its traditional role in the several native cultures as a phase of their activities that recurred only at irregular intervals, but "in well-recognized circumstances and with well-established rules and techniques. . . . War was," as Wright believed it to have been for all primitive people, "definitely within the mores."[21]

Concerning both immediate and ultimate causes of Yuman warfare, our first consideration is for the complexity of their armed conflict. It doubtless became elaborated through time and was influenced by considerable changes in other aspects of their cultures. In viewing the functions of war as being complex, we are in general accord with those who have assumed them to represent an aggregation of customs and beliefs: "Every war is fought for more than one motive, spurious or real, appreciated or unrealized. Every individual warrior joins . . . for more than one reason. It is characteristic of successful social institutions to have a bundle of functions, as every human activity has a bundle of utilities. . . . The basic function of every institution is the maintenance of the psycho-physical equilibrium of its clientele considered as individual persons. . . ."[22] And just as we may expect to find several probable causes for any particular war, so also the personal reactions of individuals swept into the "state of war" may be expected to differ.[23]

Among the Yumans and Pimas there was almost certainly a great individual difference in reactions to plans for offensive warfare and the sudden reality of attack upon one's own ranchería. We suspect that anyone physically able to do so rallied to mutual defense, and it is known that large numbers of women, even children, fought against attackers.

As for offensive warfare, it seems likely that individual subjective motivations were so varied when a battle expedition was being planned among the Maricopas, Quechans, Mohaves, or Cocopas that it is impossible to account precisely for the creation of such expeditions. As far as we know, individuals of these four groups were brought into the expedition because of their identity as members of a given clan, just as was the case with the Western Apache. Unlike the case of the Western Apache, however, participation was more voluntary than otherwise.

That the objectives and character of regional warfare changed about 1830 offers support for some of the more recent theories concerning warfare generally. The data indicate, for example, that a serious war of Quechans against Maricopas may have been rekindled in 1832 by a massacre of Quechans who were on a raiding party, followed the next year by a major retaliatory expedition of Quechans against the Maricopas. And so on until 1857.

These events fit neatly a theoretical framework proposed by Andrew Vayda. He has pointed to the usefulness of identifying stages of wars carried on among primitive peoples. He suggests finding changes in basic problems that confronted peoples from time to time—which problems in turn might indicate shifts in the nature of wars. In other words, warfare might continue in more or less the same tempo, but no longer with all the same needs, problems, and objectives. Where war was persistent and directed at territorial conquest, "such persistence need not end because of long periods without territorial conquests or because of periods during which hostilities are undertaken . . . against groups living too far away for territorial conquests for them to be feasible as the result of an escalating process."[24]

Here Vayda is discussing the benefits of considering war as a process with "recurrent, distinguishable phases." One may be able to identify conditions conducive to escalation from "one phase to another." Vayda feels it is important to be conscious of the "duration and frequency not simply of warfare but of particular phases of war processes."[25]

What we can see in the war processes as carried on by the Gila and Colorado peoples after 1830 is that some of the people—the Cocopa and the Maricopa—faced very much the same problems as before, while as time went on another tribe, the Quechan, found itself in a progressively more difficult situation. The Mohaves, in the meantime, had no further concerns of the kinds that had engaged them before 1830. They were now fortunately situated, with no enemies close at hand, no danger of invasion of their home territory, and with lands so ample that they presumably had more than they needed for use and occupancy.

Quechan difficulties stemmed from hostilities with Cocopas which became very expensive in life and goods. Neither people, however, chose to respond to the constant danger of attack by altering its ranchería style of open and widely dispersed small settlements of a few families each. The war here had entered a new phase at least to the extent that permanent invasion was no longer an objective. The two groups battered away at each other in occasional large expeditionary attacks, and they brought to bear those other means, stratagems of treachery and ambush, that can be practiced by peoples living near each other and who are acquainted and even slightly intermarried across the warring line.

As for the Quechan Maricopa rivalry, the Maricopas did not choose, if they had a choice, to remove their villages from the exposed western position they then held. Theirs was the closest of the middle Gila villages to potential attackers from the Lower Colorado. They continued to live in a state of apprehension, their settlements open to murderous attack without warning.

The Mohave took part in support of Quechan expeditions against Cocopas and Maricopas whenever they were invited and whenever they chose to go along. As for the Pimas, they were engaged more and more against their enemies to the north, the Apaches, with whom they continued to exchange serious and destructive raids and expeditions of war. The Pimas never sent detachments against the Quechans, but if time permitted them to bring their warriors to the field, they came to the defense of their Maricopa neighbors when the Quechan arrived to try to overrun them.

We concur with Vayda[26] that it is futile to attempt to discern a "specifiable, discrete cause or set of causes" for any given war. There is, however, however, a possibility of finding some causes and some objectives, the more likely "probable causes" for continuation of the long, drawn out, and damaging warfare in the Gila-Colorado country after 1830. These hostilities had continued beyond the time when the stakes were lands along the Lower Colorado. Many causes have been suggested for the phase of war characterized by destructive attacks between about 1830 and 1857. We will review the possibilities briefly and will point to some factors we believe may account for continuing hostilities during the period.

First of all, the evidence indicates that war remained prominent in the value systems of these Yuman groups through many succeeding generations. The myths and historical narratives constituting the peoples' religious literature continued to speak of militant activity on the part of the progenitors—those superhuman, human, and animal personages involved directly or indirectly in the creation of the people.

More than this, by the time the historical record can be regarded with some confidence, offensive warfare was clearly prestigious. It offered one of the very few arenas in which a male could establish respect among his own people. Taking the case of the Mohave as an example, the only other callings through which men might accumulate prestige were those of shaman *(kwathidhe)*; religious leader and festival chief *(kohota)*; and "head chief" *(yaltanack* or *huhach)*. A head chief was "one who was concerned about the welfare of all the people; who was wise and understanding; who possessed knowledge of tribal culture, tribal history, and tribal needs; who protected tribal lands against enemies and land-grabbers; who set a worthy example for his people; who was faithful to his trust and was honorable in his dealings; who always kept his word; who gave his time and means in working for the good of the tribe, and who could not be tempted or swerved by personal ambitions."[27] Moreover, among the Mohave many of "the bravest fighters [*kwanami*] became chiefs."[28]

Anthropologist C. Daryll Forde, who gathered information from Quechans in 1928 and 1929, was, as we have noted earlier, led to observe, "War expeditions are the one feature of their practical life which are considered worthy of remembrance and attention."[29] However, five of his seven informants were men, and it is likely the worthiness of remembrance of war expeditions reflects this bias.

As with Mohaves, the war leader or *kwanami*, "brave man" was an important and prestigious individual among Quechans. The religious leader and "head chief" of the Mohaves may have been combined in one status among Quechans, the *kwoxot*, "a tribal leader, an authority to whom appeal might be made on any matter of dispute, but more significant as an embodiment of spiritual power than as a lawgiver or executive."[30] Quechans also had shamans, called "doctors" by Forde, who could simultaneously be singers, funeral orators, or chiefs.[31]

One modern investigator notes that "Spanish and Anglo sources consistently reported the existence of two tribal leadership statuses [among the Quechan], one [*kwoxot*] for civil affairs, the other [*kwanami*] for war. Forde's account accepts this dichotomy, but how accurately it reflects the traditional Quechan situation—as distinct from one imposed by foreigners accustomed to executive hierarchies—is not clear."[32]

There is no question that the status of career warrior was a prestigious one among Yumans of the Lower Colorado, especially in the early and middle nineteenth century. This seems confirmed by historical and ethnographic data as well as by the fact that the warrior mystique among the Mohaves long outlasted the end of hostilities and was still present in the early decades of the twentieth century.[33]

That warfare was a pervasive theme in the lives of Lower Colorado

Yumans can be seen in scalp dances and pre-expeditionary ceremonies; in postwar victory celebrations and purification rites (described on pp. 90–92, 100); and in the commemorative Mourning Ceremony and all its stately grandeur. These were among the very few activities bringing together all the people of a tribe, and with those ceremonies came the public exercise of ritual by a tribe's most prestigious figures. The Mourning Ceremony was held in honor of any outstanding warrior. Other such ritual occasions of general importance were apparently nonexistent among Mohaves, although both Quechans and Cocopas celebrated harvest ceremonies and Quechans had a special celebration at the time of the mesquite harvest.[34]

The only organized training for boys and young men was that which introduced them and hardened them to usages of war. This simultaneously underlined the importance of the mature, skillful, and brave men who served as teachers. There was also a purely practical reason for continuing the program of training boys to fight and of selecting from among them those who promised to become career warriors. Every small settlement of people in Quechan and Cocopa lands, the disconnected southern Mohave settlements, and the Maricopa villages lay open to surprise attack. Any person and any piece of property could fall prey to raiders, and there had to be warriors in each locality who could take up arms. The same was true for Pimas.

These activities are but the visible evidence of a phenomenon which probably possessed deeper meaning. Offensive warfare and brave resistance in defense of one's people must have been upheld by a deep belief in the significance of these acts of affirmation, these ultimate acts of patriotic identity. Ethnologists became aware of such sentiments when talking both with older men who had survived the tribal wars as well as with somewhat younger men, and even women, who had never seen the battles and who had never suffered a surprise attack. William Kelly encountered this emotion when talking with the Cocopa; Leslie Spier, among the Halchidhoma, Mohave, and Maricopa; A. L. Kroeber, among the Mohave; Edward Gifford when talking with a number of these peoples; and C. Daryll Forde when studying the culture of the Quechans.

It was Forde, writing about the Quechans, who perhaps best described what might be called this sense of patriotism:

Tribal pride played a great part in the continuance of hostilities: every attack had to be repaid by a counterattack. This code was externalized and strengthened by the custom of scalping. . . . Every scalp lost had to be avenged. There is now perhaps no means of knowing how deep-seated was the scalping ritual among the Yuma but the acquisition of scalps is almost invariably adduced by the teller of war stories as one of the primary objectives of war parties and the procedure is still well known among the older men.[35]

Success in the numerous small skirmishes that constituted warfare in this region was indispensable to welfare. It was the concrete expression of spiritual strength. To be severely beaten by an enemy or to draw back sluggishly and avoid attackers would bring down scorn and shame, for Yuma mysticism was essentially directed at the acquisition and manifestation of great "power," power which should make them invincible before their enemies. . . .

The explanation of this continual fighting is to be sought in the deeply rooted tradition of warfare as a means of obtaining and demonstrating tribal strength. This tradition is associated with a definite technique of fighting, with particular criteria of bravery, and the use of feathered standards, symbols of bravery and invincibility analogous to those of the Plains [tribes]. Above all, warfare enters intimately into the creation myth and its reenactment in ritual. While it would be impossible to prove that the mythological and ritual correlates are earlier than the practice of habitual fighting among these people, the two would appear to be associated in origin. . . .

The condition of the Lower Colorado, then, would appear to conform to the postulates of Perry that primitive warfare, in the sense of organized violent behavior, is an institution, not an innate tendency, a product of human culture depending everywhere for its existence and perpetuation on a definite code of belief and practice more stable and significant than any one of the series of military activities in which it is manifested; in other words, that a warlike society must of necessity maintain a permanent tradition and apparatus without which its practices will fall into decay.[36]

Such an understanding of the basis for continuing war by the Quechans is close to George Fathauer's conclusions from long experience with the Mohaves. In the course of mentioning many causes he felt were in various ways related to tribal warfare, he also discussed what he took to be the central relationship:

The typical response of Mohave informants attempting to convey an understanding of almost any aspect of their culture was to narrate the parts of the origin myth pertaining to the subject of inquiry, and war was no exception. Warfare was instituted by *Mastaxmo*, who decreed that certain people in each generation would experience power-dreams connected with it. For the Mohave, then, warfare was a constant, inevitable part of their total way of life. . . .

The origin myth was an expression of the basic philosophical premises of Mohave culture. It embodied the fatalistic belief that all behavior was determined by the patterns established by the creators. All power was received by dreaming, and it was the identical power which had been given by *Mastaxmo* in the beginning. This resulted in a static conception of the universe. In each generation certain individuals automatically occupied the statuses which made up the social system, but the system itself remained unchanged. All of the important tribal officials were sacred specialists in the sense that they derived their power directly from the creators by means of unsought dream experiences. . . . The reason for the obsessive desire for war on the part of the braves was religion, embodied in myth and per-petuated by unsought power-dreams. They had dreamed war power, and therefore it was their nature to want war. It also explains why they constantly were able to keep the tribe embroiled in war although some of the people may have been peacefully inclined. According to Mohave philosophy the specialists who dreamed power were tribal representatives of *Mastaxmo* in their generation. The people were dependent upon them to play the roles decreed by the creator. . . .[37]

We stress Forde's and Fathauer's opinions because it seems to us that the conscious or nearly conscious motivations for Yuman battle expeditions must have been grounded in certain aspects of the value system of each culture. By "value system" we refer to the series of assumptions these people learned in childhood concerning what the world is, what it should be, and how one's life and one's existence with others is supposed to unfold. This is also to assume that personalities in those Indian societies were shaped according to the outlines and directions given in the tribal value system. How the various individuals in any one of those societies would put into his own words the importance of offensive warfare is something we cannot now recover. Nor can we see the full range of individual decisions that could be made within bounds set by values that bore on all individuals.

Basic assumptions about life and proper conduct must have been virtually unchallengeable in the conservative and repetitive round of life of
those tribal societies. Rather than questioning the values themselves, people followed their personal decisions whether to act or not to act within the
limits allowed. We wish we knew more concerning allowable personal
alternatives and more of the cultural contexts in which people were given
opportunities to decide their own courses of action. By the time ethnologists visited these people after the turn of the twentieth century, they found
few enough surviving warriors from whom they might have learned about
the realm of personal choice open to men and women even under stress of
the "state of war." What made up a warrior's mind to volunteer for battle
or not to take part? What did the women think of warfare, and what range
of opinions were to be seen in their decisions to urge their husbands to go
to battle or to avoid it? How would a wife or daughter remember the
anxious days of waiting for the warrior's return? Would she be eager to see
him go yet another time?

In our records there are only a few specific examples of widely variant
choices being made by religious and moral leaders, by warriors, and by
others. One chooses to leave the battleground; others argue bitterly as to
whether an expedition is indicated, or is prohibited, by omens and
prospects of other kinds. There is enough evidence to suggest that the
enterprise of war as such was unchallengeable by any of the people, at least
as late as the mid-nineteenth century, but that societal sanction of war
obligated no specific person to take part.

Yuman history indicates that expeditions were infrequent; they occurred
with no perceivable regularity; and no one was ever forced—beyond infor-
mal pressure exerted by peers—to accompany any expedition. Perhaps the
voluntarist nature of offensive warfare helps explain its long endurance as
an important part of the culture of each of these peoples. Their political
organization had not shifted to the point at which orders were given and
obeyed in matters of life and death.

To return to the assumption that war remained central to these cultures,
we are impressed by that view and therefore are inclined to accept the deep
conviction to be seen in Daryll Forde's statements and in those of George
Fathauer, even though these are based on suggestive information rather
than on clear proof. The fact is that the battle expeditions were from
beginning to end surrounded and penetrated by the most elaborate ritual

in the hands of the tribes' most prestigious figures. Moreover, the enterprises were carried through time after time despite the strong likelihood of defeat and of tragic loss of men. The battle expedition was an austere undertaking, and to all appearances it had a quality that reenforced values embedded in the culture.[38]

After years of study of the ethnology and known history of some of these aboriginal peoples, A. L. Kroeber offered an integrated answer to the problem of warfare, one which he found in tribal size, agriculture, and the sense of identity of the warriors:

> These peoples had a sense of set-offness. The Mohaves felt themselves to be different.
> The Yuma in the same way felt themselves to be distinctive. Other tribes were hostile to both of these but their attitude remained essentially the same. Such attitudes led to political and military lineups that ended in an indulgence of warfare which finally squeezed all but the Yumas and Mohaves off the Colorado River. They fought not for redress or maintenance of their independence but because the ambitious and brave among them looked upon war as the road to honor and prestige. This is atypical for California as a whole where the overwhelming majority of Indians looked upon warfare as a trouble, and something to be avoided if possible. There seems little doubt that the much larger size of tribes in the lower Colorado area, their subsistence by farming and the military attitude, are all connected.[39]

THE DRIVES TOWARD WAR

We move for a moment beyond the example of Yumans and Pimans to more abstract considerations. Keith Otterbein and R. Brian Ferguson have possibly done the best jobs to date in summarizing theoretical approaches of anthropologists, as well as of others, toward causes of war. Otterbein groups these causes under eight broad categories:[40]

1. *Innate aggression.* Some investigators point to an instinct of pugnacity and aggression as an explanation for fighting between groups of men. Among the more noteworthy of such proponents have been Konrad Lorenz[41] and Robert Ardrey.[42] The most outspoken critic of their views has been Ashley Montagu, whose volume on *The Nature of Human Aggression*

was written primarily to "examine in detail the facts and arguments, and in the end to refute the conclusions, presented to an enormous public in recent years by a group of popular writers who state that human beings are inescapably killers—that because of their animal heritage, they are genetically and instinctively aggressive, and cannot be otherwise." Montagu argues that "our true inheritance lies in our ability to make and shape ourselves, not the creatures but the creators of our destiny."[43] Montagu and other critics of the innate aggression idea say the idea is both a simplistic and tautological one; that fighting between two men is not warfare; and that there is no physiological evidence that man has an aggressive instinct.

2. *Frustration-aggression.* Proponents of this view assert that frustrations of everyday life create an aggressiveness that is often expressed ultimately in warfare. This is not to say that frustration causes war; it is merely to assert that the more frustrated a people become the more likely they are to go to war. As Otterbein points out, at least three anthropologists and one psychologist have advanced this notion.[44]

3. *Diffusion.* A few anthropologists regard warfare as an invention of *Homo sapiens*, and see it as being peculiar to that animal. If war is regarded as an invention, it becomes an idea capable of being diffused from group to group just as one might, for example, learn the art of agriculture from a neighboring tribe.

4. *Physical environment.* As Otterbein notes, "Few anthropologists argue that the physical environment or a culture's mode of adaptation to its environment is responsible for warfare,[45] although Geoffrey Gorer saw a correlation between war and subsistence technology.[46]

Related to this notion, however, is the concern with the ecological approach. "In the broad sense, ecology deals with the relationship of men and other animals to each other and to the physical environment. For those anthropologists who subscribe to this approach, an equitable distribution of resources is viewed as ecologically desirable. . . ."[47]

5. *Goals of War.* Many theorists believe men engage in warfare to achieve goals, many of these growing out of the culture itself. In our case, for example, Fathauer[48] argues that Mohaves were inspired to go to war to satisfy magico-religious beliefs. And Otterbein[49] lists as common goals subjugation and tribute, land, plunder, trophies and honors, defense, and revenge.

6. *Social structure.* Social structure factors involved in causes of war have been encompassed within fraternal interest group theory. Some analysts point to localized aggregates of related males who can resort to aggressive measures when the interests of their members are threatened. Margaret Mead[50] has even argued that "war can be abated if nations can develop social structures in which units resembling fraternal interest groups are absent."[51]

7. *Military preparedness.* "Military readiness can itself be considered a cause of war. That is to say, if a culture is well prepared militarily, it is more likely to become involved in wars than if it were not so well prepared."[52] Before he made this observation, Otterbein carried out a cross-cultural study for which he devised a scale of military sophistication comprised of eleven efficient military practices. His survey led him to the conclusion "that political communities with efficient military organizations are likely to engage in frequent warfare with culturally different political communities."[53]

8. *Cultural evolution.* Many students of warfare have called to our attention that the type of war fought by a people relates to the evolutionary stage in their development as a culture. Elman Service, for example, sees warfare waged in different ways and for different reasons among bands, tribes, chiefdoms, states, and empires.[54]

One of Service's statements, that hunter-gatherers are relatively peaceful, has been challenged in print by Carol Ember whose comparative survey of fifty such societies has led Ember to assert that some sixty-four percent of them engaged in warfare at least once every two years, twenty-six percent had warfare somewhat less often, and a mere ten percent could be characterized as truly "peaceful." Even eliminating from the sample hunter-gatherers who were horseback hunters and those who depended on fishing for more than half their subsistence, Ember still found that warfare was rare among only twelve percent of the remaining groups.[55]

One of the problems with this criticism is that Ember does not make a distinction, as indeed the data base on which the survey rests does not always clearly distinguish, between formal warfare and raiding or raids that become elevated into major skirmishes. Many ethnographic monographs fail to make such a differentiation, and yet such a differentiation is possibly crucial to our knowledge of war's origins. There are important qualitative, as well as quantitative, differences.

R. Brian Ferguson has more recently provided us with an excellent survey of anthropological perspectives concerning war.[56] He arranges the studies into five principal categories, those involving (1) human aggressiveness and war; (2) psychological approaches to war; (3) social structure and war; (4) political organization and war; and (5) military organization and war. He then constructs what he sees as an over-arching or integrative category, "a materialist view [that] is not necessarily opposed to other approaches to war."[57] This "materialist approach to war focuses on war's relation to the practical problems of maintaining life and living standards. Since about 1960, this usually has meant studying war in relation to local ecology. But ecology is not everything. . ."[58] He argues that both the natural environment and internal sociocultural arrangements need be taken into account, that changes in either or both can produce stress among individuals which they might attempt to alleviate through force.

Ferguson also has a discussion of "motivations" for war,[59] an aspect of the phenomenon which we regard as immediate causes or rationalizations rather than ultimate origins of war.

The classification schemes of Otterbein and Ferguson, presented here in an extremely cursory manner, are assuredly not the only ones concerned with theories of war causation. Bernice Carroll and Clifton Fink have devised what they call a "two-dimensional matrix for analyzing theories of war causation," in which one axis concerns itself with whether the analysis is at the level of the international, supra-national, or nation-state system; at that of the coalition, nation-state, or group subsystem; or at that of the individual actor. The second axis outlines theories of strict determinism; limited causality; gross predictability; indeterminacy; limited free will; and the absurd universe. In their scheme, for example, analysis occurring at the level of the subsystem has produced notions of limited causality labeled "factor theories," such as biological, environmental, psychological, sexual, structural, social-psychological, and economic factors.[60]

Simon Ottenberg, much more simply, classifies anthropological studies of war into three groups: social, cross-cultural, and intracultural.[61]

Anyone working through the plethora of published materials concerning warfare and its causes is a candidate for despair. The proposals, and even attempts to classify proposals, have been so numerous and so disparate as to make one feel the subject lies beyond human comprehension.

Our contention is that there exists a single factor common to all warfare which in some way may help explain its existence in human affairs.

TO BE MALE AND TO BE HUMAN

We are concerned here with the origins of war, that is, of what Otterbein
called "armed combat between political communities," rather than with
intragroup or interpersonal conflict or aggression. And by "origins," as
stated in Chapter 6, we mean ultimate, primary sources or causes rather
than immediate causes. Too, we stand with those who view warfare as a
cultural institution and we choose to seek its sources within the confines of
traditional, learned behavior.

Having said this, we pose the question: what is the common denomina-
tor in warfare? One answer: the conduct of war is quintessentially a male
occupation.

It can be argued that females are also warriors, as witness the roles of
women in warfare in the twentieth century, including women in combat
roles. There is no question, however, that the role of warrior is universally
one primarily linked to men and that women as actual fighters are very
much the exception—however much this may presently be changing. Even
the Amazons were not "women." Third century B.C. Athenians bestowed
on Amazons the "male prerogatives of ruling lands, enslaving neighbors,
and pursuing a reputation," thus giving Amazons male attributes even as
they retain their female bodies. "The result," says classics scholar William
Tyrrell, "is a sexual hybrid. Amazons are not women in male armor but
are androgynes—apparitions composed of male and female elements
which confuse the distinctions between the sexes and the values and categories of thought assigned to each."[62] In other words, there was no question
in Greek minds about the masculine role in pursuits of war.

Once having gotten beyond the definition of war itself, there is probably
no other fact concerning it that is so apparent. It is so obvious, indeed, that
it has been all but overlooked in the literature. We simply take for granted
that males are the principal planners and executors of war. Rarely have we
asked why.

The answers may be many. We do not believe, however, it is because of
the physical superiority of males over females. Brute strength may have
advantages in some kinds and in some stages of warfare, but in areas of
physical endurance, potential skills in handling weapons, and in mental
quickness and alertness, the curves of frequency occurrence for males and
females probably overlap near their apexes. Neither do we believe the
warrior role is a result of some instinctual perverseness in the character of

males which inclines them to acts of violence, although we are aware that males—even as children—are more aggressive in all societies in which the phenomenon has been studied and that individual aggressive tendencies are related to levels of sex hormones.[63] But it is a large step from what may be biologically innate leanings toward individual aggression to ritualized, socially sanctioned, institutionalized group warfare.

We are instead persuaded by the evidence that the reason men are the chief proponents of warfare as well as the warriors is to be discovered in the nature and evolution of culture.

A few theorists have walked to the very threshold of this simple, yet powerful, idea, but have failed to take the next step. Lynne Iglitzin, for example, has noted that "it has been *men* who have fought in wars, *men* who have committed the great majority of violent crimes, and *men* who have made up the political elite whose decisions involved the use of violent force in domestic and foreign confrontations."[64] She also observes the equating of militarism and violence with manliness, but she neglects to speculate on how or why such a link has come to pass in the unfolding of human history. So does she fail to emphasize the fact that the majority of "masculine traits" and "feminine traits" are cultural constructs rather than biological givens. But she concludes with the hope, one which we share, that "someday men and women will assert not their respective masculinity and femininity but their common humanity."[65]

In 1971, Bernard Fontana taught a course in historical archaeology at the University of Arizona. On the first day of class, eleven numbered artifacts, whole or fragmentary pieces of ordinary objects collected from the surface of an abandoned late nineteenth-century southern Arizona mining camp, were circulated to all sixty-six students. Each object was numbered and students were instructed to describe the objects in no more than one or two sentences.

Among the artifacts was a .22 caliber metallic cartridge case. The base was stamped with the letter "U," indicating it had been manufactured by the Union Metallic Cartridge Company of Bridgeport, Connecticut. A small rectangular indentation at one edge of its base indicated it was a rim-fire cartridge and that it had been fired; the casing was bent where someone or something had stepped or fallen on it after it had been ejected from the weapon in which it had been fired.

Of the sixty-six students, twenty-two were female and forty-four were male. Their descriptions of this artifact were highly revealing. Males in the class were inclined to write in detail: "cartridge case, rimfire, about .32 caliber, brass, with U. S. stamped on;" "an old bullet casing of a rim-fired bullet, apparently made for or used by the U. S. Govt. Size between .22 and .30-.30;" or ".32 cal. rim-fired cartridge casing marked U. S.; copper or brass (from pistol)." The women's accounts, in contrast, tended to be brief: "bullet shell;" "empty shell cartridge (gun);" "metal shell to a gun (small);" or "an old bent cartridge."

A careful tally indicated that half the males as opposed to thirty-five percent of the females noted "rimfire;" some forty-eight percent of the males as contrasted to twenty-seven percent of the females guessed at the caliber; seven males and one female guessed whether the weapon firing the cartridge had been a rifle or handgun; and sixty-one percent of males and only thirty-six percent of the females paid some written attention to the "U" stamped on the base.

Without belaboring the point, it is obvious, and not at all surprising, that this artifact was of far more interest to males than to females in the class. Males focused on more attributes to include in their descriptions; they were more knowledgeable about the object.

Metallic cartridges, as representatives of the entire realm of firearms and, by extension, of weapons, are clearly within the cultural domain of hunting and fighting. And hunting and fighting are clearly within the traditional realm of male activities. It is a cultural legacy that is untold thousands of years old. Students writing about the cartridge were the unconscious bearers of that tradition.

In 1932, Father Berard Haile, a Franciscan priest on the Navajo Reservation, wrote down a text dictated by Curly To Aheedliinii of Chinle, Arizona. It was a small part of the Emergence story of the Navajos, and Father Berard labelled its topics "Where People Moved Opposite" and "Where People Moved Opposite Each Other."[66] Subsequently, in 1981, Karl Luckert, a student of comparative religions, published the edited and annotated text collected by Father Berard as *Women Versus Men: A Conflict of Navajo Emergence.*[67]

This story tells of a time in the Navajos' mythic past when the sexes became separated. This occurred when they were still in the underworld before emerging to the surface of the earth in their present form. A conflict had caused all the men to go on one side of a stream, leaving all the women on the opposite bank. Eventually, the difficulties were re-solved and the women went across the stream to rejoin the men. Luckert's interpretation of these events is that they are really speaking of the time Navajos shifted from a hunting-gathering economy to one supplemented, if not supplanted, by agriculture. He writes:

> . . .The men's role and importance in the human economy has been called into question [in this myth]. Although the problem of having to adapt to a settled planter's lifestyle has caught up with some Navajo men only in relatively recent times—and with their primary adaptation to herding they never needed to face up to this problem in its full extent—a brief glance at the early dynamics of plant domestication might nevertheless be helpful. . . . The earliest planting procedures were naturally in the hands of women. Originally, perhaps, the women's success with their campsite gardens resulted in a gradual increase of the human population. In turn, this increase put pressure on the supply of food animals. An increase in the number of hungry people, and a relative decrease of available game animals, together threatened the status of men. Worldwide, this threat has produced secret men's associations which artificially tried to maintain the old glory and comradeship which formerly existed during hunting expeditions. . . .[68]
>
> . . . The division of the life processes into hunting (i.e., the wielding of death power) and nurture (i.e., the wielding of life power) was a natural one. . . . Perhaps very early already, in prehistory, the men had to keep their death power away from the camp of the family. That is, they had to keep it out there on the range and in the same context of the wider cosmos, by ceremonial methods. Feminine life power, on the other hand, has nurtured the family along at the home camp. This basic separation of death and life functions probably is what has evolved into the distinct roles of men and women today. It took at least three million years to get us to the level of problems at which we now are.[69]
>
> . . . [The fall of First Man in this Navajo myth] means the end of masculine identity. Very probably, it was the decline of their hunter economy which drove the men into forming unions and secret societies. With home life and planting in the hands of the women, what else was there for them to do? After over a million years of dignity through hunting, of having been providers as hunters, now suddenly depending on the women's economy, masculine dignity could only be salvaged by developing more inclusive ceremonialism in a cosmos-wide dimension. . . . This editor [confesses] that in his household, too, a woman rules over the necessities of daily living,

whereas he, reading the evening newspaper, judges matters of world-wide and cosmic dimensions. What will a disinherited hunter do if his woman was to claim equality also in this holdout of face-saving pretense? Mothers give birth and raise children into adults. Apart from fleeting moments of passionate surrender in procreation, what is there left for men to do which women could not do as well? What is there, in line of fully understood and controlled creativity, by which a man can establish his exclusive male identity? . . . The after-effects of having had to quit a very ancient way of life are still upon us. [70]

It appears to us that Luckert has seized on an important idea. But we would suggest that rather than emphasizing the resultant formation of male unions and secret men's societies, one might point to the domestication of plants and animals—the Neolithic Revolution—as a principal generator of warfare as a cultural institution. Before that time, males, as hunters and as gatherers who worked the distant perimeters of their group's territory, were essential partners in the maintenance of family and community life. Everyone needed the food men provided in order to survive. Indeed, in a comparative survey of 161 hunter-gatherer societies carried out by Carol Ember, in eighty-three percent (134 cases) of such societies men contributed more than the women to primary subsistence; in nine per cent (14 cases) the contribution was about equal between men and women; and in only the remaining eight per cent (13 cases) did the women contribute more than the men. By omitting the 30 equestrian societies from the sample, the percentages remained basically the same. And further reducing the sample to 77 societies by eliminating those highly dependent on fishing, Ember found that men continued to be the major contributors to subsistence in seventy percent (54) of the cases; males and females shared the work evenly seventeen percent (13 cases) of the time; and women outdistanced men in thirteen percent (10) of the societies in the sample. [71]

With the advent of farming, however, it became evident that women often could perform most or even all essential community chores: tend the hearth, bear and raise children, and plant, cultivate, and harvest the calories needed to stay alive. The worth of males, their dignity as human beings, was challenged to the utmost. A major response appears to have been a shift from man the hunter (and killer) to man the warrior (and killer); from man the physically strong hunter and gatherer working the

distant boundaries of one's own territory to man the statesman and world
diplomat. The new statuses may well be what Luckert has called "face-
saving pretense."

There seems to be plentiful archaeological evidence for a tremendous
upsurge in warfare—or at least armed conflict, whether raiding or warfare—in Europe in late Neolithic times.[72] Notwithstanding, Irenaus Eibl-
Eibesfeldt has said, "The theory that war first developed in the Neolithic
age with the development of horticulture and agriculture does not stand up
to critical examination; there is evidence of armed clashes as early as the
Paleolithic period."[73] This statement does not distinguish, however—and,
indeed, it may forever be impossible to do so on the basis of archaeological
evidence alone—among violence resulting from raiding, institutionalized
warfare, or other possible forms of conflict that might result in an "armed
clash."

Similarly, Phil Donahue has noted that "in the Saltadora cave in Cas-
tile, Spain, there's a crude painting of a man that dates from the Meso-
lithic era. He has been shot with an arrow. He drops to the ground,
clutching his own bow as he goes down: the first recorded victim of our
own species' thirst for its own blood."[74] But it is a large step from what
may well be an instance of individual aggression to socially sanctioned, organized warfare. For that matter, the Saltadora cave figure may be history's
first recorded hunting accident, a tragedy rather than a thirst for blood.

While many cultural evolutionists have noticed the correspondence between warfare and agricultural societies, virtually all of them have attributed the correlation to resultant population increases and the need for
more territory for people and agricultural pursuits. While acknowledging
that land suited to agriculture is a comparatively scarce commodity, we
suggest that hunters and gatherers—fishermen aside—require more land
for their subsistence than do farmers. If this is so, and additional pressures
for land are not the origin of institutionalized conflict, what are the sources
of the correlation?

It may also be that the Neolithic Revolution resulted in agricultural
products that became an additional motive for raiding by members of nonagricultural societies. Raiding brings with it the risk of being killed;
killing, as we have seen, can be the occasion for vengeance warfare. Once
begun, vengeance warfare can continue in a prolonged cycle.

While something like this may indeed have occurred in antiquity, we
believe that a deeper reason—and one that might help explain the persis-

tence of warfare as a modern phenomenon—may lie in the disequilibrium in the sex divisions of respected societal roles which resulted when males became less essential as hunters and gatherers.

Most "causes" that have been proposed for warfare, we suggest, are perhaps better regarded as rationales. Plunder, land, slaves, revenge, political or economic dominion over others: these may be the ex post facto formulations of males who are members of societies that give legal sanction to the killing of "enemies." Should this be so, they are better classified as manifest motives than as latent causes.

If, indeed, it was the introduction of agriculture that led ultimately to the institutionalization of warfare, how might we account for such warfare among groups for whom agriculture, or even horticulture, meant very little in terms of their subsistence? The most dramatic example of such societies in North Amercia is to be found among the Plains Indians.[75]

Here we can only guess that it was another aspect of the Neolithic Revolution—the domestication of animals—that may lie at the root of the kinds of formal hostilities characteristic of Plains groups in historic times. It is impossible to speak with any degree of confidence concerning the nature of gender roles in Plains societies in the prehistoric period, and by the time Europeans began to describe these peoples in more than a passing manner, the introduction of the Old World horse among them had already brought about revolutionary changes. Says anthropologist Bernard Mishkin, "The pastoralization of Plains culture affected the whole gamut of social relations and particularly warfare and rank," and that these were the "effects of overnight changes."[76] What those changes may have been with respect to the worth of males' roles in society can only be conjectured. What we can say is that horse-ridden warfare and raiding among buffalo-hunting Plains Indians evolved to look suspiciously similar to these same institutions as we have found them among the foot-soldier, crop-growing Yumans. Among the Kiowa, for example, warfare and raiding were separately conceptualized, the former being a revenge party of one hundred to two hundred men and the latter being carried out to get horses or to gain personal glory by from one to thirty men.[77]

Nonagricultural hunter-gathers highly dependent on fishing, such North American groups as the Aleut, Yurok, and Bellacoola, were less than peaceful in their relations with their neighbors.[78] Here, however, as in the case of many agricultural societies, the women could make large contributions to the group's subsistence without having to rely on men.

It may be that what we are looking at is some kind of energy equation. In prehistoric times, buffalo provided the chief source of food for Plains peoples, even for such horticulturalists as the Arikara, Pawnee, Osage, and Omaha. Killing buffalos must have been fairly costly in terms of human energy, especially that of the males who were most likely the hunters. The horse altered the energy equation: the horse, rather than men, did most of the work and the whole process was speeded up such that in a relatively short time more than enough meat, hides, sinew, and so forth, could be acquired to supply not only immediate needs but to provide a surplus as well. This means that men afoot, who had plenty of meaningful work to do, as men on horseback found themselves with an overabundance of leisure time and, conceivably as well, in a threatened status position vis-à-vis women.

Whatever the explanation, it is clear that equestrian hunter-gatherers, if the results of Ember's survey of such societies has produced valid results, are far more likely to be "warlike" than otherwise. A table listing thirty-one hunting-gathering societies in terms of their "warfare frequency" includes equestrian societies only among those who carry out "warfare" more than once every two years. None are shown among those for whom warfare is "less frequent" or from absent to rare.[79] Moreover, the lure of energy efficiency provided by the horse in buffalo hunting was apparently enough to entice such settled horticultural village peoples as the Arikara, Pawnee, Osage, and Omaha largely to forsake that life-style in favor of horse-raiding and increased buffalo hunting. The Cheyenne and Arapaho, believed to have been maize farmers in the protohistoric period, gave themselves over entirely to horse nomadism and hunting.[80]

On the other side of the coin, societies characterized by their peaceful nature may be those in which men and women contribute more or less equally to the maintenance of the whole, that is, in which men and women equally produce, collect, or conserve the energy needed for the society's survival. David Fabbro, drawing on Morton Fried,[81] notes that most peaceful societies are egalitarian band societies, those which "generally lack formal patterns of ranking and stratification, place no restriction on the number of people capable of exercising power or occupying positions of prestige, and have economies where exchange is based on generalised reciprocity."[82]

The examples cited by Fabbro[83] are the Semai of Malaya, [84] a people who rely at least in part on slash-and-burn agriculture; the Siriono of eastern Bolivia,[85] also hunter/gatherers who practice a small amount of slash-and-burn farming; the Mbuti pygmies of the Ituri Forest;[86] the Kung Bushmen of the Kalahari Desert;[87] the Copper Eskimo of northern Canada;[88] the Hutterites of North America,[89] a people who maintain themselves by agriculture, both for subsistence and cash; and the fishing/farming islanders of Tristan da Cunha.[90]

The data from our Lower Colorado and middle Gila Yumans and Pimans appear to support the hypothesis that warfare has its origins in an imbalance in the sex division of valued status positions within a society. Yumans on the Colorado were warlike, we suggest, because they lived in one of the best agricultural regions of the entire Southwest. The Colorado and Gila rarely failed; floodplain farmers could almost always count on a crop, especially after Spaniards introduced winter wheat. Women could do all the work necessary for society's physical survival. Males were potentially persons of great leisure. Or, put another way, males were potentially all but useless. Given these circumstances, it is small wonder that they developed warfare to a high degree. It was a way they could maintain their dignity as human beings.

Jack Forbes, writing about the Quechans, noted: "They were basically happy with their way of life, even including the intertribal warfare which provided the people with the opportunity for demonstrating and enhancing their spiritual power and the individual with the opportunity for demonstrating and developing his manhood . . ."[91] He is, of course, talking about males.

On the other hand, warfare for the Pimas was basically of a defensive nature. To be a man who had killed another in battle, and therefore to be a "ripe" person, was indeed to have a valued status. But the dangers attendant on this activity were great, and there is nothing in the literature to suggest that Pima warriors were necessarily among the most respected of human beings.

The ethnographic data available incline us to believe Pimas had worked out a mutually satisfactory adjustment in the role of sexes in their society, one which did not involve a particularly prestigious warrior status for males. Hunting (all but non-existent among Yumans), "keeping the smoke," practicing shamanism, helping to gather wild foods, clearing fields, planting, cultivating, constructing weirs, digging ditches for irrigation, and managing the water distribution system were apparently status positions sufficient to assure males of their humanity. While harvesting farmed products was normally the province of females, the harvesting of wheat—introduced by the Spaniards—was chiefly the work of men.[92]

We are not suggesting that warfare is a necessary result of agriculture. Fabbro's list of peaceful societies attests to this. Other male statuses than that of "warrior" might adequately substitute for those of hunter and far-wandering gatherer in sedentary societies. Indeed, it is less likely that "agriculture" is the key concept than "sex division of labor," "sex divisions of valued status positions," or "sex division of energy allocation." Whatever the forces may be causing severe maladaptation in this relationship, be they farming, animal husbandry, equestrian nomadism, intensive fishing, or other economic activities, it is the imbalance in the relationship that matters. All of us, males and females, need to awaken each morning believing we are worthwhile persons who have real and respected purposes for living.

Whether we are right or wrong that war has been brought about by forces unleashed through the domestication of plants and animals, the subsequent need for males to re-validate their status as dignified human beings, and a natural shift from hunting to fighting, it is certain the question is one worthy of closer examination by all who would know the origins of war. The sex division of labor; male and female status positions within a society; facts concerning the involvement of males and females in the production, allocation, and consumption of energy on which societies and individuals depend for survival: these, we suspect, are the clues to ultimate understanding.

We should like to think that when all of us comprehend the roots of warfare, and by extension, the modern tree which continues to thrive on those roots, we might be set free from its taint, including the threat of universal annihilation. We can imagine a world of societies in which warrior status is denigrated out of existence rather than respected into maintenance and growth. We should like to think that we, our progeny, and generations to come will sense the freedom from fear and anxiety fostered by a lasting peace. Ahwan-tsevarih, a Maricopa leader, said it well at a Mohave-Maricopa peace conference in the late 1850s or early 1860s:

> In the mornings, a coyote would howl and scare you: 'It is the Mohave, war is coming' you thought, and you seized your bows and clubs; now that is over. Some days, an owl would hoot in the morning—'look out, war is here,' you would say. Now there is no more fighting. Let coyote yelp; you can sleep. When we still fought, we all got up early, we were afraid to sleep late. Now we can sleep after the sun is up. . . .[93]

EPILOGUE

The year was 1940. Mary Juan didn't want the strangers, including a newspaper photographer, to see her most cherished possession. But John Thomas, headman of the Maricopa Colony on the Gila River Reservation, persuaded her it would be all right. So she brought from her house "a large heavy envelope on which was subscribed the name of 'Captain Juan Jose' in large capital letters, who was her father and a Sub-Maricopa chief. The envelope contained a number of old documents, and among them was the Treaty of Peace, badly worn, and which had been pasted on another sheet of paper to hold it together."[1]

The "treaty," never formally approved by the United States Senate, was a badly fragmented copy, one written on a single sheet of glossy foolscap in cursive script. The text read:

Treaty Between Indians of New Mexico and California, 1863

To Whom It May Concern:

Know Ye, that on the 7th, 8th, 9th, 10th and 11th of April, 1863, the Chiefs of the Pima, Maricopa, Chimehuevia, Wallapai and Yuma Indians of New Mexico Territory met at Ft. Yuma, all with the approval [name missing] Commanding officer [missing] of Ft. Yuma, and unitedly agree to a Treaty of Peace and Friendship [missing] themselves and Americans, as against tribes [names of tribes missing].

Severally agreed to protect Americans against any and all of the above Tribes. A copy of which Treaty is filed in the Adjutant General's office at Ft. Yuma.

[names of signatures missing]

Given under my hand at Ft. Yuma, California, the 11th day of April 1863.

[signed] Henry Lee.

It had been seventy-seven years since the signing of the treaty. A celebration was clearly in order, so Maricopas became the hosts. Mohaves, Quechans, Pimas, and Arizona Governor Robert T. Jones sent representatives. Guests were welcomed to the officially proclaimed "Feast of Peace"; Maricopas danced and sang accompaniment to their recently revived Buzzard, Hummingbird, and Coyote dances; there was a baseball game; and festivities concluded with social dancing during the evening.

Old enmities had been buried, remembered as history but nothing more. More than one hundred and twenty years after the Massacre on the Gila, the tribes involved persist as viable cultural and political communities.[2] The role of warrior persists, but enacted now only in the military service of the United States. But that is another problem.

NOTES TO THE CHAPTERS

PROLOGUE

1. Material in the prologue concerning Isaiah Churchill Woods is based on Loomis (1968). An extract from Woods's journal was originally published in the *Senate Executive Documents* ([Woods 1859]). According to Loomis (1968: 94), Woods's original report was submitted to the Postmaster General under the name "J. C. Wood." For a recent treatment of the history of the San Antonio and San Diego Mail Line, including Woods's role in it, see Austerman (1985).

2. The fairly extensive literature concerning both the Kearny and Cooke expeditions, including pertinent bibliographic references, is summarized in Hackenberg and Fontana ([1974] vol. 1, chap. 4:33–79).

3. Most published accounts of Forty Niners using this route are summarized and listed bibliographically in Hackenberg and Fontana ([1974] vol. 1, chap. 4:79–88). Spanish and Mexican-period use of the lower Gila trail is summarized in Corle (1951:72–123) and Martin (1954:34–91), but also see Bean and Mason (1962). Prehistoric sites along the lower Gila are documented in Haury (1976) and Vivian (1965). Paul Ezell (1968) has written an article about the use of this highway in the 1820s and 1830s by Maricopa Indian mail couriers.

4. Spier (1978: 18–22) actually lists sixteen settlements for the mid-nineteenth century rather than two, basing his information on informant data of the 1930s. Nearly all contemporary observers, however, agreed that there were two Maricopa "villages," at least in the political sense of that term.

5. Descriptions of Pima settlements, fields, and products for the late 1840s through the late 1850s are summarized in Hackenberg and Fontana [1974] vol. 1, chap 4: 33–195). Figures given for the total number of Pima villages vary, but the 1859 listing by Indian agent Silas St. John (1974: 170–71) is probably the most accurate. He gives the names of ten Pima settlements and lists their headmen, population by age grade and sex, and their numbers of cattle and horses.

6. For details, see Dunbier (1968). For changes in the Gila River environment in Pima and Maricopa country since 1857, see Rea (1983).

7. The figures given here are approximate. For the actual figures given by Lieutenant Chapman, see Russell (1975:21). It is also Russell (1975:22) who gives Pima names for two Maricopa villages.

8. Loomis (1968:106).

CHAPTER ONE. THE BATTLE:
WHITE MEN'S VERSIONS

1. Enmities among other groups of North American Indians, such as in the region of the Great Plains, led to major Indian versus Indian encounters, at least into the 1870s. For example, as many as eighty-six Pawnees died at the hands of the Sioux in August 1873, in a one-sided encounter in which no white men were directly involved (Hyde 1951: 245—47).

2. A good summary of these campaigns is in Thrapp (1967).

3. Anonymous (1857a).

4. Hinton (1906).

5. Burton (1857).

6. Anonymous (1857c).

7. Anonymous (1857d).

8. Mowry (1858:587—88).

9. St. John (n.d.). St. John's physical appearance in 1912 is attested to in a photo of him taken that year, a print of which is on file in the Southwest Museum, Los Angeles, California.

10. Ives (1861:45, 72).

11. Hinton (1906).

12. Anonymous (1857d).

13. Hamilton (1951:8).

14. St. John (n.d.).

15. Steen (1857).

16. Cremony (1969:148).

17. Oaks (1956:23).

18. Browne (1974:104). For a biography of Browne, See Dillon (1965).

19. Ives (1861:94).

20. Mowry (1858:588).

CHAPTER TWO. THE BATTLE:
INDIANS' VERSIONS

1. Russell (1975: 18 *n.*, 36—37). The description of Owl Ear is based on a photograph of him in Russell (1975:Plate IIb).

2. Russell (1975:46—47).
3. M. Kelly (1972:261).
4. The complex history of those Yuman tribes forced off the Colorado River, who ultimately came to be known as the "Maricopa," is told in Ezell (1963). Data are also presented in Dobyns, Ezell, and Ezell (1963); Ezell and Ezell (1970); Forbes (1965); and Spier (1970; 1978).
5. Spier (1978:140).
6. Spier (1978:174). The 1863 peace conference is described in Anonymous (1940:3—4).
7. Gifford (1926:65—66).
8. A. Kroeber (1925b:753).
9. A. Kroeber (1925b:753).
10. Gifford (1932:185—86).
11. Gifford (1932:181; 1936:253).
12. Shaw (1968:36—42). A second version by Shaw (1974:10—13) has been published as well.
13. Perchero (1970:3—4, 6).
14. Spier (1978:xii—xiii). Ida Redbird as a potter is featured in Sayles and Sayles (1948).
15. Redbird (1970:1—2).
16. Another problem may be the fact that most informants spoke in Quechan and Houser had to work through an interpreter. The six Quechans interviewed were Hippa Collins, Jack Kelly, Tom Kelly, Lawrence Levy, Sr., Lee Emerson, and Jefferson Miguel. Tapes are on file in the Arizona State Museum, University of Arizona, Tucson.
17. A. Kroeber (1925a:201—2).

CHAPTER THREE. ARMED CONFLICT: CONCEPTIONS, PERSONNEL, AND THE WARPATH

1. A. Wallace (1968:173).
2. Voegelin and Voegelin (1966).
3. Ezell (1963); M. Kelly (1972:261); Spier (1970; 1978).
4. Voegelin and Voegelin (1966).
5. The concept of ranchería peoples is delineated in Spicer (1962:12—13). The problem of dating canal irrigation among the Gila River Pimas is discussed by Winter (1973) and by Doelle (1981), who opt for Spanish-period introduction, and by Dobyns (1974), who disagrees.
6. See Spicer (1962:273—79) for a summary.
7. Forde (1931:164—65); too tightly condensed in Forbes (1965:75).
8. Stewart (1947b:266). He meant that only career warriors, *kwanamis*, went in the smaller raiding parties, but we have no corroboration and we doubt that small raids were exclusive to *kwanamis*.

9. Spier (1978:162).

10. Basso (1971:16—18).

11. This slave raiding is discussed in Dobyns and others (1957:49).

12. Forbes (1965:292) briefly discusses this attack on the Quechan village near Fort Yuma. It had been preceded by a heavy Cocopa attack on the same village and by a Quechan counterattack in which many Quechan warriors, probably all, were killed.

13. See Sweeny (1956:204—5) for a report of the May 1853 events, and Heintzelman (1857:43) for a brief discussion of a previous similar incident between these two tribes.

14. Sweeny (1956:209—10, 212).

15. Spier (1978:172—73).

16. Spier (1978:164—75).

17. Spicer (1962:374).

18. Spicer (1962:374).

19. Spicer (1962:375).

20. Spicer (1962:375).

21. Spicer (1962:376).

22. Spicer (1962:377).

23. This translation for *sumach* comes via personal communication with Professor Lorraine Sherer. See note 35.

24. See, for example, Fathauer (1954:98).

25. Spicer (1962:378).

26. Forde (1931:138); Gifford (1932:186—87).

27. W. Kelly (1977:133).

28. Forbes (1965:36); Forde (1931:140—41). Also see Bee (1963:209).

29. Forde (1931:166).

30. Forde (1931:173). Also see Bee (1963:220), regarding the expectation that mothers whose husbands had been killed in real battle would teach their sons the skills of war.

31. Densmore (1932:10—11). Also see Couts (1932:41—44), reporting the departure of a large Quechan expedition against the Cocopa in 1848, "some mounted, some on foot."

32. Spier (1978:166—68).

33. Forde (1931:134).

34. Harrington (1908:327). Also see Forde (1931:201). A broad discussion of the whole topic as it concerns Mohaves is in W. Wallace (1964). As A. Kroeber (1925b:755, 784) put the case for Mohave, "[T]hey admit they have learned, but insist that all this knowledge comes from dreams. . . . [T]hey would probably say that the phenomena of dreams have an absolute reality but that they exist in a dimension in which there is no time and in which there is no distinction between spiritual and mental. . . . [S]o deep are these convictions, especially as old age comes on, that most Mohave can no longer distinguish between what they have received from other men and what is their own inward experience."

Concerning Maricopas, Spier (1978:236) wrote, "Learning was displaced by dreaming, and while it was recognized that an individual acquired skill by practice or imitated songs on hearing others, his activity or knowledge would be neither wholly successful nor significant unless he had dreamed."

35. A. Kroeber (1925b:755). This explanation of *sumach ahot* comes to us via personal communication with Professor Lorraine Sherer, who served as Fort Mohave tribal historian starting in 1952 and whose research among Mohaves of the Fort Mohave Indian Reservation was both intensive and extensive. See, for example, Sherer (1965, 1966).

36. Fathauer (1954:102); Stewart (1947b:260—61); A. Kroeber (1948:61—62). Also see W. Wallace (1964:261).

37. Stewart (1947b:261).

38. Fathauer (1954:102). He points to Devereux's (1939) similar analysis of aspirants to a shaman's career. W. Wallace (1964:253) says that a youth, growing up with a firm belief in the all-sufficiency of personal revelations, was conditioned to expect a power-bestowing dream.

39. Stewart (1947b:272—74) lists forty-seven elements concerned with warfare that were shared among all four, and fifty-two other elements most of which were shared by three tribes or by differing pairs among those same four.

40. Stewart (1947b:266).

41. Fathauer (1954:98) has the conference conducted only among *kwanami* with the addition of the *ahwe sumach* who, Fathauer feels, was the "major war leader." He also has the *kohota* sitting in such conferences. Records we have seen, however, do not seem to give the *kohota* any responsibilities beyond keeping enemy scalps, calling the occasional tribal fiestas, and officiating as war parties returned to the Mohave Valley. The likelihood is that the figure known as *kohota* in anthropologists' works, and the "chief" or "head chief" of historical records, were one and the same.

42. See Stewart (1947b:266) who says that the Mohaves' reconnaissance of a prospective enemy objective was conducted months ahead of time.

43. Stewart (1947b:266). Spier (1955:11—12) gives a somewhat different sequence of events, with the decision-making conference and dance in rapid order, perhaps from one day to the next. There are enough differences in detail regarding Mohave war customs among the accounts given to Stewart, Fathauer, A. Kroeber, and Spier to suggest that few Mohaves imparting the information had ever seen war parties depart from the Mohave Valley. For instance, Oatman's account (Stratton 1858:138—39) reports "a long time" between a decision to raid the Cocopa in 1854 and departure of the war party, as well as a "convocation of nearly the whole tribe" the day of the departure.

44. Stewart (1947b:266) states that small raiding groups of ten to twelve men would all be *kwanamis*, and that battle expeditions of forty to fifty people (rarely more than a hundred) would have six or seven *kwanamis*. We suspect, however, this proportion varied a great deal, considering that any warrior was free to choose whether or not to accompany any expedition.

45. This is alleged by Mohaves who talked with Fathauer (1954:99), but it appears nowhere else in the literature. We cannot guess what proportions of a war party were clubmen, bowmen, or wielders of the longer club *(tokyeta)*. Neither can we guess how many warriors went on horseback, if any did.

46. Stewart (1947b) and Fathauer (1954:104—6) agree concerning double or triple roles. But Fathauer's sources told him that spies, *matevawe*, were of different temperament than were *kwanamis*; that they were likely to be following in their fathers' footsteps if found fit for the work; that they were "very brave"; and so on. We feel it is much more likely that scouts—although often working alone or in pairs in enemy country—fought alongside the warriors in battle expeditions.

47. Fathauer (1954:99) says young women went to tend prisoners on the return trip. Mohaves who talked with Stewart (1947b:267) said these women were relatives of *kwanami*, and added that when the Mohaves drove the Halchidhoma from the Colorado in the 1830s some women entered the fray. They also gave "pep talks" to the warriors during stopovers on the long overland travel to the Maricopa villages.

48. Fathauer (1951:605—7; 1954:107); Stewart (1970:19—20; 1974a). It is difficult to be certain of the roles assumed by the *ahwe sumach*. He may have been a soul-loss curer among his other responsibilities.

49. Forde (1931:192, 198); Fathauer (1951:606—7). Devereux (1961:128—35) studied the forms of *ahwe* illnesses during the 1930s among the Mohave. Although, as Devereux recognized, it is often impossible to regain the aboriginal atmosphere and behaviors through modern research, his discussion of *ahwe hahnock (ahwe hafnock)* illnesses from foreign contamination, and *ahwe nyevedhi* (from contact with ghosts), and others, is enlightening in showing how serious these matters were.

50. Spier (1978:154—86).

51. Ezell (1963).

52. Spier (1978:154).

53. Spier (1978:154).

54. Spier (1978:156—57).

55. Spier (1978:236).

56. Spier (1978:237).

57. Spier (1978:238—39).

58. Spier (1978:248).

59. Spier (1978:167, 176).

60. Spier (1978:320).

61. Spier (1978:322).

62. Spier (1978:322).

63. Spier (1978:338—39).

64. Spier (1978:177).

65. Fathauer (1954:110) reminds us that a Mohave fighter may have had more than one role to play in a war party, and it seems possible that Yara tav, a *kwanami*, *pipa tahone*, and possibly a shaman as well, was revealing his power of magic when talking to his fellow warriors. See Kroeber and Kroeber (1973:8—9,

17, 94). W. Kelly (1977:133) found that the Cocopa war leader could likewise conjure rain and dust storms, using power gained from a dream experience while a war expedition was impending.

66. Fontana (1981:33—41).

67. Underhill (1939:57—58).

68. Underhill (1939:70, 72). One is reminded of similar titles used for the Halchidhoma leader: "adviser," "big man," "one who has the name [of honor]," "one who tells things," "well-known," and "praised" (Spier 1978:157).

69. Underhill (1939:73).

70. Underhill (1939:73—75, 77).

71. Underhill (1939:77).

72. Underhill (1939:76—77).

73. Underhill (1939:78—79).

74. Underhill (1939:80—81).

75. Bringas (1977:67); Dobyns and others (1957; 1960); Ezell (1961:118).

76. Kino (1948 [I]:179).

77. Summarized in Fontana (1981:52—60).

78. Lopez (1981).

79. Underhill (1939:128—29).

80. Underhill (1939:132).

81. Ezell (1961:125).

82. Ezell (1961:125—28).

83. Underhill (1939:85).

84. Quoted in Hackenberg and Fontana ([1974], vol. 1, chap. 4:178).

85. Hackenberg and Fontana ([1974], vol. 1, chap. 4:170—71). A genealogy of the Azul family beginning with Culo Azul, whom she identifies as "Anton" Azul and who was Antonio's father, is given by Parsons (1928:447 *n.* 4, Genealogy II following p. 448). Also see note 92, below.

86. Russell (1975:20, note b); St. John (n.d.).

87. Bartlett (1965 [II]:254); Kessell (1976:316 *n*86); Russell (1975:196). Also see Ramírez (1837).

88. Kessell (1976:317).

89. Spier (1978:157), who says Malai was a Halchidhoma chief who died at age 70, offers a partial genealogy for this Maricopa leader.

90. Hackenberg and Fontana ([1974] vol. 1, chap. 4:140).

91. Russell (1975:196).

92. Emory (1859:96), quoted in Hackenberg and Fontana ([1974] vol. 1, chap. 4:140).

93. Hackenberg and Fontana ([1974] vol. 1, chap. 4:105). St. John (n.d.) gives the Maricopa chief's name as Echevaria; Spier, who uses "Chevereah," says the Maricopas spoke of *wantcavarí* (Juan Chevereah) (Spier 1978:156 *n*3). There is a photograph of him in Kroeber and Kroeber (1973:Plate 5), where his name is given as Juan Chivaria.

94. See, for instance, Bringas (1977:89) and Gallego (1935:77).

95. Ezell (1961:126).

96. Grossmann (1873:418).

97. Densmore (1929:114—16) gives an excellent account of one such female curer, Juana Manuel or "Owl Woman," who lived on the San Xavier Indian Reservation in 1920.

98. Dobyns and others (1957:48).

99. H. Wood (1955:13—14).

100. Trippel (1889:8). Two were killed for the funeral of the chief, Pascual, in May 1887 (Woodward 1955:152).

101. By 1874 some horses were being bred in the Mohave Valley (see responses by Captain E. F. Thompson and Lieutenant Allen to the questionnaire, from Camp Mohave, Arizona Territory [United States Army 1874]). We have no knowledge that Quechans were yet breeding horses at that time, and a report from Arizona City dated February 11, 1872, stated they had only a few "if indeed any" (Meigs 1872:163). Walapais were breeding horses on the Colorado River Reservation in 1874 (Crook 1936:98).

102. Castetter and Bell (1951:92).

103. Forbes (1965:264) reports that those herds were stolen by a party of beaver trappers of which Kit Carson and Ewing Young were members.

104. In 1851—52. See Heintzelman (1857:37).

105. Olive Oatman, who lived there as a captive in the early 1850s, mentions no such thing. She was brought overland to the Mohave Valley in 1852 by a party of Mohave traders which included two mounted men (Stratton 1858:166), and the Mohaves left two horses behind with the Yavapais as part of the price paid for Olive and her sister. Travelers generally encountered very few mounted warriors when entering Mohave country, and these are assumed by us to have been the mounted scouts who served as guardians of the approaches to the valley. Möllhausen (1858(II):253) said all three horses he saw here in 1854 "seemed to be regarded rather in the light of things sacred than intended for use."

106. Gifford (1932:205, 216).

107. Forbes (1965:77—79) traces this history for the late eighteenth century. Also see Dobyns and others (1957, 1960) and Kroeber and Kroeber (1973:3—4) for further discussion.

108. Forde (1931:169—70) for Quechans; A. Kroeber (1925b:744) for Mohaves; and Goodwin (1969:96) for Western Apaches.

109. See, for example, Bringas (1977:73—75, 120).

110. Silas St. John, in Hackenberg and Fontana ([1974]vol. 1, chap. 4:171).

111. Gifford (1933a:300) mentions twenty in one battle expedition by Maricopas and Cocopas against Quechans. A narrative of another such expedition says "twenty or fewer," and Spier (1978:173, 175) concluded, "Half the party was said to have been mounted in these engagements." In one expedition to the Colorado about a hundred men were said to have gone on horseback and about the same number on foot (Spier 1978:245).

112. According to Spier (1978:171), "[T]hey would finally charge through the mass composed of friends and foes together, depending on the weight of their steeds, rather than any finesse of their arms." Two accounts of Maricopa horsemen

in battle on the Colorado state that both groups managed to ride through the mass of Quechan footmen, but in one case only a few came back and in the other no rider returned (Spier 1978:173, 245—46). In the 1841 expedition against Quechans, one rider survived a charge through the enemy's lines while the other did not (Russell 1975:41).

113. Forbes (1965:304, 307). Tradition later argued to the effect that Quechans made little use of horses in warfare (Forde 1931:93).

114. Heintzelman (1851: Jan. 20), while his fellow travelers had found mounts among the Cocopas (1851:Jan. 14). There may have been steady losses for still another reason. As an Army officer reported in 1874, "being deprived of the advantages of shoeing, horses never last long in Arizona" (responses to the questionnaire, from Camp Mohave, Arizona Territory [United States Army 1874]).

115. Stewart (1947b:265, 268).

116. Fathauer (1954:100—101) was told of four mounted men who always stood guard at separate points within the Mohave Valley. Several visitors there in the 1850s saw mounted guards at widely separated points in the valley, but it may be too much to insist that four were always there or that each of those horses always had the same given name. (See, for instance, the same names given for horses which participated in the final campaign against the Halchidhoma on the Colorado many years earlier [Spier 1955:15].) When Lorenzo Sitgreaves' small expedition entered the valley from the east late in 1851, a surprise to the Mohaves, among the first people he saw were "three . . . mounted on fine horses . . . ," and all together (Sitgreaves 1962:17).

117. Forbes (1973:21).

118. Bringas (1977:89).

119. N. Michler, in Hackenberg and Fontana ([1974] vol. 1, chap. 4:136).

120. Hackenberg and Fontana ([1974] vol. 1, chap. 4:171).

121. Russell (1975:241—42). By the time John P. Harrington (1908) heard the Quechan origin story in 1902 it also contained the origin of the horse. A crucial difference, however, lies in the fact that the Pima narrative has the animal created in Pima territory by Pimas; the Quechan narrative says that Kumastamxo awarded the horse to white people, along with such other novelties as guns and steamboats.

122. Couts (1961:67) reported that the Pima "chief" asked his expedition which passed through the Pima villages in October 1848 for a thousand guns (and for 1,000 to 2,000 spades for good measure) for the purpose. In 1857 a deputation of Pimas and Maricopas visiting the commandant at Fort Buchanan in southern Arizona asked for 500 guns in the hope that thus armed they could stop Apache depredations for all time (Steen 1857).

123. See Ezell (1961:118—20). Benjamin B. Harris (1960:81) said after visiting the Pimas in July 1849 that "each able-bodied man was required to keep a horse for war purposes."

124. Russell (1975:84) believed Pimas could mount only a fraction of the warriors raiding the Apache; the calendar stick accounts bear him out (Russell 1975:38—55) as do war narratives related to Spier (1978).

125. Russell (1975:84).

126. Gifford (1936:305).

127. Densmore (1932:10—11).

128. Stewart (1947b:268). It should be pointed out there are differences in data on Mohave warfare as collected by Stewart (1947b), Fathauer (1954), and Spier (1955).

129. Gifford (1926:64—65).

CHAPTER FOUR. ARMED CONFLICT: TOOLS, TECHNIQUES, VICTORY, AND DEFEAT

1. Forde (1931:170); Gifford (1936:287); W. Kelly (1977:131); Spier (1955:9—10), among others who have discussed and illustrated the weapons. Much of this material is also summarized in both tabular and note form in Drucker (1941:118—20, 183—85). Descriptions indicate a considerable range in length of the various clubs, staves, and lances then in use. It appears that anything called a "spear" or "lance" was from five to six feet long, and the only long pole known is the Yavapais' ten- or twelve-foot lance which they sometimes used in hand-to-hand combat. The handles of the short mallet clubs were probably about two inches in diameter, the same as for the *tokyeta [to'kyet]*, both being wielded in one hand.

2. Gifford (1932:225; 1936:287—88); Goodwin (1971:238).

3. Forde (1931:170); W. Kelly (1977:131); Spier (1978:171).

4. Mohave and Quechan arrows are said not to have had foreshafts. But Lorenzo Sitgreaves (1962:18) in 1851 described a Mohave arrow the forward quarter (7 inches) of which was of hardened wood, the rest of "a light weed." Robert Eccleston (1950:230), who amused himself by shooting Quechan arrows in December of 1849, said they were "cane with a piece of harder wood inserted & a piece of flint, cut sharp for the head, ingeniously fastened on." Lieut. Tom Sweeny (1956:71) in 1852 saw Quechan shafts of which the forward half was wooden, the rest of "cane." And finally, boundary surveyor Nathaniel Michler (1857:108), who was among Quechans in 1855, said "the arrows are of reed, part of the shaft of arrow-wood—the point tipped with a hard stone, jasper or agate, small, but neatly and sharply edged; they are winged with the gay feathers of the various birds of this country."

5. Gifford (1932:223—25; 1936:287). Also see Corbusier (1886:331). The Maricopa used a much simpler mixture based on deer's blood. We do not know that Quechans or Mohaves poisoned their arrow tips.

6. Densmore (1932:11).

7. Sweeny (1956:71) reports this dimension, and that the Quechans were "never without" this weapon.

8. Forde (1931:167) was told by Joe Homer that Quechans had only one shield in a battle, that carried by one of the stavebearers.

9. Gifford (1932:223—25).

10. Spier (1955:8).

11. Gifford (1932:223—25).

12. Gifford (1936:303).

13. The anthropological accounts in some cases report only a pair of feathers or down worked into the back hair of warriors and leaders; but Cave Couts (1932:42 —43) reports the Quechan leader's helmet in specific detail.

14. Sweeny (1956:72). In 1854 Lieutenant Michler (1857:110) saw vermilion, black, and blue in Quechan war paint. He also noted that some of the men were tattooed.

15. Taylor and Wallace (1947:193).

16. Details differ in descriptions given to anthropologists to such a degree as to raise the question whether warriors had several options in painting and decorating for battle. For instance, the Mohave face paint described above as distinctive for warriors much resembles the old man's style shown in A. Kroeber (1925b:730). The old man's color was red, and the warrior's was supposed to have been black; but we feel there is uncertainty in such specific detail when the large number of people giving the descriptions may only have seen a few aged warriors dressed and painted for tribal ceremonials—and certainly never saw a large number of warriors departing on a major battle expedition.

17. Spier (1978:163).

18. See p. 38—39 for an account of this event.

19. Russell (1975:120).

20. Russell (1975:95).

21. Burrus (1965:Plate 9).

22. Russell (1975:Plate 8a).

23. Russell (1975:96).

24. Castetter and Underhill (1978:71).

25. Russell (1975:86).

26. Woodward (1933:166—67).

27. Russell (1975:111).

28. Grossmann (1873:416).

29. Castetter and Underhill (1978:70—71).

30. Russell (1975:96).

31. Grossmann (1873:416).

32. Russell (1975:120—21).

33. Russell (1975:96).

34. Whittemore (1893:69).

35. Russell (1975:116, Figure 40).

36. Burrus (1965:Plate 9). Also see Kino (1971:frontispiece) for an enlargement of the sketch.

37. Ormsby (1942:97).

38. Russell (1975:202).

39. Grossmann (1873:417).

40. Underhill (1939:131—32). For illustrations of Papago war headdresses and face paint, see Underhill (1968:71).

41. Underhill (1939:131). For further discussion and illustrations, also see Underhill (1951:83—91; 1979:28—31).

42. Devereux (1961:523); Gifford (1926:66).

43. To avoid this, in June 1853, Pasqual, the Quechan leader, took a sizeable party some sixty miles into Cocopa country to the spot at which Quechans and Kamias had recently suffered heavy losses in a treacherous ambush. The ceremonies were conducted even in the face of the fact that the Cocopas could have attacked the party. See Sweeny (1956:205).

44. Grossmann (1873:416).

45. Russell (1975:202).

46. Underhill (1939:190).

47. Spier (1978:170).

48. Spier (1978:173).

49. Spier (1978:162, 169—70). The Mohaves who talked with Kenneth Stewart (1947b:268) firmly denied any such single combat.

50. The best description we have seen is in Couts (1932:43—44), and illustrated in the manuscript of the diary. For discussion, see Forde (1931:232, Figure 14); Spier (1955:12—14, Plate 1); and Stewart (1947b: 265—66). Most examples known in the present century had to be made to order under the direction of old tribesmen at the behest of anthropologists, and some of these were copied from versions of the stave still in use during the 1920s and 1930s in the old-style mourning *(keruk)* ceremonies then still being conducted by some of these peoples. Accordingly there is much uncertainty concerning how many such poles were carried into battle (one, two, or more), how many feathers were attached, the length of the stave, and how many other similarly symbolic objects may have been used in the same situation.

51. Forde (1931:167); Spier (1978:165); Stewart (1947b: 265—66).

52. Forde (1931:170). Also see Densmore (1932:10) for Charles Wilson's brief explanation.

53. Spier (1978:135). He was told that the Maricopa only struck downward with the club. There is a record, however, of a Maricopa's killing a Quechan in battle with the sharp end of the club piercing his enemy's side (Russell 1975:41).

54. A. Kroeber (1925a:202).

55. Harrington (1929:17) has clubmen ahead and bowmen "in the background." Stewart (1947b:264, 268) has it as presented here. Fathauer (1954:99) has the formation of Mohaves running from left to right, bowmen on the wings, mallet-clubmen in the center, and the war leader directing from the rear. Battle accounts include one that reports Quechan archers firing over the line of their own clubmen. It may be there was confusion in reporting and recording formations, since clubmen at the front backed up by other warriors would be a reasonable alignment for surprise attacks whether or not it might also be used in ritual warfare.

56. Spier (1978:132) said he was told of this repeatedly, and it is clear in one of the narratives he presents.

57. Bartlett (1965 [II]:249—50).

58. In Hackenberg and Fontana ([1974], vol. 1, chap. 4:167, 169, 171).

59. In Hackenberg and Fontana ([1974], vol. 1, chap. 4:178).

60. Farish (1915—1918 [VI]:261—62).

61. Ezell (1961:119).

62. Russell (1975:200).

63. Woodward (1933).

64. Russell (1975:202).

65. This is the report of all authorities except John P. Harrington (1929:17), who stated that the first Mohave to touch one of the enemy would gain possession of his scalp if it were taken. One of the most detailed discussions of scalping by Quechans and all that it entailed is that of Charles Wilson as told to Frances Densmore (1932:11—13).

66. Spier (1978:180—82) for many specific details.

67. Spier (1978:182—86, 300—309).

68. Forde (1931:168) concerning Quechan observances. As for hanks of hair, see Bartlett (1965(II):221) and Russell (1975:45).

69. Stratton (1858:220—23) has Olive Oatman reporting her account of the messenger's arrival, the war party's return, and ensuing relief and rejoicing. This was in 1854 when a Mohave war party made a successful attack against the Cocopas and suffered no losses among themselves.

70. Stewart (1947b:270).

71. Fathauer (1954:100), who does not add that fiestas of this scale, and with the same general purpose in view, were also held during the autumn harvest season. Stratton (1858:202—5) rigidly and scornfully discusses the autumn party of 1854 in blistering moralistic terms, making the party sound as if it were an utter debauch, but without giving any of the salacious details.

72. Which events occurred in exactly which sequence during the fiestas is not discoverable at this late date. The information here follows most closely Stewart (1947b:270) and to some extent Fathauer (1954:99—100) and Spier (1955:14). No two accounts, however, are quite the same.

73. Stratton (1858:22) has Olive Oatman report that meat-salt denial continued for a "moon"; but as so often is the case, this may be the writer's bending whatever Olive Oatman said to fit his own categories of symbols supposedly representing Indian culture.

74. Spier (1955:14) describes a sixteen-day purification period for warriors who had killed enemies. Stewart (1947b:270) was told of four to eight days for all warriors returning from war parties. Sources differ as well on other aspects of this very ritualized phase that was fraught with danger for all concerned.

75. W. Kelly (1949b:85, 88).

76. Yuman cremation and mourning rites have been described in considerable detail in the anthropological literature. For Quechan, see Forde (1931:207—51);

for Mohave, Forde (1931:252—53), Key (1970), A. Kroeber (1925b:749—51), and Stewart (1974b); for Cocopa, Forde (1931:254—56) and W. Kelly (1949a; 1977:86—98); for Yavapai, Gifford (1932:232; 1936:302—3); for Halchidhoma (included among the "Maricopas" of the 1857 battle), Forde (1931:253—54) and Spier (1978:300—308); and for Maricopa, Forde (1931:254) and Spier (1978:300—304, 308—9).

77. Grossmann (1873:416).

78. See Ezell (1961:88—89) for a discussion.

79. Russell (1975:116, Plate 40).

80. Densmore (1929:33, 103, 195—97); Underhill (1939:137; 1946:185—90).

81. Densmore (1929:190, 193, 195—97).

82. Densmore (1929:103).

83. Ezell (1961:88); Gifford (1936:335—38).

84. Underhill (1939:137).

85. Underhill (1946:210).

86. Bahr et al. (1974:65—69).

87. Bourke (1969:203).

88. Russell (1975:204—5).

89. Grossmann (1873:416—17).

90. Bahr et al. (1974:65—69); Ezell (1961:88).

91. Brennan (1959:232—33); Densmore (1929:187—99), Gunst (1930:34—37); Underhill (1939:136—38; 1946:196—210; 1968:93—103; 1979:44—46); and Underhill et al. (1979:126—36).

92. Densmore (1929:186—87).

93. Cremony (1969:106—7).

94. Russell (1975:205—6).

95. Underhill (1939:137; 1946:186; 1968:85—92; 1979:45—46).

96. Gunst (1930:34); Underhill et al. (1979:137).

97. Densmore (1929:187, 193).

98. Ezell (1961:97). Ezell (1961:95—97) also offers a lengthy discussion of the history of cremation among Pimans. Cremation of Papago warriors killed in battle is documented by Jose Lewis Brennan (1959:227) and in Underhill (1939:136, 188, 190).

99. Allyn (1974:110—11). Russell (1975:193—95) also describes Pima funeral rites. He notes that near relatives of the deceased, both men and women, cut their hair shorter, women more so than men. During the mourning period, which in theory could last up to four years, widows "were compelled to remain at home, to refrain from washing their hair, and to cry aloud the name of the deceased every morning at daybreak." Once mourning ended, the name of the deceased was never supposed to be mentioned again (Whittemore 1893:60).

100. Hinton (1906). Also see Fish (n.d.:241).

101. Anonymous (1857b).

CHAPTER FIVE. YUMAN ANTAGONISTS: MARICOPAS, QUECHANS, AND MOHAVES TO 1857

1. Spicer (1962:262—66, Map 17).
2. Some of these distributions are shown and discussed in Ezell (1963:1—3, Map 2). Also see Dobyns and Euler (1970:70; 1976:3); Forbes (1965:12—40); and the maps in Gifford (1932; 1936).
3. McGuire (1982:216—222)
4. Waters (1982).
5. Schroeder (1979).
6. Spier (1970).
7. C. Kroeber (1965:173); Sherer (1966).
8. See Manners (1959) for a discussion.
9. See, for instance, DuBois (1906); Gifford (1931:12, 75—81; 1933b); Gifford and Lowie (1928); Harrington (1908); W. Kelly (1977); and A. Kroeber (1948; 1951; 1972). See discussion of some of these and others by Spier (1978) and by Forbes (1965:17—30, 34 ff.). Forbes makes an excellent effort to discern to what extent origin narratives reflect the factual history of the tribes involved.
10. Ezell (1963:23—24) presents and discusses the only specific evidence we have seen in any of these tribal literatures for important changes in mythological content. He uses an account of 1775, comparing it with another dating from about 1900. He raises questions of possibilities of differing longevity for various kinds of historical facts where these have been transmitted either in tribal mythology or in personal memory. For a further discussion of the problem of historicity of mythological texts, see Fontana (1969).
11. Spicer (1962:373—79).
12. Devereux (1961:118—19, 136—37).
13. Forbes (1965:86—88).
14. A. Kroeber (1920:477).
15. Dobyns and others (1963:109—12, 135—37); Forbes (1965:81).
16. This history is summarized in Dobyns (1972:20—32).
17. Gifford (1932:181; 1936:253).
18. Forbes (1965:12—133) discusses development of slave trading and the effects it presumably had on inter-tribal relationships. Also see Dobyns et al. (1957; 1960).
19. We have no absolute proof of such a major shift, but we venture the thought because Spanish chroniclers, and such thoroughgoing scholars as Forbes and Spicer (1962), leave the impression that earlier warfare was frequent but neither of a scale nor intensity to suggest wars of annihilation. Forbes (1965:125—26) reviews data for 1699—1701 that seem not to indicate the same bitterness or

fear toward each other that later, before the end of the 1700s, became common among Gila-Colorado peoples.

20. Although to give a specific date seems impossible. Forbes (1965:76—79, 97 —98, 110—11, 126) discusses in detail this question of shift in intensity of warfare, coming at some time between the earliest whites' visits in the 1540—1604 period and the nineteenth century when warfare was "constant." He concludes that "warfare assumed an increasingly serious form after 1782, when the Quechans had very great scores to settle with the Maricopas, Gila Pimas, Halchidhomas, and Kohuanas because the latter aided the Spaniards in an invasion [actually, punitive expeditions] of Quechan territory" (Forbes 1965:78—79). He also believes the slave trade had shown serious and continuing effect in alienating peoples. Ezell and Ezell (1970) agree. Also see W. Kelly (1977:130) who inclines to date increasing intensity of warfare at some time between 1605 and 1701. At a later date in the eighteenth and nineteenth centuries, the outcome was withdrawal of some of the peoples from the vicinity of the Colorado River.

21. The best summary of this entire episode is in Forbes (1965:175—220). The punitive efforts are described on pages 212—20 of Forbes (1965). Also see Bringas (1977:96—97, 100—111).

22. Dobyns et al. (1963).

23. One of Spier's Halchidhoma informants even specifically stated that the 1857 attack first hit the Maricopa village, and that the Maricopa subsequently "sent word to the Halchidhoma, who lived [to the east] near Sacate" (Spier 1978:173). For the modern Halchidhoma, see M. Kelly (1972).

24. Some of the incidents cited in Table 1 may be duplications (possibly numbers 12, 13, and 14; 17 and 18; and 20 and 21). Undatable incidents include the Quechans' challenging the Maricopas to battle on the Colorado, perhaps before 1800 (Spier 1970:16); a Maricopa collision with Quechans part way between the two homelands (Spier 1978:173); a Maricopa victory at the Quechan villages (possibly the same as number 15 in the table) (Spier 1978:172); and a Maricopa victory on the Colorado, an arranged battle sometime before 1854 (possibly the same as number 15 in the table) (Froebel 1895:511—12).

25. "That it [warfare among Colorado River tribes] was both highly destructive of human life and tribal existence seems indicated by direct account, in part, by the heavy reduction in population estimates, and the disappearance of tribal groups before the period of direct European influence . . .," states W. Kelly (1977:129), referring to the whole history of that warfare from earliest Spanish explorations through the 1850s.

26. Forbes (1965:77) cites Father Jacobo Sedelmayr.

27. Kutox, the Halchidhoma born about 1847, explained to Leslie Spier (1978:171) a sort of short version of a creation or origin tale which states that the Halchidhoma sided with "Mission Indians," assumed by Spier to have been Cahuillas. Lowell Bean (1972:131) mentions Cahuilla traditions of two war expeditions the Cahuillas launched against the Quechans, although for accidental reasons neither of them arrived on the Colorado.

28. See Forbes (1965:325—40) for a summary.

29. Hackenberg and Fontana (1974: I: Chapter 4:138—40), giving William Emory's account of being visited by a delegation of concerned Pima, Papago, and Maricopa leaders who wanted assurances concerning their status under the United States. Kessell (1976:317) also reports an 1855 visit to Mexican authorities in Sonora by Papagos and Gila Pimas who had the same concerns.

30. The first U.S. Army post in the region was established at Camp Moore, near the junction of Potrero Creek and the Santa Cruz River (Serven 1965:27).

31. Hackenberg and Fontana (1974: I: Chapter 4: 165-66, 167, 171-72).

32. See C. Kroeber (1965).

33. In all, we have seen thirteen mentions of Maricopa aggression against Quechans. They are to be found in Couts (1961:64—65, 73); Forbes (1965:291 ff.), using the diary of Sweeny (1956); Franco Coronel (1877); Froebel (1859: 511 —12); Gifford (1932:185); Hall (1907:418); Russell (1975:40—41); and Spier (1955:16; 1978:171—73, 245—46).

The fourteen mentions of Quechan attacks (some accompanied by allies) on the Maricopa villages or against Gila Bend saguaro fruit gatherers are found in Cremony (1969:111—12); Bartlett (1965:II:221); Hall (1907:418, 420); Russell (1975:38, 41-42, 44-45, 46-47); Smith (1942:23); Spier (1978:173); and Suárez (1832).

It is our feeling that the thirteen mentions of Maricopa aggression refer to seven different attacks; the fourteen mentions of Quechan aggression against Maricopas refer to eight different attacks.

34. Enrique Tejeda was a Caborca, Sonora, Papago, who for many years had been captain of the Sixth Infantry Company of Pimans. See Fontana (1981:57), where the name is misspelled "Tejada."

35. Suárez (1832).

36. Gifford (1933a:301—2).

37. In Spier (1955:16). That series of engagements occurred just at the time the Kohuana were departing from the Colorado River.

38. For the inner complexities of Indian and Indian-white relationships in that region from the eighteenth through the mid-nineteenth centuries, see Phillips (1975).

39. Forbes (1965:268—69, 274—87).

40. The war chief was killed attacking Maricopas in 1842 (Russell 1975:41); Pablo Coclum, tribal leader, was deposed in 1849 (Couts 1932:34—36); a great warrior was killed in a Cocopa raid about 1848 (Forbes 1965:292); a chief was killed attacking the Maricopas in 1850 or 1851 (Russell 1965:44); Antonio, a *pipa taxan*, was murdered at the Maricopa villages in December 1851 (Forbes 1965:329 —31); Macedon, the tribal leader, was killed in a Cocopa ambush in May 1852 (Forbes 1965:337); and the "principal chief of the Yumas," perhaps Santiago, who by that time had been deposed by act of the U.S. Army commandant, died in 1856 (Ives 1861:45). In the meantime, "old" Pasqual had been killed by a white man near Fort Yuma in 1851 (Woodward 1955:47, 85—86, 140).

A few leaders survived all attempts by Indians and whites to betray, assassinate, depose, confine, or kill them on the field of battle. Caballo en Pelo was already a redoubtable warrior in the 1830s and was tribal war leader at least until the middle 1850s; and Pasqual, a famous fighter and *pipa taxan* in the 1840s, became tribal leader in the early 1850s and lived until 1887 (Forbes 1965:337 *n* 62, 343).

41. Kroeber and Kroeber (1973:7—11).

42. Heintzelman (1851:January 4 entry; 1857) believed that by summer of 1853 the Quechan and New River Kamia could not field 400 warriors between them. In 1851 he had underestimated the Cocopa as numbering only 250 people in all; but by 1853 he thought they had 300 warriors.

43. Their defense system is described on pages 85—87. Spier (1978:22) says that by mid-century Maricopas were settling more compactly because of "accumulated losses from Yuma-Mohave attacks."

44. See Phillips (1975), discussing leadership by Juan Antonio, Antonio Garra, and other Southern California band leaders assuming new roles. In Kroeber and Kroeber (1973) Yara tav of the Mohaves is described as exerting this kind of double role; and Pasqual of the Quechans is another of the same kind. Little as we know about them, Quashackama of one of the Yavapai bands and Ah-pan-kuh-ya ("Pan Coyer") of the Chemehuevi probably played the same part, both of traditional leader and of go-between. In some cases they may also have been independent clients of the whites. Something like this may also have been the case with Antonio Azul of the Gila River Pimas.

CHAPTER SIX. MOTIVES AND ORIGINS: WARFARE AND PEACE ON THE COLORADO AND GILA

1. Burton (1857).
2. Ives (1861:45*n*).
3. A. Kroeber (1948:4—5).
4. For a list, see Castetter and Bell (1951:30—33).
5. Hicks (1974:141).
6. C. Kroeber (1980).
7. Stone (1981:184). She is aware Mohaves also fished and hunted.
8. Stone (1981:191).
9. Stone (1981:191—93). She further argues those peoples knew nothing of irrigation or other means for efficient use of river water; also, that individuals or families would not settle at the best farming locations because "the acquisition of superior agricultural land was not the sole or even primary determinant of settlement location" (p. 193).
10. Stone (1981:183, 187, 190).
11. Stone (1981:187).
12. Stone (1981:186—87, 189).
13. Stone (1981:193).

14. Graham (1975).
15. Graham (1975:451–52).
16. Graham (1975:460).
17. Graham (1975:451).
18. Graham (1975:460). This is in spite of the fact that his analysis seems to suggest the Halchidhoma left the Colorado not because of losing a long series of wars, but simply because they needed more food.
19. Stone (1981:187).
20. W. Kelly (1977:17).
21. See Castetter and Bell (1951) for a series of food-getting activities we represent as Table 2 (p. 127). Data on seasons of cropping and food collecting are on pages 131–37 (seasonal fluctuations in volume of water in the river, etc.); 148 (peak water periods and various planting times); 144–46 (second flooding on the river, multiple plantings, household plots); and 181 (mesquite bean and screwbean seasons). For other important semicultivated and wild crops, see pages 165–204ff. Details of harvest time are on pages 157ff; wheat, pages 124–26; and long trips outside the valley to locate food, page 74. For data on cattail seasons, see Niethammer (1974:88–89). For additional data on Mohave agriculture, see Stewart (1966).
22. Gifford (1936:263); A. Kroeber (1925b:594).
23. Dobyns et al. (1963:132).
24. Dobyns et al. (1957:51). In this connection, the "Origin of War" myth collected by A. L. Kroeber (1972:80ff), recounts the beginning of Mohave warfare as involving the exploits of a fearsome cannibal, Kwayu. His killing and eating of Kohuana Indians is followed by the remark: "So began the fighting between the tribes, by killing others to eat." Later, when Halkutata, who lived in the sea "beyond the Kohuana" had killed the cannibal and the creator figure, Mastamho, had gone from Mohave country to kill Halkutata, the final remark is: "That was the beginning of war."
25. Ezell and Ezell (1970:171). They specify that Gila River Pimas' belligerence was "utilized basically as a means of territorial defense."
26. Ezell and Ezell (1970:170); Dobyns et al. (1957:61). The latter also mention theft of food as a purpose of war which may have originated in aboriginal or later times.
27. Dobyns et al. (1957:50–61); Ezell and Ezell (1970:174–75).
28. Dobyns et al. (1957:61); Ezell and Ezell (1970:178).
29. Dobyns et al. (1957:50).
30. Ezell and Ezell (1970:181–82, 184).
31. Forbes (1965:78–288, 343). Data are here concerning horse stealing and trade, slave trading, and intensified hostilities as a result of these activities. Forbes also documents the decline in Quechan population (p. 343).
32. A. Kroeber (n.d.:6).
33. See Forbes (1965:76, 97–98, 110, 126, 163, 172, 234, 271) to this same effect.

34. Forbes (1965:234). He dates a period of renewed war by Quechans against their neighbors in the years 1783—1800, just following the hostilities attendant upon the Spanish attempt to settle a colony among the Quechans.

35. Bailey (1963:164—67).

36. Brady (1860).

37. White (1974).

38. Dobyns et al. (1963:110). Also see White (1974).

39. See Forbes (1965:80—81; 1973). Dobyns et al. (1963:141—45) lean toward this sort of vision in drawing analogies between southwestern Indian relationships and Western nation-states' alliances and power blocs.

40. A. Kroeber (1925b:596).

41. In conversation, Robert Heizer reminded us of such possibilities—that warfare in what is now Arizona could have come about through reverberations originating in some ancient Mexican imperial influences. If reclaimable at all, indications of such influences will be found only in archaeological remains. As Heizer recognized, such influences are unlikely ever to become clear. But to those who ponder the ultimate causes of warfare, the possibilities of origins outside the immediate zone of conflict must be kept in mind. C. Daryll Forde, for one, believed that war usages and customs of Lower Colorado River peoples "indicate that the warfare of this region is related to the wider militancy of the south and east and is probably as intrusive as their agriculture and the metate" (Forde 1931:175).

42. See Forbes (1965:27ff) for the only thoroughgoing attempt to sort out origins of the various Lower Colorado Indian peoples by analyzing accounts recorded by the people themselves.

43. These communications and trade are discussed in Dobyns and others (1957, 1963); Forbes (1965); and Spier (1935, 1978).

44. Spier (1978:20—22).

45. Fathauer's 1952 letter to George Devereux (1961:429) included the statement that "revenge appears to have been one of the main motives for warfare among the tribes."

46. For the earlier period of these wars—before about 1830—statements abound in the record indicating that members of these tribes took horses from each other and trafficked in slaves, many of whom were captured originally from nearby peoples. See, for instance, Forbes (1965) and Dobyns et al. (1957). But the records themselves, and their presentation, fail to inform which of the cases involve ordinary trade, which refer to raids, and whether any refer to taking property on battle expeditions.

Another difficulty with the assumption that slave trading was a major motive for war expeditions is the fact that the few captives taken by Yumans were often kept within the tribe rather than being sold. In the discussion between Maricopa and Mohave leaders making peace, Ahwan-tsevarih asked Yara tav what had happened to the prisoners captured by the Mohaves in war. Yara tav's answer was that they had grown up in the tribe and had married there (Kroeber and Kroeber 1973:15—16).

After reviewing the record of a number of these peoples, Homer Aschmann (1974:207—211) concluded that economic return from "regular warfare" was unlikely. Donald Calloway (1978:40) arrived at a similar opinion: ". . . raiding for booty (including food) and territory . . . seems less applicable to the River Yumans who seldom, if ever, raided for food. . . ."

47. Russell (1965:38). The meteoric fall (the Leonid Shower) occurred November 13, 1833, and many American Indians dated events from that "Day the Stars Fell."

48. Russell (1965:41).

49. Antonio Azul spoke for the Pimas; Juan Chivaria (Ahwan-tsevarih) for the Maricopa; Yara tav for some of the Mohaves; Ah-pan-kuh-ya ("Pan coyer") for the Chemehuevis; and Quashackama for one of the Yavapai bands. The meeting occurred in April 1863, and among the agreements was one asserting the peoples "would forget any thought of retaliating against each other for reason of any past 'difficulties'" (Kroeber and Kroeber 1973:57).

Although there is no record of the appearance of a Quechan at this meeting, a holograph copy of the "treaty" says the "chiefs" of the "Pima, Chimehuavia, Wallapai and Yuma Indians" agreed to its terms, and the probability of Quechan presence seems high (Anonymous 1940; see also pp. 176—77).

50. The Halchidhoma was Kutox, born in 1847, who could not have known of these events at firsthand (Spier 1978:173).

51. See Chapter 5, note 40. For Pasqual, see Forbes (1965:337 *n* 343).

52. Some of the Mohaves left the field during the battle. Many years later George Devereux (1961:427) was told that the "senior Mohave warriors (who wield short mallet-shaped clubs) ordered the adolescents and young men (who wield straight clubs) to retire, while they and the Yuma stood fast and were wiped out."

53. Kroeber and Kroeber (1973:27—32).

54. The importance of Gila River peoples, especially Pimas, as suppliers of wheat is summarized in Fontana (1976:51).

55. Kroeber and Kroeber (1973:56 *n*13).

56. In 1874 several responses to the Army's questionnaire mentioned that chiefs-and-council was the form of government among the Mohaves (United States Army 1874).

CHAPTER SEVEN. THE FOURTH AGE: ON THE ORIGINS OF WAR

1. Thoreau (1960:7—8).
2. Otterbein (1973:923).
3. Malinowski (1941:523).
4. Mead (1940:402).

5. Mead (1968:215—16).
6. Ferguson (1984:2).
7. Otterbein (1973:923).
8. Newcomb (1960:328).
9. Newcomb (1960:329).
10. Ferguson (1984:5).
11. Netting (1974:139).
12. Netting (1974:140).
13. Netting (1974:140).
14. See, for example, M. Harris (1974) and Vayda (1968a, 1968b).
15. Turney-High (1949:172); Wright (1942 [I]:59, 75).
16. A. Wallace (1968).
17. Newcomb (1960: 326—27).
18. Newcomb (1960:320).
19. Wright (1942 [I]:87, 88—100).
20. Wright (1942 [I]:87).
21. Wright (1942 [I]:61).
22. Turney-High (1949:141). Also see Vayda (1968b:471).
23. For a discussion, see Leeds (1963:69, 79).
24. Vayda (1976:3—5, 103—4).
25. Vayda (1976:2).
26. Vayda (1976:2).
27. A. Kroeber (1925b:745); Sherer (1966:2—3); Stewart (1983:62, 64, 66).
28. A. Kroeber (1902:278).
29. Forde (1931:134).
30. Forde (1931:134).
31. Forde (1931:182).
32. Bee (1983:92).
33. While one of us (Kroeber) worked with Lorraine Sherer and Frances Malika Stillman on matters relating to Mohave history and culture, we spoke of warfare and warriors *(kwinemi),* and Mrs. Stillman noted that her late husband, Luke, had been known as a *kwinemi* among the Fort Mohave people. "He became one," she said, and added that his warrior status had to do with his having volunteered for service with the U. S. Army in wartime. For information concerning Mrs. Stillman, see Sherer (1965:3—4, 22, 37, and photo on p. 36).
34. The data are summarized in Castetter and Bell (1951:224—35). Also see Stewart (1947a) and Stratton (1858:202—05) for the Mohave Mourning Ceremony.
35. Forde (1931:165).
36. Forde (1931:134, 174—75). The authority he mentions is Perry (1917; 1924:191 ff). Perry's view was a very strong version of diffusionism. Forde stressed his feeling that war should not be interpreted as a reflection of pugnacious personality, but rather as a result of assimilation and diffusion of the cultural elements of which a pattern of warfare comes to be composed.

37. Fathauer (1954:110, 114—15). He felt his conclusions were the same as those Forde had come to after studying the Quechans. Fathauer's whole discussion of Mohave warfare, pages 110—18, is worthy of close attention in its own right and also for his attempt to compare Mohave data with then-current theories concerning the causation of war among primitive peoples.

38. We have worded this statement carefully because it is a guess on our part, and therefore not the firm assertion made by so many theorists of primitive war to the effect that one of the main functions of warfare, manifest as well as latent, is to foster the unity of the tribe or nation.

39. A. Kroeber (1963:104—5).

40. The discussion which follows is based almost wholly on Otterbein (1973:927 — 48).

41. Lorenz (1966).

42. Ardrey (1966).

43. Montagu (1976:3, 325).

44. Otterbein (1973:930).

45. Otterbein (1973:934).

46. Gorer (1938).

47. Otterbein (1973:934).

48. Fathauer (1954:115).

49. Otterbein (1973:936).

50. Mead (1963).

51. Otterbein (1973:940).

52. Otterbein (1973:942).

53. Otterbein (1973:942).

54. Service (1968).

55. Ember (1978:443).

56. Ferguson (1984).

57. Ferguson (1984:22).

58. Ferguson (1984:23).

59. Ferguson (1984:37—42).

60. Carroll and Fink (1975:62 — 66).

61. Ottenberg (1978).

62. Tyrrell (1984:18).

63. Mitchell (1981:152).

64. Iglitzin (1978:63).

65. Iglitzin (1978:63, 69).

66. Haile (1981:vii—viii).

67. Haile (1981).

68. Haile (1981:17 *n*).

69. Haile (1981:18 *n*).

70. Haile (1981:19 *n*).

71. Ember (1978:442).

72. See Childe (1941), Newcomb (1960:328), and Roper (1975).

73. Donahue (1985:237).
74. Donahue (1985:237).
75. A summary of Plains Indian warfare is in Mishkin (1940:1–4).
76. Mishkin (1940:58, 57).
77. Mishkin (1940: 28).
78. Ember (1978:444).
79. Ember (1978:444).
80. Mishkin (1940:57).
81. Fried (1967).
82. Fabbro (1980:181).
83. Fabbro (1980:182–97).
84. Dentan (1968).
85. Holmberg (1966).
86. Moore (1972).
87. Lee (1968); Marshall (1965); Thomas (1969).
88. Jenness (1922); Palmer (1965); Rasmussen (1932).
89. Hostetler and Huntington (1967).
90. Loudon (1970); Munch (1964; 1970; 1971; 1974).
91. Forbes (1973:21).
92. Castetter and Bell (1942:180).
93. Kroeber and Kroeber (1973:17).

EPILOGUE

1. Information concerning the "treaty" and subsequent "Feast of Peace" is taken from Anonymous (1940).

2. For recent reviews of the histories, ethnographies, and contemporary situations of the various tribes involved in the 1857 battle, see Bee (1983, for Quechans); Ezell (1983, for Pimas); Fontana (1983, for Pimas); Harwell and Kelly (1983, for Maricopas); Khera and Mariella (1983, for Yavapais); Pablo (1983, for Pimas); Stewart (1983, for Mohaves); and Williams (1983, for Cocopas).

REFERENCES

ALLYN, JOSEPH P.
1974   *The Arizona of Joseph Pratt Allyn: letters from a pioneer judge.* Edited by John Nicolson. Tucson: The University of Arizona Press.

ANONYMOUS
1857a   The Great Overland Mail. *San Diego Herald* [newspaper], September 12. San Diego, California.
1857b   [Untitled.] *San Diego Herald* [newspaper], September 26. San Diego, California.
1857c   From Arizona. *Daily Alta California* [newspaper], September 28. San Francisco, California.
1857d   Further news from the Pimos Villages. *San Diego Herald* [newspaper], October 3. San Diego, California.
1940   Maricopa Indians celebrate "Feast of Peace." *The Genealogical and Historical Magazine of the Arizona Temple District* (July), pp. 1–7, 15–16. Mesa, Arizona: Church of Jesus Christ of Latter Day Saints.

ARDREY, ROBERT
1966   *The territorial imperative.* New York: Dell.

ASCHMANN, HOMER
1974   Environment and ecology in the "Northern Tonto" claim area. In *Apache Indians,* vol. 5, pp. 167–260. New York: Garland Publishing, Inc.

AUSTERMAN, WAYNE R.
1985   *Sharps rifles and Spanish mules: the San Antonio-El Paso mail, 1851–1881.* College Station: Texas A&M University Press.

BAHR, DONALD M., JUAN GREGORIO, DAVID I. LOPEZ, and ALBERT ALVAREZ
1974   *Piman shamanism and staying sickness (ka:cim mumkidag).* Tucson: The
        University of Arizona Press.

BAILEY, L.R., editor
1963   *The A.B. Gray report.* Los Angeles: Westernlore Press.

BARTLETT, JOHN R.
1965   *Personal narrative of explorations and incidents in Texas, New Mexico, Cali-
        fornia, Sonora and Chihuahua.* Two volumes. Chicago: The Rio Grande
        Press, Inc. [Reprint of the 1854 edition.]

BASSO, KEITH H.
1971   Introduction. In *Western Apache raiding and warfare,* by Grenville Good-
        win. Edited by Keith H. Basso, pp. 9—25. Tucson: The University of
        Arizona Press.

BEAN, LOWELL
1972   *Mukat's people: the Cahuilla Indians of Southern California.* Berkeley: Uni-
        versity of California Press.

BEAN, LOWELL J., and WILLIAM M. MASON, editors
1962   *Diaries and accounts of the Romero expeditions in Arizona and California,
        1823—1826.* Los Angeles: W. Ritchie Press, for the Palm Springs Desert
        Museum, Palm Springs, California.

BEE, ROBERT L.
1963   Changes in Yuma social organization. *Ethnology,* vol. 2, no. 2 (April), pp.
        207—27. Pittsburgh: University of Pittsburgh Press.
1983   Quechan. In *Handbook of North American Indians,* edited by William C.
        Sturtevant, vol. 10 (*Southwest*), edited by Alfonso Ortiz, pp. 86—98.
        Washington, D.C.: Smithsonian Institution.

BOURKE, JOHN G.
1969   *On the border with Crook.* First indexed edition. Glorieta, New Mexico:
        Rio Grande Press, Inc. [Reprint of the 1892 edition.]

BRADY, PETER R.
1860   [Report to Major G.O. Haller, 4th Infantry, Commanding, Fort Mojave,
        New Mexico, dated October 9.] In the National Archives of the United
        States, Washington D. C. Records of the War Department. U. S. Army
        Commands. From Department of California—Fort Mohave. Misc.

BRENNAN, JOSE L.
1959   Jose Lewis Brennan's account of Papago "customs and other references,"

edited by Bernard L. Fontana. *Ethnohistory*, vol. 6, no. 3 (Summer), pp. 226–37. Bloomington, Indiana: American Indian Ethnohistoric Conference.

BRINGAS DE MANZANEDA Y ENCINAS, DIEGO MIGUEL
1977   *Friar Bringas reports to the King.* Translated and edited by Daniel S. Matson and Bernard L. Fontana. Tucson: The University of Arizona Press.

BROWNE, JOHN R.
1974   *Adventures in the Apache country.* Re-edition with introduction, annotations and index by Donald M. Powell. Tucson: The University of Arizona Press. [Republication of a portion of the 1869 first edition of the book. The Arizona and Sonora articles initially appeared in *Harper's Monthly* between October 1864 and March 1865.]

BURRUS, ERNEST J.
1965   *Kino and the cartography of northwestern New Spain.* Tucson: Arizona Pioneers' Historical Society.

BURTON, H.S.
1857   [Letter to Thomas H. Henley, Superintendent of California Indian Affairs, datelined Fort Yuma, California, September 16.] *National Archives Microfilm Publications,* microcopy 234, *Letters Received by the Office of Indian Affairs, 1824-81,* roll 35, California Superintendency, 1856 – 1857. Washington: National Archives and Records Service.

CALLOWAY, DONALD G.
1978   "Raiding and feuding among western North American Indians." Unpublished Ph.D. dissertation. Ann Arbor: University of Michigan.

CARROLL, BERENICE A., and CLINTON F. FINK
1975   Theories of war causation: a matrix for analysis. In *War: its causes and correlates,* edited by Martin A. Nettleship and others, pp. 55–71. The Hague and Paris: Mouton Publishers.

CASTETTER, EDWARD F., and WILLIS H. BELL
1942   *Pima and Papago Indian agriculture.* Albuquerque: University of New Mexico Press.
1951   *Yuman Indian agriculture.* Albuquerque: University of New Mexico Press.

CASTETTER, EDWARD F., and RUTH M. UNDERHILL
1978   *The ethnobiology of the Papago Indians.* New York: AMS Press. [Reprint of the 1935 edition.]

CHILDE, V. GORDON
1941   War in prehistoric societies. *Sociological Review*, vol. 33, nos. 3–4 (July–October), pp. 126–38. Malvern, Worcestershire, England: The Institute of Sociology.

CORBUSIER, WILLIAM M.
1886   The Apache-Yuma and Apache-Mohaves. *American Antiquarian and Oriental Journal*, vol. 8, no. 5 (September), pp. 276–84; no. 6 (November), pp. 325–38. Chicago: F. H. Revell.

CORLE, EDWIN
1951   *The Gila.* New York and Toronto: Rinehart & Company, Inc.

COUTS, CAVE J.
1932   *From San Diego to the Colorado in 1849: the journal & maps of Cave J. Couts.* Edited by William McPherson. Los Angeles: Zamorano Club.
1961   *Hepah, California! The journal of Cave Johnson Couts from Monterey, Nuevo Leon, Mexico, to Los Angeles, California, during the years 1848 – 1849.* Edited by Henry F. Dobyns. Tucson: Arizona Pioneers' Historical Society.

CREMONY, JOHN C.
1969   *Life among the Apaches.* Glorieta, New Mexico: Rio Grande Press, Inc. [Reprint of the 1868 edition.]

CROOK, GEORGE
1936   Extract from report of Gen. George Crook, Commanding, Department of Arizona, August 31, 1874. In *Walapai Papers*, pp. 97–98, *Senate Executive Documents*, no. 273, 74th Congress, 2nd session. Washington, D.C.: United States Government Printing Office.

DENSMORE, FRANCES
1929   Papago music. *Bulletin of the Bureau of American Ethnology*, no. 90. Washington: United States Government Printing Office.
1932   Yuman and Yaqui music. *Bulletin of the Bureau of American Ethnology*, no. 110. Washington: United States Government Printing Office.

DENTAN, ROBERT K.
1968   *The Semai: a nonviolent people of Malaya.* New York: Holt, Rinehart and Winston.

DEVEREUX, GEORGE
1939   Mohave culture and personality. *Character and Personality*, vol. 8, no. 2 (December), pp. 91–109. Durham, North Carolina: Duke University Press.
1961   Mohave ethnopsychiatry and suicide. *Bulletin of the Bureau of American*

Ethnology, no. 175. Washington: United States Government Printing Office.

DILLON, RICHARD H.
1965   *J. Ross Browne, confidential agent in old California.* Norman: University of Oklahoma Press.

DOBYNS, HENRY F.
1972   *The Papago people.* Phoenix, Arizona: Indian Tribal Series.
1974   The Kohatk: oasis and ak chin agriculturalists. *Ethnohistory*, vol. 21, no. 4 (Fall), pp. 317–27. Tucson: American Society for Ethnohistory.

DOBYNS, HENRY F., and ROBERT C. EULER
1970   Wauba Yuma's people: the comparative socio-political structure of the Pai Indians of Arizona. *Prescott College Studies in Anthropology*, no. 3. Prescott, Arizona: Prescott College Press.
1976   *The Walapai people.* Phoenix, Arizona: Indian Tribal Series.

DOBYNS, HENRY F., PAUL H. EZELL, and GRETA EZELL
1963   Death of a society. *Ethnohistory*, vol. 10, no. 2 (Spring), pp. 105–61. Bloomington, Indiana: American Indian Ethnohistoric Conference.

DOBYNS, HENRY F.; PAUL H. EZELL, ALDEN W. JONES, and GRETA EZELL
1957   Thematic changes in Yuman warfare. In *Cultural stability and cultural change* [Proceedings of the 1957 Annual Spring Meeting of the American Ethnological Society], edited by Verne F. Ray, pp. 46–71. Seattle: American Ethnological Society.
1960   What were Nixoras? *Southwestern Journal of Anthropology*, vol. 16, no. 2 (Summer), pp. 230–58. Albuquerque: University of New Mexico.

DOELLE, WILLIAM H.
1981   The Gila Pima in the late seventeenth century. *Anthropological Research Papers*, no. 24, pp. 57–70. Tempe: Arizona State University.

DONAHUE, PHIL
1985   *The human animal.* New York: Simon and Schuster.

DRUCKER, PHILIP
1941   Yuman-Piman. *Anthropological Records*, vol. 6, no. 3, pp. 19–230, *Culture Element Distributions*, no. 17. Berkeley: University of California Press; London: Cambridge University Press.

DuBOIS, CONSTANCE C.
1906   Mythology of the mission Indians. *Journal of American Folk-lore*, vol. 19, no. 72 (January – March), pp. 52–58; no. 73 (April–June), pp. 145–64. Boston and New York: Houghton, Mifflin and Company.

DUNBIER, ROGER
1968   *The Sonoran Desert: its geography, economy and people.* Tucson: The University of Arizona Press.

ECCLESTON, ROBERT
1950   *Overland to California on the southwestern trail, 1849. Diary of Robert Eccleston.* Edited by George P. Hammond and Edward H. Howes. Berkeley and Los Angeles: University of California Press.

EMBER, CAROL R.
1978   Myths about hunter-gatherers. *Ethnology,* vol. 17, no. 4 (October), pp. 439–48. Pittsburgh: University of Pittsburgh.

EMORY, WILLIAM H.
1859   Sketch of territory acquired by treaty of December 30, 1853. In *Report on the United States and Mexican Boundary Survey,* by William H. Emory, *House Executive Documents,* no. 135, 34th Congress, 1st session, vol. 1, pt. 1, pp. 93–100. Washington: Cornelius Wendell, Printer.

EZELL, GRETA S., and PAUL H. EZELL
1970   Background to battle: circumstances relating to death on the Gila, 1857. In *Troopers west: military and Indian affairs on the American frontier,* edited by Ray Brandes, pp. 169–87. San Diego, California: Frontier Heritage Press.

EZELL, PAUL H.
1961   The Hispanic acculturation of the Gila River Pimas. *Memoirs of the American Anthropological Association,* no. 90. Menasha, Wisconsin: American Anthropological Association.
1963   The Maricopas. An identification from documentary sources. *Anthropological Papers of the University of Arizona,* no. 6. Tucson: The University of Arizona Press.
1968   The Cocomaricopa mail. *Brand Book of the San Diego Corral of the Westerners,* no. 1, pp. 28–34. San Diego, California.
1983   History of the Pima. In *Handbook of North American Indians,* edited by William C. Sturtevant, vol. 10 (*Southwest*), edited by Alfonso Ortiz, pp. 149–60. Washington, D.C.: Smithsonian Institution.

FABBRO, DAVID
1980   Peaceful societies. In *The war system: an interdisciplinary approach,* edited by Richard A. Falk and Samuel S. Kim, pp. 180–203. Boulder, Colorado: Westview Press.

FARISH, THOMAS E.

1915 — *History of Arizona.* Eight volumes. Phoenix, Arizona: State Historian.
1918

FATHAUER, GEORGE H.

1951 The Mohave "ghost doctor." *American Anthropologist,* vol. 53, no. 4 (October–December), pp. 605–07. Menasha, Wisconsin: American Anthropological Association.
1954 The structure and causation of Mohave warfare. *Southwestern Journal of Anthropology,* vol. 10, no. 1 (Spring), pp. 97–118. Albuquerque: University of New Mexico Press.

FERGUSON, R. BRIAN

1984 Introduction: studying war. In *Warfare, culture, and environment,* edited by R. Brian Ferguson, pp. 1–81. Orlando: Academic Press, Inc.

FISH, JOSEPH

n.d. "History of Arizona." Manuscript on file in the library of the Arizona Historical Society, Tucson.

FONTANA, BERNARD L.

1969 American Indian oral history: an anthropologist's note. *History and Theory,* vol. 8, no. 3, pp. 366–70. Middletown, Connecticut: Wesleyan University Press.
1976 The faces and forces of Pimería Alta. In *Voices from the Southwest,* edited by Donald C. Dickinson, W. David Laird, and Margaret F. Maxwell, pp. 45–54. Flagstaff, Arizona: Northland Press.
1981 *Of earth and little rain: the Papago Indians.* With photographs by John P. Schaefer. Flagstaff, Arizona: Northland Press.
1983 Pima and Papago: introduction. In *Handbook of North American Indians,* edited by William C. Sturtevant, vol. 10 *(Southwest),* edited by Alfonso Ortiz, pp. 125–36. Washington, D.C.: Smithsonian Institution.

FORBES, JACK D.

1965 *Warriors of the Colorado. The Yumas of the Quechan nation and their neighbors.* Norman: University of Oklahoma Press.
1973 Nationalism, tribalism, and self-determination: Yuman-Mexican relations, 1821–1848. *The Indian Historian,* vol. 6, no. 2 (Spring), pp. 18–22. San Francisco: American Indian Historical Society.

FORDE, C. DARYLL
1931   Ethnography of the Yuma Indians. *University of California Publications in American Archaeology and Ethnology,* vol. 28, no. 4, pp. 83—278. Berkeley: University of California Press; London: Cambridge University Press.

FRANCO CORONEL, ANTONIO
1877   "Cosas de California." Unpublished manuscript, a dictation taken in 1877. Cal ms. C-D 61, Bancroft Library, University of California, Berkeley.

FRIED, MORTON H.
1967   *The evolution of political society: an essay in political anthropology.* New York: Random House.

FROEBEL, JULIUS
1859   *Seven years' travel in Central America, northern Mexico, and the Far West of the United States.* London: Richard Bentley.

GALLEGO, HILARIO
1935   Reminiscences of an Arizona pioneer. *Arizona Historical Review,* vol. 6, no. 1 (January), pp. 75—81. Tucson: The University of Arizona.

GIFFORD, EDWARD W.
1926   Yuma dreams and omens. *Journal of American Folk-lore,* vol. 39, no. 151 (January—March), pp. 58—69. New York: American Folk-lore Society.
1931   The Kamia of Imperial Valley. *Bulletin of the Bureau of American Ethnology,* no. 97. Washington: United States Government Printing Office.
1932   The Southeastern Yavapai. *University of California Publications in American Archaeology and Ethnology,* vol. 29, no. 3, p. 177—252. Berkeley: University of California Press; London: Cambridge University Press.
1933a   The Cocopa. *University of California Publications in American Archaeology and Ethnology,* vol. 31, no. 5, pp. 257—334. Berkeley: University of California Press; London: Cambridge University Press.
1933b   Northeastern and Western Yavapai myths. *Journal of American Folk-lore,* vol. 46, no. 182 (October—December), pp. 347—415. New York: American Folk-lore Society.
1936   Northeastern and Western Yavapai. *University of California Publications in American Archaeology and Ethnology,* vol. 34, no. 4, pp. 247—354. Berkeley: University of California Press; London: Cambridge University Press.

GIFFORD, EDWARD W., and ROBERT H. LOWIE
1928   Notes on the Akwa'ala Indians of Lower California. *University of California Publications in American Archaeology and Ethnology,* vol. 23, no. 7, pp. 339—52. Berkeley: University of California Press.

GOODWIN, GRENVILLE
1969   *Social organization of the Western Apache*. Tucson: The University of Arizona Press. [Reprint of the 1942 edition.]
1971   *Western Apache raiding and warfare*. Edited by Keith H. Basso. Tucson: The University of Arizona Press.

GORER, GEOFFREY
1938   *Himalayan Village: an account of the Lepchas of Sikkim*. London: Michael Joseph, Ltd. [2nd edition, 1967; New York: Basic Books.]

GRAHAM, EDWARD E.
1975   Yuman warfare: an analysis of ecological factors from ethnohistorical sources. In *War, its causes and correlates*, edited by Martin A. Nettleship and others, pp. 451–62. The Hague and Paris: Mouton Publishers.

GROSSMANN, FREDERICK E.
1873   The Pima Indians of Arizona. *Annual Report of the Smithsonian Institution, 1871*, pp. 407–19. Washington: United States Government Printing Office.

GUNST, MARIE L.
1930   "Ceremonies of the Papago and Pima Indians, with special emphasis on the relationship of the dance to their religion." Unpublished Master's thesis. Tucson: The University of Arizona.

HACKENBERG, ROBERT A., and BERNARD L. FONTANA
1974   *Aboriginal land use and occupancy of the Pima-Maricopa Indians*. Two volumes. New York and London: Garland Publishing Company.

HAILE, BERARD
1981   Women versus men. A conflict of Navajo emergence. Edited by Karl W. Luckert. *American Tribal Religions*, vol. 6. Lincoln and London: University of Nebraska Press.

HALL, SHARLOT M.
1907   The story of a Pima record rod. *Out West*, vol. 26, no. 5 (May), pp. 413–23. Los Angeles: Out West Magazine Company.

HAMILTON, JAMES G.
1951   *"My dear Cornelia." A series of letters written by James Gillespie Hamilton to his wife, Cornelia Bernard Hamilton, during an overland trip from Westport, Missouri to California; and return by steamer via New York; August 26, 1857 –April 15, 1858*. Copied and mimeographed by his granddaughter, Katherine Jones Moore. Fresno, California.

HARRINGTON, JOHN P.
1908   A Yuma account of origins. *Journal of American Folk-lore*, vol. 21, no. 82 (October–December), pp. 324–48. Boston and New York: Houghton Mifflin Company.
1929   The Mojave. *El Palacio*, vol. 27, nos. 1–7 (July 6–August 17), pp. 16–19. [Santa Fe], School of American Research, the University of New Mexico, and the Museum of New Mexico.

HARRIS, BENJAMIN B.
1960   *The Gila trail: The Texas argonauts and the gold rush.* Edited by Richard H. Dillon. Norman: University of Oklahoma Press.

HARRIS, MARVIN
1974   *Cows, pigs, wars, & witches: the riddle of culture.* New York: Random House.

HARWELL, HENRY O., and MARSHA C. S. KELLY
1983   Maricopa. In *Handbook of North American Indians*, edited by William C. Sturtevant, vol. 10 (*Southwest*), edited by Alfonso Ortiz, pp. 71–85. Washington, D.C.: Smithsonian Institution.

HAURY, EMIL W.
1976   *The Hohokam: desert farmers and craftsmen.* Tucson: The University of Arizona Press.

HEINTZELMAN, SAMUEL P.
1851   [Journal]. Unpublished original in the Library of Congress, Washington, D. C. Microfilm copies of the period 1847–1860 in the library of the Arizona Historical Society, Tucson.
1857   Report to Major E. D. Townsend, Assistant Adjutant General, U.S.A., Pacific Division, San Francisco, California, datelined Fort Yuma, California, July 15, 1853. *House Executive Documents*, vol. 9, no. 76, pp. 34–58, 34th Congress, 3rd session. Washington: Cornelius Wendell, Printer.

HICKS, FREDERIC
1974   The influence of agriculture on aboriginal socio-political organization in the Lower Colorado River Valley. *Journal of California Anthropology*, vol. 1, no. 2 (Winter), pp. 133–44. Banning, California: Malki Museum, Inc.

HINTON, JOHN N.
1906   "Notes of statement by John N. Hinton. San Diego, November, 1906. Reminiscences of life in Arizona and California during the years 1853 to 1856." Unpublished 9-page typescript on file in the Sharlot Hall Museum, Prescott, Arizona.

HOLMBERG, A. R.
1966   *Nomads of the longbow: the Siriono of eastern Bolivia.* New York: Natural History Press.

HOSTETLER, J. A., and G. E. HUNTINGTON
1967   *The Hutterites of North America.* New York: Holt, Rinehart and Winston.

HYDE, GEORGE E.
1951   *Pawnee Indians.* Denver: The University of Denver Press.

IGLITZIN, LYNNE B.
1978   War, sex, sports, and masculinity. In *War: A historical, political, and social study,* edited by L. L. Farrar, Jr., pp. 63–69. Santa Barbara, California, and Oxford, England: ABC Clio, Inc.

IVES, JOSEPH C.
1861   Report upon the Colorado River of the West, explored in 1857 and 1858. *House Executive Documents,* no. 90, 36th Congress, 1st session. Washington: United States Government Printing Office. [Reprinted in 1969; New York: Da Capo Press.]

JENNESS, DIAMOND
1922   The life of the Copper Eskimos. *Report of the Canadian Arctic Expedition, 1913–1918,* vol. 12a. Ottawa: F.A. Acland.

KELLY, MARSHA C.
1972   The society that did not die. *Ethnohistory,* vol. 19, no. 3 (Summer), pp. 261–65. Tucson: American Society for Ethnohistory.

KELLY, WILLIAM H.
1949a   Cocopa attitudes and practices with respect to death and mourning. *Southwestern Journal of Anthropology,* vol. 5, no. 2 (Summer), pp. 151–64. Albuquerque: University of New Mexico Press.
1949b   The place of scalps in Cocopa warfare. *El Palacio,* vol. 56, no. 3 (March), pp. 85–91. Santa Fe, School of American Research, Museum of New Mexico, Archaeological Society of New Mexico, and the Laboratory of Anthropology.
1977   Cocopa ethnography. *Anthropological Papers of the University of Arizona,* no. 29. Tucson: The University of Arizona Press.

KESSELL, JOHN L.
1976   *Friars, soldiers, and reformers.* Tucson: The University of Arizona Press.

KEY, HAROLD
1970   A Mohave cremation. *The Kiva,* vol. 36, no. 1 (Fall), pp. 23–38. Tucson: Arizona Archaeological and Historical Society.

KHERA, SIGRID, and PATRICIA S. MARIELLA
1983   Yavapai. In *Handbook of North American Indians,* edited by William C.
        Sturtevant, vol. 10 *(Southwest),* edited by Alfonso Ortiz, pp. 38–54.
        Washington, D.C.: Smithsonian Institution.

KINO, EUSEBIO F.
1948   *Kino's historical memoir of Pimería Alta.* Translated, edited, and annotated
        by Herbert E. Bolton. Two volumes in one. Berkeley and Los Angeles:
        University of California Press. [Reprint of the two-volume 1919 edition.]
1971   Kino's biography of Francisco Javier Saeta, S.J. Translated, with an epi-
        logue, by Charles W. Polzer; original Spanish text edited by Ernest J.
        Burrus. *Sources and Studies for the History of the Americas,* vol. 9. St. Louis,
        Missouri, and Rome, Italy: Jesuit Historical Institute.

KROEBER, ALFRED L.
n.d.   Mohave chiefs and bands in 1860: the Brady report, with discussion.
        Unpublished manuscript; copy on file with Clifton B. Kroeber, Los An-
        geles, California.
1902   Preliminary sketch of the Mohave Indians. *American Anthropologist,* vol.
        4, no. 2 (April–June), pp. 276–85. New York: G.P. Putnam's Sons.
1920   Yuman tribes of the Lower Colorado. *University of California Publications
        in American Archaeology and Ethnology,* vol. 16, no. 8, pp. 475–85.
        Berkeley: University of California Press.
1925a   Earth-tongue, a Mohave. In *American Indian life,* edited by Elsie Clews
        Parsons, pp. 189–202. New York: B.W. Huebsch.
1925b   Handbook of the Indians of California. *Bulletin of the Bureau of American
        Ethnology,* no. 78. Washington, D.C.: Government Printing Office.
        [Reprinted in 1953; Berkeley: California Book Company.]
1948   Seven Mohave myths. *University of California Anthropological Records,* vol.
        11, no. 1, pp. 1–70. Berkeley and Los Angeles: University of California
        Press.
1951   A Mohave historical epic. *University of California Anthropological Records,*
        vol. 11, no. 2, pp. 71–176. Berkeley and Los Angeles: University of
        California Press.
1963   The nature of land-holding groups in aboriginal California. In *Aboriginal
        California,* edited by Robert F. Heizer, pp. 81–120. Berkeley: University
        of California Press.
1972   More Mohave myths. *University of California Anthropological Records,* vol.
        27. Berkeley, Los Angeles, and London: University of California Press.

KROEBER, ALFRED L., and CLIFTON B. KROEBER
1973   A Mohave war reminiscence, 1854–1880. *University of California Publica-
        tions in Anthropology,* vol. 10. Berkeley, Los Angeles, and London: Univer-
        sity of California Press.

KROEBER, CLIFTON B.

1965   The Mohave as nationalist, 1859—1874. *Proceedings of the American Philosophical Society*, vol. 109, no. 3 (June), pp. 173—80. Philadelphia: American Philosophical Society.

1980   Lower Colorado River peoples: hostilities and hunger, 1850—1857. *Journal of California and Great Basin Anthropology*, vol. 2, no. 2 (Winter), pp. 187—98. Banning, California: Malki Museum, Inc.

LEE, R.B.

1968   What hunters do for a living: or how to make out on scarce resources. In *Man the hunter*, edited by R. B. Lee and I. Devore, pp. 30—48. Chicago: Aldine.

LEEDS, ANTHONY

1963   The functions of war. In *Violence and war, with clinical studies [Science and Psychoanalysis*, vol 6], edited by Jules H. Masserman, pp. 69—82. New York and London: Grune and Stratton.

LOOMIS, NOEL M., editor

1968   Journal of I. C. Woods on the establishment of the San Antonio and San Diego mail line. *Brand Book of the San Diego Corral of the Westerners*, no. 1, pp. 94—125. San Diego, California.

LOPEZ, FRANK

1981   'Al Wiapoi [The Boy Who Gets Revenge]. Translated by Ofelia Zepeda. In *The south corner of time*, edited by Larry Evers, pp. 130—49. Tucson: The University of Arizona Press.

LORENZ, KONRAD

1966   *On aggression.* New York: Harcourt, Brace & World.

LOUDON, J.B.

1970   Teasing and socialisation on Tristan da Cunha. In *Socialisation: the approach from anthropology*, edited by P. Mayer, pp. 293—331. London: Tavistock.

McGUIRE, RANDALL H.

1982   Problems in culture history. In *Hohokam and Patayan. Prehistory of southwestern Arizona*, edited by Randall H. McGuire and Michael B. Schiffer, pp. 153—274. New York, London: Academic Press.

MALINOWSKI, BRONISLAW

1941   An anthropological analysis of war. *American Journal of Sociology*, vol. 46, no. 4 (January), pp. 521—50. Chicago: University of Chicago Press.

MANNERS, ROBERT

1959   Habitat, technology, and social organization of the Southern Paiute. *América Indígena*, vol. 19, no. 3 (Julio), pp. 179—97. México, D.F.: Instituto Indigenista Interamericano.

MARSHALL, L.
1965   The Kung Bushmen of the Kalahari Desert. In *Peoples of Africa*, edited by J. L. Gibbs, pp. 241–78. New York: Holt, Rinehart and Winston.

MARTIN, DOUGLAS D.
1954   *Yuma crossing.* Albuquerque: University of New Mexico Press.

MEAD, MARGARET
1940   Warfare is only an invention—not a biological necessity. *Asia*, vol. 40, no. 8 (August), pp. 402–05. New York: Editorial Publications, Inc.
1963   The psychology of warless man. In *A warless world*, edited by A. Larson, pp. 131–42. New York: McGraw-Hill.
1968   Alternatives to war. In *War: the anthropology of armed conflict and aggression*, edited by Morton Fried, Marvin Harris, and Robert Murphy, pp. 215–28. Garden City, New York: Natural History Press.

MEIGS, M.C.
1872   Letter to William W. Belknap, Secretary of War, Washington, D.C., datelined February 11, 1872, Yuma Depot, Arizona. In *Annual report of the Commissioner of Indian Affairs to the Secretary of the Interior for the year 1872*, pp. 162–63. Washington: United States Government Printing Office.

MICHLER, NATHANIEL
1857   From the 111th meridian of longitude to the Pacific Ocean. In *Report on the United States and Mexican Boundary Survey*, by William H. Emory [*House Executive Documents*, no. 135, 34th Congress, 1st session], vol. 1, part 1, pp. 101–25. Washington: Cornelius Wendell, Printer.

MISHKIN, BERNARD
1940   Rank and warfare among the Plains Indians. *Monographs of the American Ethnological Society*, no. 3. New York: J. J. Augustin.

MITCHELL, G.
1981   *Human sex differences: a primatologist's perspective.* New York: Van Nostrand Reinhold Company.

MÖLLHAUSEN, BALDWIN
1858   *Diary of a journey from the Mississippi to the coasts of the Pacific with a United States exploring expedition.* Translated from the German by Mrs. Percy Sinnett. Two volumes. London: Longman, Brown, Green, Longmans & Roberts. [Reprinted in 1969; New York: Johnson Reprint Corporation.]

MONTAGU, ASHLEY
1976   *The nature of human aggression.* New York: Oxford University Press.

MOORE, B., JR.
1972   *Reflections on the causes of human misery and upon certain proposals to elimi-nate them.* London, Allen Lane: The Penguin Press.

MOWRY, SYLVESTER
1858   Report on the Indian tribes of Arizona Territory. *Senate Executive Docu-ments,* no. 11, vol. 1, pp. 584–93, 35th Congress, 1st session. Washington: William A. Harris, Printer

MUNCH, PETER A.
1964   Culture and superculture in a displaced community: Tristan da Cunha. *Ethnology,* vol. 3, no. 4 (October), pp. 369–76. Pittsburgh: University of Pittsburgh Press.
1970   Economic development and conflicting values: a social experiment in Tristan da Cunha. *American Anthropologist,* vol. 72, no. 6 (December), pp. 1300–1318. Washington, D.C.: American Anthropological Association.
1971   *Crisis in Utopia: the ordeal of Tristan da Cunha.* New York: Thomas Y. Crowell.
1974   Anarchy and anomie in an anachronistic community. *Man,* vol. 9, no. 2 (June), pp. 243–61. London: Royal Anthropological Institute.

NETTING, ROBERT M.
1974   Kofyar armed conflict: social causes and consequences. *Journal of Anthropo-logical Research,* vol. 30, no. 3 (Autumn), pp. 139–63. Albuquerque: University of New Mexico.

NEWCOMB, WILLIAM W., JR.
1960   Toward an understanding of war. In *Essays in the science of culture,* edited by G. Dole and R. Carneiro, pp. 317–35. New York: Crowell.

NIETHAMMER, CAROLYN
1974   *American Indian food and lore.* New York: Collier Books; London: Collier Macmillan Publishers.

OAKS, GEORGE W.
1956   *Man of the West. Reminiscences of George Washington Oaks, 1840–1917.* Recorded by B. Jaastad; edited by Arthur C. Woodward. Tucson: Arizona Pioneers' Historical Society.

ORMSBY, WATERMAN L.
1942   *The Butterfield Overland Mail.* Edited by Lyle H. Wright and Josephine M. Bynum. San Marino, California: The Huntington Library.

OTTENBERG, SIMON
1978   Anthropological interpretations of war. In *War: A historical, political, and social study,* edited by L. L. Farrar, Jr. Santa Barbara, California, and Oxford, England: ABC Clio, Inc.

OTTERBEIN, KEITH
1973   The anthropology of war. In *Handbook of social and cultural anthropology,* edited by J. J. Honigmann, pp. 923–58. Chicago: Rand McNally and Company.

PABLO, SALLY G.
1983   Contemporary Pima. In *Handbook of North American Indians,* edited by William C. Sturtevant, vol. 10 (*Southwest*), edited by Alfonso Ortiz, pp. 212–16. Washington, D.C.: Smithsonian Institution.

PALMER, STUART
1965   Murder and suicide in forty non-literate societies. *Journal of Criminal Law, Criminology, and Police Science,* vol. 56, no. 3 (September), pp. 320–24. Baltimore: Williams and Wilkins Company for the Northwestern University School of Law.

PARSONS, ELSIE C.
1928   Notes on the Pima, 1926. *American Anthropologist,* vol. 30, no. 3 (July–September), pp. 445–64. Menasha, Wisconsin: American Anthropological Association.

PERCHERO, LUKE
1970   "Nicholas P. Houser interviewing Luke Perchero, Maricopa Colony, September 16." Unpublished 21-page transcript of a tape-recorded interview, on file in the Arizona State Museum Library, Tucson, The University of Arizona.

PERRY, WILLIAM J.
1917   An ethnological study of warfare. *Memoirs and Proceedings of the Manchester Literary and Philosophical Society,* vol. 41, pp. 1–16. Manchester, England.
1924   *The growth of civilization.* New York: Dutton.

PHILLIPS, GEORGE H.
1975   *Chiefs and challengers: Indian resistance and cooperation in Southern California.* Berkeley: University of California Press.

RAMÍREZ, TEODORO
1837   [Letter to Rafael Elías Gonzáles, dated September 6.] Unpublished; on file in Cuaderno 9, Papago section, Archivo Histórico del Estado de Sonora, Hermosillo, Sonora, México.

RASMUSSEN, K.
1932   Intellectual culture of the Copper Eskimo. *Report of the Fifth Thule Expedition to Arctic North America,* vol. 9. Copenhagen: Gyldendalske Boghandel, Nordisk Forlag.

REA, AMADEO M.
1983   *Once a river: bird life and habitat changes on the middle Gila.* Tucson: The University of Arizona Press.

REDBIRD, IDA
1970   "Nicholas P. Houser interviewing Mrs. Ida Redbird of Maricopa Colony, Gila Reservation. July 29." Unpublished 17-page transcript of tape-recorded interview, on file in the Arizona State Museum Library, Tucson, The University of Arizona.

ROPER, MARILYN K.
1975   Evidence of warfare in the Near East from 10,000−4,300 B.C. In *War, its causes and correlates,* edited by Martin A. Nettleship and others, pp. 299−340. The Hague and Paris: Mouton Publishers.

RUSSELL, FRANK
1975   *The Pima Indians.* Re-edition with introduction, citation sources, and bibliography by Bernard L. Fontana. Tucson: The University of Arizona Press. [The first edition appeared in 1908; Washington, D.C.: United States Government Printing Office.]

ST. JOHN, SILAS
n.d.   "The establishment of the transcontinental mail service upon the Overland Stage route." Unpublished manuscript on file in the Sharlot Hall Museum, Prescott, Arizona. [Portions of this manuscript, edited by Sharlot Hall, appeared in the Prescott *Journal-Miner* newspaper of March 5, 1912, probably near the time it was written.]
1974   Report to A. B. Greenwood, Commissioner of Indian Affairs, Washington, D. C., from St. John, Special Agent Pimo and Maricopa Inds., Pimo and Maricopa Agency, Pimo Villages, New Mexico, 16th of September, 1859. In *Aboriginal land use and occupancy of the Pima-Maricopa Indians,* by Robert A. Hackenberg and Bernard L. Fontana, vol. 1, chap. 4, pp. 167−72. New York and London: Garland Publishing Company.

SAYLES, GLADYS, and TED SAYLES
1948   The pottery of Ida Redbird. *Arizona Highways,* vol. 24, no. 1 (January), pp. 28−31. Phoenix: Arizona Highway Department.

SCHROEDER, ALBERT H.
1979   Prehistory: Hakataya. In *Handbook of North American Indians,* edited by
        William C. Sturtevant, vol. 9, *(Southwest),* edited by Alfonso Ortiz, pp.
        100–07. Washington, D.C.: Smithsonian Institution.

SERVEN, JAMES E.
1965   The military posts on Sonoita Creek. *The Smoke Signal,* no. 12. Tucson:
        Tucson Corral of the Westerners.

SERVICE, ELMAN R.
1968   War and contemporary ancestors. In *War: the anthropology of armed conflict
        and aggression,* edited by Morton Fried, Marvin Harris, and Robert Mur-
        phy, pp. 160–67. Garden City, New York: Natural History Press.

SHAW, ANNA M.
1968   *Pima Indian legends.* Tucson: The University of Arizona Press.
1974   *A Pima past.* Tucson: The University of Arizona Press.

SHERER, LORRAINE M.
1965   *The clan system of the Fort Mojave Indians.* Los Angeles: The Historical
        Society of Southern California.
1966   Great chieftains of the Mojave Indians. *Southern California Quarterly,* vol.
        48, no. 1 (March), pp. 1–35. Los Angeles: Historical Society of South-
        ern California.

SITGREAVES, LORENZO
1962   *Report of an expedition down the Zuñi and Colorado rivers.* Chicago: The
        Rio Grande Press, Inc. [Reprint of the 1853 edition.]

SMITH, [MRS.] WHITE MOUNTAIN
1942   Time marches on in Pimeria. *Desert Magazine,* vol. 5, no. 6 (April), pp.
        22–24. El Centro, California: Desert Publishing Company.

SOUTHWORTH, C.H.
1931   A Pima calendar stick. *Arizona Historical Review,* vol. 4, no. 3 (July),
        pp. 44–51. Tucson: The University of Arizona.

SPICER, EDWARD H.
1962   *Cycles of conquest.* Tucson: The University of Arizona Press.

SPIER, LESLIE
1955   Mohave culture items. *Bulletin of the Museum of Northern Arizona,* no. 28.
        Flagstaff: Northern Arizona Society of Science and Art, Inc.
1970   Cultural relations of the Gila River and Lower Colorado tribes. *Yale*

University Publications in Anthropology, no. 3. New Haven, Connecticut: Human Relations Area Files Press. [Reprint of the 1936 edition.]

1978   *Yuman tribes of the Gila River.* New York: Dover Publications, Inc. [Reprint of the 1933 edition.]

STEEN, ENOCH

1857   Letter to J. W. Denver, Commissioner of Indian Affairs, datelined Ft. Buchanan, N. M., November 2. *National Archives Microfilm Publications,* microcropy 234, *Letters received by the Office of Indian Affairs, 1824—81,* roll 548, New Mixico Superintendency, 1856—1857. Washington: National Archives and Records Service.

STEWART, KENNETH M.

1947a   An account of the Mohave mourning ceremony. *American Anthropologist,* vol. 49, no. 1 (January—March), pp. 146—148. Menasha, Wisconsin: American Anthropological Association.

1947b   Mohave warfare. *Southwestern Journal of Anthropology,* vol. 3, no. 3 (Summer), pp. 257—78. Albuquerque: University of New Mexico Press.

1966   Mojave Indian agriculture. *The Masterkey,* vol. 40, no. 1 (January—March), pp. 4—15. Los Angeles: Southwest Museum.

1970   Mojave Indian shamanism. *The Masterkey,* vol. 44, no. 1 (January—March), pp. 15—24. Los Angeles: Southwest Museum.

1974a   Mojave shamanistic specialists. *The Masterkey,* vol. 48, no. 1 (January—March), pp. 4—13. Los Angeles: Southwest Museum.

1974b   Mortuary practices of the Mohave Indians. *El Palacio,* vol. 79, no. 4 (March), pp. 2—12. Santa Fe: Museum of New Mexico.

1983   Yumans: introduction. In *Handbook of North American Indians,* edited by William C. Sturtevant, vol. 10 (*Southwest*), edited by Alfonso Ortiz, pp. 1—3. Washington, D.C.: Smithsonian Institution.

STONE, CONNIE L.

1981   Economy and warfare along the Lower Colorado River. *Anthropological Research Papers,* no. 24, pp. 183—97. Tempe: Arizona State University.

STRATTON, ROYAL B.

1858   *Captivity of the Oatman girls: being an interesting narrative of life among the Apache and Mohave Indians.* 3rd edition. New York: Carlton and Porter.

SUÁREZ, FRANCISCO

1832   [A report on the part of the Ayuntamiento of the Altar District of Sonora to Sonoran Vice-Governor José Ignacio Bustamente, datelined Guadalupe del Altar, October 1.] On file in the Archivo Histórico del Estado de Sonora, Papagos, Cuaderno 3. Hermosillo, Sonora, México.

SWEENY, THOMAS W.
1956   *Journal of Lt. Thomas W. Sweeny, 1849–1853.* Edited by Arthur Wood-
        ward. Los Angeles: Westernlore Press.

TAYLOR, EDITH S., and WILLIAM J. WALLACE
1947   Mohave tattooing and face-painting. *The Masterkey,* vol. 21, no. 6
        (November), pp. 183–95. Los Angeles: Southwest Museum.

THOMAS, ELIZABETH
1969   *The harmless people.* New York: Penguin Books.

THOREAU, HENRY D.
1960   *H. D. Thoreau: A writer's journal.* Edited by Laurence Stapleton. New
        York: Dover Publications, Inc.

THRAPP, DAN L.
1967   *The conquest of Apachería.* Norman: University of Oklahoma Press.

TRIPPEL, EUGENE J.
1889   The Yuma Indians. *The Overland Monthly,* 2nd series, vol. 13, no. 78
        (June), pp. 561–84; vol. 14, no. 79 (July), pp. 1–11. San Francisco:
        Overland Monthly Publishing Company.

TURNEY-HIGH, HARRY H.
1949   *Primitive war: its practices and concepts.* Columbia, South Carolina:
        University of South Carolina Press.

TYRRELL, WILLIAM B.
1984   *Amazons: a study in Athenian mythmaking.* Baltimore: Johns Hopkins
        University Press.

UNDERHILL, RUTH M.
1939   Social organization of the Papago Indians. *Columbia University Contribu-
        tions to Anthropology,* vol. 30. New York: Columbia University Press.
1946   Papago Indian religion. *Columbia University Contributions to Anthropology,*
        no. 33. New York: Columbia University Press.
1951   *People of the crimson evening.* Riverside, California: Department of the
        Interior, United States Indian Service, Branch of Education.
1968   *Singing for power.* Berkeley and Los Angeles: University of California
        Press. [Reprint of the 1938 edition.]
1979   *The Papago and Pima Indians of Arizona.* Palmer Lake, Colorado: The
        Filter Press. [Reprint of the 1941 edition of *The Papago Indians of Arizona
        and their relatives the Pima.*]

UNDERHILL, RUTH M., DONALD M. BAHR, BAPTISTO LOPEZ, JOSE PANCHO, and DAVID LOPEZ
1979   Rainhouse and ocean. Speeches of the Papago year. *American Tribal Religions*, vol. 4. Flagstaff: Museum of Northern Arizona Press.

UNITED STATES ARMY. *Department of Arizona.*
1874   "Report on Arizona Indians." Unpublished manuscript, Ms P-D 3, Bancroft Library, University of California, Berkeley.

VAYDA, ANDREW P.
1968a   Hypothesis about functions of war. In *War: the anthropology of armed conflict and aggression*, edited by Morton Fried, Marvin Harris, and Robert Murphy, pp. 85–91. Garden City, New York: Natural History Press.
1968b   Primitive war. In *International encyclopedia of the social sciences*, edited by David L. Sills, vol. 16, pp. 468–72. New York: Macmillan.
1976   *War in ecological perspective. Persistence, change, and adaptive processes in three Oceanian societies.* New York: Plenum Press.

VIVIAN, R. GWINN
1965   An archaeological survey of the lower Gila River, Arizona. *The Kiva*, vol. 3, no. 4 (April), pp. 95–146. Tucson: Arizona Archaeological and Historical Society.

VOEGELIN, CARL F., and FLORENCE M. VOEGELIN
1966   *Map of North American Indian languages.* N.p., American Ethnological Society.

WALLACE, ANTHONY F. C.
1968   Psychological preparations for war. In *War: the anthropology of armed conflict and aggression*, edited by Morton Fried, Marvin Harris, and Robert Murphy, pp. 173–88. Garden City, New York: Natural History Press.

WALLACE, WILLIAM J.
1964   The dream in Mohave life. *Journal of American Folk-lore*, vol. 60, no. 237 (July–September), pp. 252–58. Menasha, Wisconsin: American Folklore Society.

WATERS, MICHAEL R.
1982   The lowland Patayan ceramic typology. In *Hohokam and Patayan. Prehistory of southwestern Arizona*, edited by Randall H. McGuire and Michael B. Schiffer, pp. 537–70. New York, London: Academic Press.

WHITE, CHRIS
1974   Lower Colorado River area aboriginal warfare and alliance dynamics. In
        Antap. California Indian political and economic organization, edited by
        Lowell J. Bean and T. F. King, pp. 111–35. Ramona, California: Ballena
        Press.

WHITTEMORE, ISAAC T.
1893   *Among the Pimas or the mission to the Pima and Maricopa Indians.* Albany,
        New York: The Ladies Union Mission School Association.

WILLIAMS, ANITA ALVAREZ DE
1983   Cocopa. In *Handbook of North American Indians,* edited by William C.
        Sturtevant, vol. 10 (*Southwest*), edited by Alfonso Ortiz, pp. 99–112.
        Washington, D.C.: Smithsonian Institution.

WINTER, JOSEPH
1973   Cultural modifications of the Gila Pima: A.D. 1697–A.D. 1846. *Ethnohis-
        tory,* vol. 20, no. 1 (Winter), pp. 67–77. Tucson: American Society for
        Ethnohistory.

WOOD, HARVEY
1955   *Personal recollections of Harvey Wood.* Introduction and Notes by John B.
        Goodman III. Pasadena, California: privately printed.

[WOODS, ISAIAH C.]
1859   Extract of report made in March, 1858, to the Postmaster General by the
        superintendent of the route from San Antonio, Texas, to San Diego,
        California. *Senate Executive Documents,* no. 1, part 4, vol. 4, pp. 744–52,
        35th Congress, 2nd session. Washington: William A. Harris, Printer.

WOODWARD, ARTHUR
1933   A man's way. *The Masterkey,* vol. 7, no. 6 (November), pp. 165–67. Los
        Angeles: Southwest Museum.
1955   *Feud on the Colorado.* Los Angeles: Westernlore Press.

WRIGHT, QUINCY
1942   *A study of war.* Two volumes. Chicago: University of Chicago Press.

INDEX

ahive sumach. *See* Mohave Indians,
  shamans
Ah-pan-kuh-ya (Chemehuevi Indian),
  194n. 44, 197n. 49
Ahwan-tsevarah (Maricopa Indian), 174,
  196n. 46, 197n. 49
ahwe sumach. *See* Mohave Indians,
  shamans
Akwa'ala Indians, 34, 101, 104, 109
Alakwisa Indians, 101, 104, 106, 140
Alarcón, Hernando de, 104
Aleuts, 171
Algodones (Quechan settlement), 24, 31,
  69–71, 120, 145
alliances. *See* military alliances
Allen, William, 184n. 101
Allyn, Joseph P., 99
Altar, Sonora, 112
Amazons, 165
Antonio (Quechan Indian), 97, 193n. 40
Antonio, Jose, 61
Antonio, Juan, 194n. 44
Apache Indians, 26, 27, 28, 49, 53, 67,
  76, 80, 85, 86, 92, 93, 94, 96, 98,
  105, 108, 112–13, 137, 146, 155,
  185nn. 122, 124; battle expeditions,
  113, 115; ceremonial purification after
  battle, 95; in the battle of 1857, 107
  (Table 1); settlements, 52; weapons,
  87, 113. *See also* Apaches, Western;
  Tonto Apache Indians, Apaches,
  Western, 55, 84, 105, 109, 184n. 108;

in battle of 1857, vii, 13–14, 28, 33;
  raiding, 35–36; warfare, 35–36;
  weapons, 73.
See also Apaches; Tonto Apaches
Arapaho Indians, 172
Archie (Papago village), 55
Ardrey, Robert, 161
Aretava. *See* Yara tav
Arikara Indians, 172
Ariza Aqua Bolando (Pima Indian), 60
Armistead, Lewis A., 133, 134
Aschmann, Homer, 197n. 46
As-pan-ku-yah (Mohave Indian), 134
Avi-kwa-hasala (Mohave placename), 26
Avikwame (placename), 45, 103
Avivava. *See* Pima Butte
Aztec-Tanoan (linguistic phylum), 34
Azul, Antonio, 17, 60, 61, 63, 183n. 85,
  195n. 44, 197n. 49
Azul, Culo, 61, 183n. 85

Bahr, Donald, 94, 97
Bartlett, John R., 61, 85
battle of 1857, vii–viii, 34, 49, 61, 63,
  67, 72, 79, 106, 107 (Table 1), 111,
  117, 129, 141, 144, 145, 147, 148, 151,
  153, 177; accounts of by Indians,
  21–32, 69–71, 81–82, 192n. 23,
  197n. 52; accounts of by non-Indians,
  6–9, 11–20, 100, 118–19
Bell, Willis, 123, 124, 125
Bellacoola Indians, 171

Steen, Enoch, 19
Stewart, Kenneth ,188n. 49
Stillman, Frances M., 198n. 33
Stillman, Luke, 198n. 33
Stone, Connie L., 121−24, 126
Suárez, Francisco, 112−13
Suástegui, Francisco, 113
sumach (Mohave concept), 41, 181n. 35
sumach ahot. *See* Mohave Indians, dreams
Sweeny, Tom, 186nn. 4, 7

Tabacaro. *See* Tabaquero
Tabaquero (Pima Indian), 60, 61
Tcókŭt Nak (Pima Indian), 21−23, 178n. 1
Tcóûtcïk Wútcïk. *See* Sacaton (Maricopa village)
Tejeda, Enrique, 112−13, 193n. 34
Tepecano Indians, 34
Tepehuan Indians, 34
Thomas, John, 176
Thompson, Edmund F., 184n. 101
Ti'ahiatam. *See* Azul, Culo
Tonto Apache Indians, 105, 188; in the battle of 1857, 7, 8, 14, 16, 17, 28, 119. *See also* Apache Indians; Apaches, Western
To-pi-ko-na-ho (Mohave Indian), 134
Treaty of Guadalupe Hidalgo, 15
Tristan da Cunha peoples, 173
Tubac, Sonora, 61
Tübatulabal Indians, 137
Tucson, New Mexico, 3, 4, 12, 62, 132
Tyrrell, William, 165

Underhill, Ruth M., 53, 54, 55, 56, 57, 59, 76, 78, 79, 81, 94, 97, 98
United States Army, 108, 109, 110, 115, 116, 129, 131, 141, 145, 146, 147, 193n. 30, 198n. 33
University of Arizona, viii; Doris Duke American Indian Oral History Project, viii
University of Arizona Library, Special Collections, viii
Uva-a'tuka. *See* Azul, Antonio

Vayda, Andrew, 151, 154, 155
Verde Valley, Arizona, 139
Vicente (Quechan Indian), 115
viva'vis. *See* Pima Butte

Walapai Indians, 11, 26, 34, 101, 109, 131, 137, 147, 176, 197n. 49; government, 102; horses, 184n. 101
Wallace, Anthony, 33, 151
warfare, 11−12, 35−39, 51−53, 112, 149−67, 169−74, 197n. 49; acculturation theories of, 127−31; classification of causation theories of, 161−64; cultural evolution and, 150, 152, 163, 166, 168; definition, 33, 149; diffusion of, 162, 196n. 41, 198n. 36; environmental explanations for, 121−27; female status and, 165−74; frustration-aggression and, 162; innate aggression and, 152, 158, 161−62, 164, 165−66, 198n. 36; male status and, 165−74; materialist approach to the study of, 164; military preparedness and, 163; military organization and, 164; motives for, 118, 123−24, 128, 139−43, 153, 162, 164, 171; origins of, 118, 128, 149, 164, 165; physical environment and, 162; political organization and, 164, 172; psychological approaches to the study of, 164; sex division of labor and, 174; social structure and, 162−63, 164
Waters, Michael, 102
Weaver, Paulino, 20
Western Yavapai. *See* Yavapai Indians
Whipple, Amiel W., 62
White, Ammi, 307
White, Chris, 136
Whittemore, Isaac T., 77−78
Wilson, Charles, 69, 189n. 65
Wood, Harvey, 64
Woods, Isaiah C., 3−9, 11, 12, 13, 19, 120, 177n. 1
Woodward, Arthur, 87, 88
Wright, Quincy, 151, 153

Xavier (Pima Indian), 60
xelyetsxa'm cama'. *See* Mohave Indians, shamans

Yampais. *See* Yavapai Indians.
Yara tav (Mohave Indian), 18, 20, 130, 134, 145, 146, 182n. 65, 194n. 44, 196n. 46
Yavapai Indians, 11, 34, 37, 49, 51, 52, 55, 56, 67, 68, 84, 93, 95, 105, 108,

ACKNOWLEDGMENTS

T he authors wish to acknowledge the following publishers and individuals for permission to quote materials for which they hold the copyright: The American Anthropological Association (Ezell 1961); The University of Arizona Press; The University of California Press; Columbia University Press (Underhill 1946); Greta and Paul Ezell (1970); George H. Fathauer and the *Journal of Anthropological Research* (1954); John B. Goodman, III (Wood 1955); The University of Nebraska Press (for materials from *Women versus Men: A Conflict of Navajo Emergence*, by Father Berard Haile, 1981); and the Southwest Museum (Woodward 1933).

DATE DUE

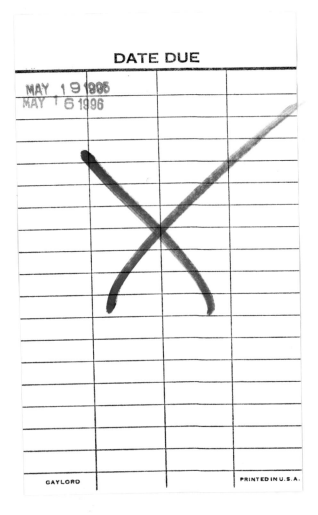